Scotland and Ulster

A Note on the Cover

Everywhere you travel in the 'Six Counties' you find demarcations of territory: flags of red white and blue, of green white and orange.

These striking abstract motifs interest me for their formal structures, and more importantly for their complexity of meanings. For several years now I have used the Union flag and the Irish flag in my work, and I have tried to break them down, to disentangle their parts, and to set up a series of processes resulting in new images.

The St Andrew's Cross, the St George's Cross and the St Patrick's Cross are all brought together in the Union flag, whilst the white of peace separates the Nationalist green from the Loyalist orange in the Irish flag. In the using of these separate elements in different configurations I was seeking to arrive at new motifs with their own worked harmonies.

With this merging of flags, the overlaying, the scraping back, the substitution of one colour for another, there are readings of cultural imposition, confusion, and mistaken identities, but more importantly and intentionally, there is the implication of new identities.

MARCEL O'CONNOR

SCOTLAND AND ULSTER

edited by

Ian S Wood

THE MERCAT PRESS
EDINBURGH

First published in 1994 by Mercat Press
James Thin, 53 South Bridge, Edinburgh EH1 1YS

© The contributors, 1994

ISBN 1873644 191

The publisher acknowledges subsidy from
the Scottish Arts Council towards the
publication of this volume.

Set in Palatino 10/12 point from author generated discs by
Servis Filmsetting Limited
Printed in Great Britain by
Athenaeum Press, Newcastle upon Tyne

Contents

Acknowledgements

A book of this type is always a team effort, so it's appropriate for an editor to thank all the contributors for their patience, industry and cooperation. Seán Costello, Tom Johnstone and Allan Boyd of Mercat Press have been a pleasure to work with and the end product owes everything to their expertise and guidance. Thanks are also due to Judie Krebs whose sharp eye and word processing skills were vital at an early stage in this project's evolution into book form.

There are too many people to name individually in and around Belfast who have provided good crack, good Guinness and hospitality during my many visits. However I would like to mention particularly Seán McKeown, Bob Purdie, Ken and Dorine Logue, Brendan Leckie, the late Maurice Kinley and his widow Muriel Kinley.

Jim Seaton, Bob Cowan, Ian Bell, and Bob Campbell – at different times Features Editors of the *Scotsman* in recent years – all gave me the chance to write, sometimes at length, on Northern Ireland, and David Lindsay, my former Head of Department at Napier University, and his successor John Troy, supported my work there, so it's appropriate to thank them.

Ian S Wood,
Editor

Editor's Preface

'A dour, ill-natured den, but our own folk all the same',[1] was a view of Ulster given by a character in John Buchan's novel *Mr Standfast* in a virulent diatribe against the Catholic Irish in Glasgow during the First World War. Anyone with experience of Ulster hospitality will reject the first part of his remark, but the claim of kinship and historical affinity is still made often enough to justify the publication of this book. *Mr Standfast* was published in 1919, so neither its author nor its characters had to define the word 'Ulster' in the way which the partition of Ireland now requires us to do.

The first charge against this collection and against me as editor is, however, likely to be that it is concerned overmuch with the statelet of Northern Ireland rather than the larger historic entity called Ulster. As far as my own contribution is concerned, I must plead guilty because of the subject I chose to write about, namely the experiences of Scottish soldiers in the current Troubles. Robbie Dinwoodie, though he has written elsewhere of a larger Ulster straddling the 1920 border, has had to limit himself to the rôle of the press in Northern Ireland. The charge cannot as easily be laid against others, least of all Owen Dudley Edwards, in his wide-ranging reflections of the final chapter, or Bob Purdie's treatment of how the Labour movement on both sides of the water addressed the Irish national question before 1914. Linde Lunney writes of an authentic Ulster literary culture already having a life of its own in the eighteenth century, and Ian Adamson's contribution also transcends partition by claiming an Ulster identity which pre-dates it.

Gerry Finn's examination of sporting links between Ulster and Scotland is not imprisoned within the confines of Northern Ireland, nor could it have been, when the opening of Glasgow Celtic's present stadium just over a century ago was marked by the laying of a symbolic square of Ulster turf. The turf came from Donegal, a county whose place in the larger process of migration to Scotland was movingly commemorated in the novels of Patrick MacGill. Loyalist flute bands continue to cross the border each year to join Orange lodges on July parades in what they still see as part of a historic Ulster dismembered only out of political expediency. Republican parades always carry the Red Hand of Ulster as emblematic proof of commitment to an all-Ireland republic, but 1920 was in fact a partition of Ulster as much as of Ireland, which the Unionists accepted as a lesser evil. One of them, H F Montgomery, wrote to his son in 1916: 'We should be in a better position to hold our own and help our friends with only six counties excluded returning 16 Unionists and nine nationalists than we should be with nine counties excluded returning 17 nationalists and 16 Unionists.'[2]

It is of course this truncated Ulster with which Unionists have had to identify themselves, and the working class Loyalists who were recruiting in the Shankill heartland during Sarah Nelson's time there did not hesitate to include the word 'Ulster' in the names of the paramilitary organisations they had set up. The new regiment raised in 1970 to replace the RUC's B-Special force could only have been called the *Ulster* Defence Regiment and the symbolism of its conversion, in 1991, into the Royal *Irish* Regiment was not lost upon the majority community.

The proper relationship of the word 'Ulster' to both the title and purpose of this book has been discussed at some length by me with my colleagues Seán Costello and Tom Johnstone from Mercat Press and also with Owen Dudley Edwards. 'Scotland and the Irish North' was considered then turned down, as was 'Scotland and the North of Ireland'. The latter title would of course have come as close as makes no difference to the coded language of republicanism, so we came back to 'Ulster' in the certain knowledge that it will anger some readers, though we hope they will still enjoy the book itself.

Inflexible republicans are always ready to take umbrage at 'Ulster' being used in contexts where, for them, 'Ireland' or 'Irish' is politically correct. I recall a bizarre and doubtless drink-fuelled argument in the Felons' Club in West Belfast one night, with a young woman who objected to my reference to the *Ulster* People's College, where I was staying with a student group from what is now Napier University. She went further, to deny that we had eaten any such thing as 'Ulster fry' that day. She insisted that she only cooked 'Irish fry' for her family, even though I was able to argue that Bobby Sands, in his hunger strike diary, had fantasized about '*Ulster* fry'.

Elsewhere in his prison poetry, he invoked the name of Ulster in celebration of Roddy McCorley, the United Irish hero hanged at Toomebridge for his part in the 1798 rebellion, though for Bobby Sands and all republicans, Ulster was simply one of the 'four green fields' which constitute the indivisible republic for which they were, and still are, ready to kill and to die.

Six years after the H-Block hunger strikes, Ulster's part in the events of 1798 was commemorated in a way which might have baffled Bobby Sands. In June 1987, 16 Loyalist flute bands and many Unionists, especially young ones, travelled the road from Carrickfergus in Antrim to Ballycarry, to honour the memory of a Presbyterian martyr, the 16-year-old Willie Nelson, whom the British crown forces hanged outside the door of his home on 30 June 1798, for his part in the rising.

He was one of many Ulster co-religionists who paid the full price for supporting the creation of a secular Irish republic, but of course the 1987 commemoration was planned by Unionists preoccupied with what they saw as the injustice to their Ulster of the 1985 Hillsborough agreement. The *Ulster Young Unionist* magazine justified the march to Ballycarry by declaring:

> Like it or not, we are rebels once more, striving for nothing more than justice. It will be a courageous step, taking the history of the United Irishmen and seeking to explain why they did what they did in Ulster. Let us play every card we hold in our struggle for justice. Let us reclaim our heritage from the Gael.[3]

The contribution of a Gaelic culture to Ulster's heritage is however something which, increasingly, Unionists and Loyalists are beginning to recognise. As Billy Kay points out in his contribution to this collection, Ulster Gaelic is much closer to the tongue still spoken in Scotland's highlands and islands than it is to that spoken further south in Ireland itself.

There has lately been a conscious effort within the majority community to prise the language away from republicanism's political hold over it. And it is now going beyond the language. Cuchulain, the legendary warrior hero of Celtic Ulster, has a statue to himself in Dublin's GPO, in celebration of the 'terrible beauty' born there in 1916, but he also commands a place of honour on a prominent new UDA mural in East Belfast. This superimposes the Red Hand and the Union flag on the image of Cuchulain who is claimed by the mural's creator to be the 'ancient defender of Ulster from Irish attacks over 2,000 years.' Alongside him, and with combat gear and assault rifle, appears a figure described as one of 'Ulster's present day defenders'.

The Gaelic Ulster tradition is not necessarily alien to or incompatible with an Ulster Protestant culture created by Reformation and Plantation. Some Ulstermen who remained thirled to the Protestant and Presbyterian Home Rule tradition realised the fact. One of them was John Ferguson, the Belfast man who in 1882 founded the Irish National League in Scotland, to campaign constitutionally for his homeland's self-government. He also published a volume of songs and poetry celebrating the rebel tradition and named his house outside Glasgow as Benburb, after the great victory over the Scottish covenanting armies won by Owen Roe O'Neill and the Gaelic earls of Ulster in 1646.

Relationships remain complex and overlapping between two communities which have each suffered much in a British mini-state still called Ulster by many of the majority. If, as a new century beckons to a Europe scarred by rekindled hatreds and ethnic cleansing, there is to be any future for Northern Ireland, Ulster, the Six Counties or the North of Ireland, it will depend upon what Graham Walker has called here a 'plurality of identities' achieving the recognition they merit.

This was surely the vision which influenced John Hewitt in half a century of prose and verse that honoured both the Gaelic and Planter/Scottish traditions of his native place.

> Ulster, considered as a region and not as the symbol of any particular creed can, I believe, command the loyalty of every one of its inhabitants. For regional identity does not preclude, rather it requires, membership of a larger association. And, whether that association be, as I hope, of a federated British Isles, or a federal Ireland, out of that loyalty to our own place, rooted in honest history and familiar folkways and knowledge, phrased in our own dialect, there should emerge a culture and an attitude individual and distinctive, a fine contribution to the European inheritance and no mere echo of the thought and imagination of another people or another land.[4]

John Hewitt wrote those words in 1947, but it is that spirit which has guided me as well in the preparation of this book.

1

The Ulster-Scottish Connection

IAN ADAMSON

The connection between the north of Ireland and western Scotland – or more specifically between what W C Mackenzie described as 'two great and intimately associated peoples'[1] – can not only be traced back to the Stone Age, but is readily seen to be, as G M Trevelyan pointed out, 'a constant factor in history'.[2] This unique connection has not only proved to be extremely productive – historically and culturally – within the area, but has made its influence felt much further afield.

The first settlers arrived in Ireland around 6,500 BC in the period known as the Mesolithic or Middle Stone Age, archaeological evidence suggesting that they probably came from the Galloway region of Scotland or Cumbria in northern England to the east coast of Ulster.[3] Their culture is therefore named Larnian. In the Neolithic period, when farming was introduced to Ireland, the population erected numerous stone burial monuments such as court cairns and dolmens. The court cairns, which are mainly distributed around the northern half of Ireland, are also found in south-west Scotland, leading Seán O Ríordáin to comment: 'The tombs and the finds from them form a continuous province joined rather than divided by the narrow waters of the North Channel'.[4] Indeed, archaeologists have labelled these tombs the 'Clyde-Carlingford cairns' to highlight the definite link between the two regions.

Such a link is hardly surprising. With north-east Ireland and south-west Scotland separated, at their closest points, by only 13 miles, and considering that much of the land would then have been covered with dense forest, the North Channel of the Irish Sea would have acted not as a barrier but rather as an effective means of communication between the islands. Continuity of population was maintained through the 'Bronze' and 'Iron' Ages.

Between 330 and 300 BC the Greek geographer and voyager Pytheas, in his *Concerning the Ocean*, gave us the earliest reference to the British Isles, calling them the 'Isles of the Pretani' (*Pretanikai nesoi*). The Pretani are thus the most ancient inhabitants of Britain and Ireland to whom a definite name can be given. As there is no evidence of any major immigrations into Ireland after the neolithic period, the Pretani would appear to be the direct descendants of the earlier peoples, or at least a dominant section within the native population.

In the later Irish literature 'Pretani' became 'Cruthin' and when medieval Irish writers referred to these people it is clear they considered them to inhabit both Ireland and Scotland. One writer stated that: 'thirty kings of the Cruthin ruled Ireland and Scotland from Ollam to Fiachna mac Baetáin' and that 'seven kings of the Cruthin of Scotland ruled Ireland in Tara' (*secht rig do Chruithnibh Alban rofhallnastair Erind i Temair*) – thereby identifying, as T F O'Rahilly notes, 'the Cruthin of Ireland with those of Scotland'.[5] Others refer to Scotland as the 'land of the Cruthin', while in a poem written in the eleventh or twelfth century, the author tells us that the *Cruthnig* made up a section of the population of Scotland. The Annals of Tigernach, the Pictish Chronicle, St Berchan, the Albanic Duan, the Book of Deer and John of Fordun plainly show that the name Cruthin was applied to the inhabitants of both Scotland and Ireland.

Eventually, the Pretanic people of Scotland were to be more generally labelled Picts, though the Pretani of Ireland were never given this appellation by those writing in Latin; later writers however have quite freely interchanged the terms 'Irish Pict' and 'Cruthin'.[6] The Picts of Scotland did not disappear from history; as Liam de Paor points out: 'The Picts undoubtedly contributed much to the make-up of the medieval kingdom of Scotland, forming probably the bulk of its population.'[7]

We cannot be certain as to when the first groups of Celtic peoples arrived in Ireland – there is no evidence which can place Celtic settlement there before the first century BC. However, it is now generally accepted that they did not displace the native population. Indeed, a seminar held by the Irish Association of Professional Archaeologists in 1984 acknowledged that any Celtic 'invasions' were more than probably carried out by numbers 'far inferior to the native population(s)'.[8] The archaeologist Peter Woodman has pointed out:

> The gene pool of the Irish was probably set by the end of the Stone Age when there were very substantial numbers of people present and the landscape had already been frequently altered. The Irish are essentially Pre-Indo-European, they are not physically Celtic. No invasion since could have been sufficiently large to alter this fact completely.[9]

Yet though they had arrived as a minority within the population, the Celts, particularly those we call the 'Gaels' – which derives from the

Old British for 'raider' – eventually achieved a dominant position in the areas which came under their sway, establishing themselves as a warrior aristocracy.

Eventually Gaelic dynasties became ascendant in many parts of Ireland, in particular the Uí Néill, who later became synonymous with the O'Neills, a situation due not only to their remarkable military achievements and the prestige accorded to their positions of 'political' power, but because their language had gradually become widely accepted among the population, especially among the learned classes and within the developing Church. To legitimise their power, the Gaelic aristocracy, through the efforts of their learned men, set about constructing suitable pedigrees for their ancestors. One of the main products of these efforts was the *Lebor Gabála*, the 'Book of Invasions', in the earliest version of which the Gaels are said to have sprung from two sons of Míl, a warrior who had come to Ireland from Spain. Then, in a later version, a third son, Ir, suddenly appears. O'Rahilly commented: 'This invention of Ir was probably due in the first instance to the genealogists, who were favourably disposed towards the Cruthin and determined to provide them with a highly respectable Goidelic [Gaelic] pedigree.'[10] This rewriting of history, as he noted, was eventually to have its desired result:

> The Cruthin or Priteni are the earliest inhabitants of these islands to whom a name can be assigned ... The combined influence of Bede, Mael Mura, and the genealogical fiction of Ir, caused *Cruithni* to lose favour as the name of a section of the Irish population. This disuse of *Cruithni* as a name is doubtless connected with the rise of a new genealogical doctrine which turned the Irish Cruthin into Goidels (Gaels) and thus disassociated them from the Cruthin of Scotland. Nevertheless the fact that there were Cruthin in Ireland as well as Scotland was, as might be expected, long remembered; and so it is not surprising to find writers occasionally suggesting, in defiance of Mael Mura, that the Cruthin of both countries formed one people in remote times.[11]

Among the great works of early Irish literature is a group of tales known as the Ulster Cycle, traditionally felt to depict the North of Ireland in the first centuries AD. While some scholars suggest that certain of the episodes enshrined within these tales have some bearing on actual historical events, this can only be speculation. The most we can say is that the whole structure of society as shown in the sagas, the weapons and characteristics of the warriors and their methods of warfare, agree precisely with the descriptions by classical authors of life among the Britons and Gauls before the Roman invasions. So while we cannot take them as 'historical' evidence, these stories nevertheless give us a glimpse, albeit romanticised, into Ireland's Iron Age – its 'Heroic' Age – and are a rich ingredient of the country's cultural heritage.

One fascinating aspect of these tales is the regularity with which characters move between Ulster and Scotland. Cuchulain, perhaps the greatest of all Ireland's legendary heroes, travels to Alba (Scotland) to receive his martial training under the tutelage of the renowned female warrior, Scáthach, and overcomes another formidable heroine, Aife, who bears him a son. One legend would also have it that the Cuillin mountains of Skye are named after the Ulster hero.

But no mention of the Ulster Tales would be complete without reference to one of the oldest stories of romance, adventure and treachery in Western European literature: the story of the 'Fate of the Children of Usnach', more popularly known as 'Deirdre of the Sorrows' after the play by J M Synge. In the story, the two main characters, the beautiful Deirdre and her lover Naisi, accompanied by the latter's two brothers, are forced to flee to Scotland after having incurred the wrath of Conor MacNessa, King of Ulster. They set up home in the lovely Glen Etive, but are enticed to return to Ulster. Deirdre is stricken with unhappiness at what is to prove a fatal decision, and sadly laments her departure from Scotland:

> Delightful land, yon eastern land,
> Alba, with its wonders;
> I would not have come hither out of it
> Had I not come with Naisi.
>
> The Vale of Láid, oh, the Vale of Láid!
> Often I slept there under soft coverlet;
> fish and venison and the fat of the badger
> were my repast in the vale of Láid.
>
> The Vale of Etive, oh, the Vale of Etive!
> In it I raised my first house;
> lovely was its wood (when seen) on rising;
> the milking house of the sun was the Vale of Etive.

While these sagas are believed to describe an Ulster of the first few centuries AD, and probably had a long oral existence, they only took literary form in the eighth and ninth centuries. The development of Irish writing which made this flowering of culture possible followed the arrival in Ireland of a new and invigorating force: Christianity.

In 398 AD St Ninian had established the first Christian Church in Scotland at Candida Casa (now Whithorn) in Galloway. Although little is known about this great Christian Saint of the Novantes, or the earliest history of his foundation, it is clear that in the fifth and sixth centuries Candida Casa was an important centre of evangelism to both Britain and the northern part of Ireland. Then in 432 AD, the ancient *Annals of Ulster* record the arrival of Saint Patrick. While most of the 'evidence' for Patrick's mission comes from his own writings, there is no doubting the zeal with which the Irish pursued the development of their church in the period after his death.

By far the most important of the many monastic settlements which sprang up was Bangor, on the coast of present-day County Down, founded in 555 by Comgall, perhaps the most famous Cruthin of all. It was Bangor which gave the largest number of great names to Irish religious history, figures such as Columbanus, Gall, Moluag, Maelrubha, Dungal and Malachy. At Bangor were compiled, in all probability, the original *Chronicles of Ireland* and the beautiful poetry 'The Voyage of Bran'. In this region too, the old traditions of Ulster were preserved and these were moulded into the Gaelic masterpiece, the *Táin Bó Cuailgne* (Cattle Raid of Cooley).

One of the great religious figures of Ireland was Columba (Columb-Cille) a prince of the Northern Uí Néill. Columba studied under St Finnian at Movilla, where he was ordained deacon, and according to the *Annals of Ulster*, founded Derry in 545. He became a close friend of Comgall, even though the political and ethnic rivalries between their respective kinsmen must at times have sorely tested their shared Christianity. The saint's legend would have us believe that it was these political and ethnic distractions which finally persuaded Columba to leave Ireland and set up a new community out of sight of its shores. Yet although Columba had not stood aloof from political intrigue, or even inciting warfare, such involvement would not have been exceptional for the clergy at that time, some of whom carried weapons to the synods. As J T Fowler wrote:

> It is no marvel then if Columba, a leading spirit in the great clan of the northern Uí Néill, incited his kinsmen to fight about matters which would be felt most keenly as closely touching their tribal honour. But at the same time, such a man as he was may very well, upon calm reflection, have considered that his enthusiasm and energies would be more worthily bestowed on missionary work than in maintaining the dignity of his clan.[12]

Whatever the reasons for his departure, the history of the Church was to be so much the richer, for the community he founded, on the small island of Iona, close to the coast of Argyll, was destined to be the cultural apotheosis of Scotland, and the place where some scholars believe the magnificent *Book of Kells* was executed.

The northern Irish monastic settlements, whether their influence emanated from Bangor or Iona, were not only to be directly responsible for the spread of Christianity to Scotland and northern England, but were to carry their missionary zeal to the very heart of Europe itself. Of all the numerous personalities who sought 'to renounce home and family like Abraham and seek a secluded spot where the ties of the world would not interfere with their pursuit of sanctity',[13] none stands out more prominently among these *peregrini* than Columbanus. In 589 AD, he set off from

Bangor on what was to become one of the great missionary journeys of history. Pope Pius XI has said:

> The more light that is shed by scholars in the period known as the Middle Ages the clearer it becomes that it was thanks to the initiative and labours of Columbanus that the rebirth of Christian virtue and civilisation over a great part of Gaul, Germany and Italy took place.[14]

More recently, Robert Schuman, the French Foreign Minister who was a driving force behind the establishment of the European Economic Community, said: 'Columbanus is the patron saint of those who seek to construct a united Europe.'

With the arrival of the Christian period and the intensive missionary activity which spread to Scotland, initiated by men of vision and energy such as Comgall and Columba, the cross-fertilisation between Scotland and Ulster was to reach new heights, particularly in respect to the flowering of literary creativeness. As Proinsias MacCana wrote:

> Isolation tends towards stagnation, or at least a circumscribed vision, while conversely intercourse and cultural commerce encourage a greater intellectual curiosity and awareness, a greater readiness to adapt old ways and experiment with new ones. For such intercourse the east-Ulster region was ideally situated. It was a normal landing-place for travellers from northern Britain, which during the sixth and seventh centuries probably presented a more dramatic clash and confluence of cultures than any other part of Britain or Ireland; and, in addition, the religious, social and political ties that linked north-eastern Ireland and north-Western Britain – particularly in that period – were numerous and close. Archaeologists speak of an 'Irish Sea culture-province' with its western flank in Ireland and its eastern flank in Britain; one might with comparable justification speak of a North Channel culture-province within which obtained a free currency of ideas, literary, intellectual and artistic.
>
> One recalls particularly those tales which relate in one way or another to the commerce that existed between east-Ulster and Scotland: for instance, the story of Suibne Geilt, whom the later evolution of his legend makes king of Dál Riata – by James Carney's reasoning it must have passed from Scotland to Ireland before c.800; or the several thematically related tales which make up what one might call the 'Tristan complex' and which also link Irish and north British tradition.[15]

Once Gaelic power had consolidated itself in the centre of Ireland, the Uí Néill embarked upon the conquest of the North. However, a determined resistance was made to these designs by the pre-Celtic Cruthin in alliance with the Celtic Ulaid (from whom the name 'Ulster' derives). Nevertheless, Uí Néill pressure was relentless, and the ancient Ulster capital at Emain Macha was destroyed or abandoned in 450 AD, and the leaders retreated east of the River Bann. A massive earthwork wall was erected to delimit part of the now much reduced boundary of Ulster, within which the

Ulstermen managed to retain a degree of independence for the next 700 years.

Possibly because of the pressure of the Uí Néill territorial gains and the contraction of Old Ulster, groups within the Northern population began to move across the North Channel, in particular the Dál Riata, who settled in Argyll and the islands along the western seaboard. The Venerable Bede, writing in his eighth century *A History of the English Church and People*, states that this land was obtained from the local Pictish people by a combination of force and treaty. The kings of the Dál Riata soon claimed sovereignty over territory on both sides of the North Channel, and when Fergus MacErc forsook his Irish capital of Dunseverick around 500 and established his main residence in Argyll, we may assume that by this time the colony had ousted the mother-country in importance. After their defeat alongside the Ulster Cruthin king Congal Cláen at the great battle of Moira in 637 however, the Dalriadan kings were finally to lose their Ulster territories to the Uí Néill.

Groups from Ireland had been raiding Roman Britain, according to Roman writers, as early as 343. The Romans called the Irish raiders 'Scotti' and Ireland became known as Scotia. However, while Ireland was eventually to lose that appellation, the new settlers crossing the North Channel were to bequeath the name to their new homeland. From the kings of Dál Riada there is a direct link to the kings of what would become 'Scotland'.

The settlement of northern Irish in Argyll has tended to overshadow a later movement across the North Channel – that of a migration of Cruthin to Galloway. As Charles Thomas wrote:

> An admirable guide to the early Irish settlement could be constructed from the distribution of certain place-name elements – particularly those relating to simple natural features. [Such names are found in] an intense localized concentration in the double peninsula of the Rhinns of Galloway, opposite Antrim. No special historical sources describe what now looks like another early Irish colony here – possibly of the sixth century. But isolated archaeological finds from Galloway, the spread of a type of early ecclesiastical site (the enclosed developed cemetery) which may be regarded as Irish-inspired, and several minor pointers in the same direction, are mounting to reliable evidence for a separate settlement in this south-western area.[16]

The church at Bangor would have had strong links with this area, indeed a Bangor monk became Abbot of St Ninian's old monastery of Candida Casa at the end of the sixth century. Churches in Galloway were often dedicated to saints popular in Ulster. Chalmers dated the main Cruthnic movements into the Galloway region to the eighth century 'followed by fresh swarms from the Irish hive in the ninth and tenth centuries.'[17]

Such a settlement by Ulster Cruthin may help to explain the references in old texts such as those of Reginald of Durham, Jocelyn of Furness and

Richard of Hexham, to the 'Picts of Galloway'. Such references had troubled some historians, for the Scottish Picts were not believed to have dwelt so far south of the Antonine Wall, erected by the Romans to keep them at bay. However, place-name, linguistic and archaeological evidence indicating the link with Ulster provides an answer to the problem. In Galloway these Cruthin would eventually be called 'Kreenies'.[18]

These settlers had already absorbed the Gaelic while in Ulster, and they were to carry it with them to Scotland, throughout which this new language, over the succeeding centuries, was eventually to spread. The ancient traditions of Ulster which the settlers brought with them remained strong among the ordinary people long after they had disappeared from many parts of Ireland. Evidence of pre-Celtic and Celtic customs also abound throughout the Scottish-Irish 'culture province' and much Ulster Folk material could still be collected in the Highlands and Islands well into the twentieth century.

Because the ancient Irish themselves considered the older inhabitants of Scotland and the Northern part of Ireland to be from the same ethnic stock, it would be fascinating to know just how close that kinship really was. Certainly, many factors lend weight to the probability that it was very close. The geographical proximity of Scotland and Ulster would certainly facilitate the same people establishing themselves on both sides of the North Channel.

Scholars also acknowledge that the older population groups of Europe, if they survived reasonably intact at all under the impact of the 'Indo-European' invasions – of which the Celts were a part – would have done so mainly at the fringes of the Continent, such as Ireland and Scotland. Further, archaeologists now believe that the inhabitants of the 'Highland zone' of the British Isles, which includes both these countries, are primarily of pre-Celtic stock. There are even indications of language similarities: when Saint Columba went to Scotland to try and convert the King of the Picts, he took with him Saint Comgall, the Cruthin abbot of Bangor, and Saint Canice, 'who, being Irish Picts, were the better able to confer with the Picts [of Scotland].'[19]

So, even if the archaeological and historical evidence may not as yet allow us to establish the exact extent of the kinship between the pre-Celtic peoples of Scotland and Ulster, there is at the same time nothing that necessarily contradicts the assertion of the ancient writers themselves that 'the Cruthin of both areas formed one people in remote times.' As Liam de Paor commented:

> The gene pool of the Irish . . . is probably very closely related to the gene pools of highland Britain . . . Within that fringe area, relationships, both cultural and genetic, almost certainly go back to a much more distant time than that uncertain period when Celtic languages and customs came to dominate both Great

Britain and Ireland. Therefore, so far as the physical make-up of the Irish goes
. . . they share these origins with their fellows in the neighbouring parts – the
north and west – of the next door island of Great Britain.[20]

Ireland was to play host to further groups of 'invaders': the Vikings in
795 and then, in 1169, the Anglo-Normans, some of whose adventurers
marched north, gained a strong foothold along the eastern coast and styled
themselves 'Earls of Ulster'. They were soon well integrated into the ethnic
and dynastic feuding which so preoccupied the local inhabitants, allying
with the Ulstermen against the O'Neills.

On 24 June 1314 the Scots, under Robert the Bruce, defeated the English
at the battle of Bannockburn. The natural extension of the victory of
Scottish independence was O'Neill of Tyrone's invitation to Robert offering to make his brother Edward – then Lord of Galloway – King of Ireland.
Robert readily accepted, for the fierce ambition of his brother was a threat
to the King of Scots himself. And so, on 25 May 1315, Edward Bruce landed
at Larne Harbour on the Antrim coast. He was joined by Robert Bisset with
the Scots of Antrim and by Donald O'Neill, son of Brian of Tyrone.

In response to this threat and in spite of his age, Richard, the Red Earl of
Ulster, representing the 'English' cause, assembled his retainers in
Roscommon and marched to Athlone, where he was joined by Felim
O'Connor and the army of Connacht. This 'English' army then marched
into Ulster laying waste the country of the O'Neill. Meanwhile, Bruce had
overrun Down and Louth, and both armies then faced each other across the
troubled waters of the bridgeless Bann. At this point, O'Connor deserted
the Red Earl who was thus forced to retreat and was subsequently defeated
in battle near Ballymena on 10 September 1315.

Following a campaign of devastation, Edward was eventually crowned
King of Ireland on 1 May 1316, in the presence of a large assembly of Irish
and Scottish nobles. He was finally defeated by an 'English' force under
John de Birmingham at Faughart near Dundalk in 1318. Edward was killed
in this battle, and with the death of this cruelly ambitious but exceptionally
brave Lord of Galloway, the Scottish invasion came to an end.

Edward Bruce had brought with him some six thousand Scottish mercenaries, called 'galloglasses', and over the next few centuries the importation by the Irish of a constant stream of these Scots, many of whom were
to remain as settlers, was to have a crucial effect on Irish warfare:

In the military and political history of Ireland the galloglass proved a turning
point. Up to this the Irish, though brave enough, in their light dress were no
match for the heavily armed Normans, but now they found in these Scottish
mercenaries trained and traditional soldiers who could endure the Norman
arrows and repulse their foot, and who before long turned the tide of battle
against them. To them we may attribute much of the resurgence of Gaelic
Ireland in the next three centuries.[21]

Yet even with the aid of the galloglasses, the Gaelic Irish proved unable to stem the relentless English attempt at total conquest, particularly during the reign of Elizabeth I, and in 1607, following the failure of a major rebellion by the Ulster chiefs, many members of the leading Ulster Gaelic families chose voluntary exile in Europe. The ravages of the cruel and bloody war fought by the Elizabethan English against O'Neill left large areas of Ulster virtually uninhabited. In addition, the Crown now controlled the vast territory confiscated following the 'Flight of the Earls'. King James I decided to plant settlers in Ulster, hoping that at the very least it might prove a way of 'civilising' this most rebellious part of Ireland once and for all.

In 1610, Sir Arthur Chichester was to be 'the chief architect of the Plantation in Ulster'.[22] Yet he was not completely happy with his task. He complained that while good English settlers were being sent to the territories now opening up in the new land of America, most of those coming to Ulster were to be Scots. Chichester, who cared little for the Irish, thought no more favourably towards the Scots. 'He had no special affection for Scotsmen, high or low, gentle or simple, and besides he had spent much of his time and ingenuity ever since his coming to Ireland, in the work of repelling and expelling Islesmen and other Northern Scots from the coasts of Ulster.'[23]

Chichester could have saved himself much wasted effort in his attempts to 'repel' such immigrants from across the North Channel if he had realised just how much coming and going there had been between Ulster and Scotland throughout history. As P L Henry pointed out:

> The mould was fixed in ancient times and modern developments continue ancient associations. We need but think of the Pictish Kingdoms in both areas, of the Ulster-Scottish Kingdom of Dalriada from the last quarter of the fifth to the close of the eighth century, of the Scottish Kingdom founded under Gaelic leadership in 842, of Irish relations with the Kingdom of the Hebrides and Argyll from the twelfth century, particularly the immigration of Hebridean soldiers (galloglasses) from the thirteenth to the sixteenth century. There was a constant coming and going between North East Ireland and Western Scotland. The Glens of Antrim were in the hands of Scottish Macdonalds by 1400, and for the next two hundred years Gaelic-speaking Scots came in large numbers. The seventeenth century immigration of a numerous Scots element need not be considered outside the preceding series.[24]

Many of these Scots, particularly those who came from areas which in previous centuries had been populated by immigrants from Ulster, may be justly considered as returning to the home of their ancestors. Thus F J Bigger has written that 'When the Galloway planters came to Ulster they were only returning to their own lands like emigrants returning home again.'[25] However, there was to be one fundamental characteristic which would stamp these new arrivals as different from the local population: the Reformation had swept Scotland and most of the newcomers were Protestants. The Reformation there had brought a social as well as a religious transformation. The development of a strong peasant movement against the feudal lords was expressed politically in democratic ideals, as well as culturally in the form of Presbyterianism. When these Lowland Scots came to Ulster they were determined to leave feudalism behind them.

The new settlers rapidly transformed the Ulster countryside, draining in particular the drumlin country which had stood as a barrier to communication between Ulster and the rest of Ireland since prehistoric times. It is wrong to assume, however, that all the settlers were Protestants, since there were Scottish Catholics as well, some of whom were ultimately of English origin. Thus a letter written by the Bishop of Derry to the Lord Chancellor in the year 1692 says: 'Sir George Hamilton since he got part of the Earl of Abercorn's grant of the Barony of Strabane has done his best to plant Popery there, and has brought over priests and Jesuits from Scotland.' It further laments that 'all the Hamilton lands are now in the hands of Papists.' A Perceval-Maxwell has confirmed that, since both Abercorn's and Sir Claud Hamilton's children were converted to Roman Catholicism through Sir George's influence, within a generation one of the most successful parts of the Scottish Plantation was led by Roman Catholics.

The new Scots settlers differed from the English in language on two counts. Firstly there was a significant group who spoke Gaelic and it seems that Scottish Gaelic speakers were intelligible to the Irish at this period. Indeed, the first book ever to be printed in Irish Gaelic was a translation of the Calvinist *Book of Common Order*, commonly called John Knox's Liturgy, published in Edinburgh in 1567 for the use of Presbyterians. Secondly, the language of the others was not the standard English of today, but Lallans, which is derived from the Central Scots language, known in Scotland as 'Inglis'. Lallans is still spoken in the north-east of Ulster and in Donegal, where contact with Scotland through settlement and commerce has been close. The Scottish speech is in some ways an older form of the English language grouping than standard English. Church and state have been just as antagonistic to Lallans as they have been to Gaelic itself, leading to as great a contraction of the Scots-speaking districts as the Gaelic-speaking areas of Ulster.

Ussher's *Discourse of the Religion anciently professed by the Irish* (London, 1631) also shows that many Protestants in the seventeenth century felt that several important points of doctrine and discipline in the early Irish church were closer to their own religious views than those of contemporary Roman Catholicism. These sentiments continued to be expressed by prominent Protestants down to modern times, notably by the Presbyterian historian James Seaton Reid in his *History of the Presbyterian Church in Ireland* (1833) and by the Gaelic scholar Nigel Mac Neill in his *Literature of the*

Highlanders (1892). Mac Neill described the early Irish church as 'the primitive Free Church'. For him there was no doubt that:

> The Gaels of Ireland and Scotland were the same people, having the same language and music; and all the elements of civilisation about them were the common property of both. At the same time there are evidences that the Gaels of the North of Ireland stood in closer relationship to those of Scotland than those in the South of Ireland. And this holds true even to this very day.

However, although the plantation never proved to be the radical transformation the Crown might have originally intended, those Irish who were dispossessed had sufficient cause to harbour a deep-seated resentment. In 1641, with civil unrest in England between Parliamentarians and Royalists, an opportunity was offered to the Catholic Irish to redress the balance, and open rebellion was declared.

It was the declared policy of the rebels at the beginning of the uprising that the Scottish Presbyterians should be left alone because of their 'Gaelic' origins. Thus Colonel Audeley Mervyn, in a report presented to the House of Commons in June, 1642, stated that: 'In the infancy of the Rebellion the rebels made open proclamations, upon pain of death, that no Scotchman should be stirred in body, goods or lands, and that they should to this purpose write over the lyntels of their doors that they were Scotchmen, and so destruction might pass over their families.'

Furthermore, he related that he had read a letter, 'sent by two of the rebels, titulary colonels, Colonel Nugent and Colonel O'Gallagher . . . which was directed to, "Our honourable friends, the gentlemen of the never conquered Scotch nation".' However, the conflict quickly became a sectarian one, and the distinction between the Scottish and English Protestant settlers was not maintained.

The rebels, despite forming themselves into a Catholic Confederacy, were disunited in their tactics and objectives, and loyalties on all sides were further complicated by the outbreak of Civil War in England between King and Parliament. As if this was not enough, by beheading the king in 1649 the Puritan government in England outraged and alienated their former Presbyterian allies in Scotland. These Presbyterians had entered into a 'Solemn League and Covenant' to protect their religion not so much against Catholicism as against the impositions demanded of them by the English High Church, and whatever political and religious grievances the 'Covenanters' may have harboured against Charles as King of England, he was also King of Scots, and more importantly, a Stuart. The Stuart (Stewart) family, descended from the Old British (Brêton) nobility, had in the main occupied the ancient throne of the Scots for upwards of three hundred years.

In August 1649, with Irish resistance already on the wane, Oliver Cromwell landed in Dublin with the intention of restoring this 'Bleeding Nation of Ireland to its former happiness and tranquillity.' However, little of this 'happiness and tranquillity' was to be engendered by his methods: his campaign was exactly what he intended it to be – quick, cruel and effective. When Cromwell, the Lord Lieutenant and General for the Parliament of England, left Ireland on 26 May 1650, he was confident that his deputies would soon be able to finish the war and that the Gaelic aristocracy was doomed, its caste system of social order destroyed for all time. Now Cromwell and his New Model Army could turn their attention to subduing his new adversaries, the Presbyterian Covenanters of Scotland.

Cromwell's designs for the conquered Ireland were embodied in an Act of Settlement passed in August 1652 by the 'Long Parliament' in England. This provided for an extensive forfeiture of land in Ulster, Leinster and Munster, ten counties of which were set aside to remunerate the Parliamentary soldiers and those who had contributed funds to the war effort. Catholic priests were transported to the West Indies. The Episcopalians also suffered, as did the Presbyterians of Antrim and Down, for it was decided that they should be transported south, away from the Scottish mainland and continued support from Ayrshire (Carrick) and Galloway. Cromwell indeed drove all the Anglican bishops out of Ireland and every Presbyterian minister with the exception of five.

In April 1653 Cromwell dismissed the Rump Parliament and ruled as Lord Protector, and a change of policy towards the leading Ulster Scots meant that their transportation south was not carried into effect. Neither was the subsequent settlement of Ireland by Cromwellian soldiers a success, for not only did they need the Irish tenants, but, despite strict attempts to prevent them, they inter-married with the Catholic Irish and within a generation many of them would become Catholics and fight for the Jacobite cause.

In 1645 Cromwell dispatched his son, Henry, to be ruler of Ireland and under his firm but mild government an increase in liberty was granted to Catholic, Presbyterian and Episcopalian alike, and Ireland began to prosper again. During the remaining years of the Protectorate, the ministers of the devout Covenanting sect gained a tremendous hold over the people of Galloway and Ayrshire. This was to have a profound influence on following events. Ministers were allowed to return to Ulster. An Irish State paper of 1660 states that 'there are 40,000 Irish and 80,000 Scots in Ulster ready to bear arms, and not above 5,000 English in the whole province besides the army.'

Following the death of Cromwell there was a year of turmoil, brought to a close by the restoration of the monarchy in 1660. Charles II's first act was to restore the Episcopalian Church in the Three Kingdoms and in 1661 an Act of Conformity was passed which required every minister who officiated in a parish church to conform to the Episcopalian Church and the Prayer Book. 'Nonconformist' ministers were ejected from their churches, and the Parliament of 1662 confirmed the return of prelacy. Throughout most of Scotland the ministers submitted, but not in Galloway, where the people resisted and government troops were sent to occupy and terrorise the whole area. Courts of High Commission were reintroduced and hundreds of Covenanters were fined, imprisoned, tortured or deported to the Colonies. Eventually this could no longer be borne, and on 13 November 1666 the 'Pentland Rising' was initiated at Dalry. Eight days later a Covenanter force of about a thousand men assembled at the Brig O'Doon near Ayr and marched on Edinburgh. On 28 November, at Rullion Green at the foot of the Pentland hills, they were routed and many fled to Ulster and Holland. Following the Rising, the persecution of Galloway was increased under Sir William Bannatyne, whose followers' murders, rapes and robberies were so numerous that the Government itself became sickened. In 1669 the Act of Indulgence was proffered to the Gallowegians, but it was not enough for them and only four ministers in the whole of Galloway subscribed to it.

In Ulster, on the other hand, the Presbyterians had learnt to live with the prelacy as they had done before, and because of this, Charles II was so well disposed towards them that he granted to the Ulster ministers a Regium Donum, or Royal Bounty. So for the 12 years following 1670, there was nothing that could remotely be described as persecution in Ulster. It was this difference between the two regions which resulted in an influx from Galloway of many of her poverty-stricken citizens.

On 13 August 1670, the Scottish Government passed the notorious 'Black Act' which made field preaching an offence punishable by death. To this barbarous legislation the increasingly impoverished Hill Folk of Galloway uttered a defiance whose fire the Government attempted to extinguish in blood. In 1678 the arrival of the Highland Host under James Graham of Claverhouse marked the beginning of a grim final decade of persecution in Galloway. These Highlanders were 'authorised to take free quarter, to seize all horses for carrying their sick men, ammunition and other provisions and are indemnified against all pursuits, civil and criminal, for anything they do whether killing, wounding, apprehending, or imprisoning such as shall make opposition to authority.'

When the Highlanders returned to their homes at seedtime, as was the custom of such Gaelic raiding parties, their place was taken by English dragoons under their own officers, who gave orders to shoot on sight. On Sunday 1 June 1679, Claverhouse and his troops attacked a field meeting or conventicle at Drumclog, but were defeated by the Covenanters. On 22 June, however, a badly-led army of Covenanters was overcome at Bothwell Bridge. Following this, a merciless persecution of Galloway was initiated. A Test Act was passed in August 1681 which obliged them to accept the complete authority of the King in all matters civil and ecclesiastical and to renounce Presbyterianism. Courts were set up to enforce this, and the innocent, suspected and guilty alike were subjected to extreme torture and then either imprisoned on the Bass Rock or in Blackness Castle. Many others were transported to the colonies to be sold as slaves.

In October 1684 James Renwick assumed the leadership of the Covenanters and published his 'Apologetical Declaration' against the king and his ministers. The Privy Council responded with an Act which stated: 'The Lords of his majesty's Privy Council do hereby ordain any person who owns, or will not disown, the late treasonable document (the Apologetical Declaration) whether they have arms or not, to be immediately put to death.'

This opened the way for summary execution without trial, and the following period, covering the autumn of 1684 and the whole of 1685 became known as the 'Killing Times'. The growing prosperity and relative tolerance of Ulster during this period attracted not only many of the impoverished Galloway people, but also Puritans, Quakers and other Dissenters, mainly from the northern counties of England and especially from Yorkshire and Durham.

On 6 February 1685, Charles II of England died. When his brother James ascended the throne the inhabitants of the growing town of Belfast (population around 2,000) sent a congratulatory address to the new king. But while 'government in the last years of Charles II had been based upon a close understanding between the Court on the one hand and the High Church and Tory Party on the other',[26] James was an avowed Roman Catholic who was determined to adopt rapid methods of Romanizing the country.

The fears of Protestants in Ireland were first engendered by the recall of Ormonde, the Lord Lieutenant, whose Protestant sympathies were not in accord with James's design for the island. According to Lord Macaulay, James also 'obtained from the obsequious estates of Scotland, as the surest pledge of their loyalty, the most sanguinary law that has ever in our island been enacted against Protestant Nonconformists.'[27] With this law and the dragoons of Claverhouse he wasted and oppressed Galloway still more, the atrocities culminating in the foul murder of the Wigton Martyrs, Margaret Maclachan and Margaret Wilson in May 1685. In England itself, before James could proceed with implementing any of his designs, a rebellion was raised by the Duke of Monmouth, natural son of Charles II and a claimant to the throne. Among the radical exiles in Holland who financed his expedition was the great philosopher John Locke. However, this ill-fated rebellion was crushed at the Battle of Sedgemoor on 15 July 1685.

Although thus far triumphant, James's Catholic Design was ironically thwarted by anti-Protestant legislation enforced by his cousin Louis XIV of France. The Revocation of the Edict of Nantes suppressed all the privileges granted by Henry IV and Louis XII to the Huguenots, inhibited the exercise of the Protestant religion, enjoined the banishment of all its ministers within 15 days, held out rewards for converts and prohibited keeping schools, or bringing up children, in any but the Catholic religion. Dragoons were sent into Languedoc, Dauphine and Provence to enforce the decree, and it has been estimated that some half-million Huguenots left France as a result. They migrated mostly to the British Isles, Holland and Germany, and brought with them their arts, industry and resentment. Their most persistent memories were the wholesale massacre of Huguenots on St Bartholomew's Day, 24 August 1572, by order of the Queen Mother, Catherine de'Medici, and the Siege of La Rochelle, 1628, where out of a population of 25,000, at least 10,000 died rather than surrender to the Catholic army under Cardinal Richelieu. This flood of persecuted Protestants into England made James's Romanizing intentions well-nigh impossible to implement.

Loyalty to James in England eventually collapsed and he fled the country in 1688, to be succeeded as King of England by his Protestant son-in-law and nephew, William of Orange. In Ireland, Presbyterians in Ulster, fearful of a repeat of the massacres of 1641, thwarted James's plans by refusing entry to his troops into Derry and Enniskillen, forcing him to commence the Siege of Derry which lasted a total of 105 days, the longest in British history, and in which one third of the city's 30,000 inhabitants died of injuries, famine and disease.

Finally, on 14 June 1690, King William himself landed at Carrickfergus, and at Loughbrickland, County Down, he reviewed an army composed of Protestants from all over Europe: Dutch, Danes, French, Germans, English, Scots, Irish, Swiss, Italians, Norwegians and Poles. His army also included an élite unit, the Dutch Blue Guards, who were Catholics. The European dimension was to be completed by James's Jacobite force of Irish, French, English, Germans and Dutch. On 1 July (corresponding to 12 July in modern calendars) the two armies met at the River Boyne where William defeated James's troops. When news reached Pope Alexander VIII, who was delighted at what was in effect a French defeat, he ordered celebratory torchlight processions in Rome, and *Te Deums* were sung in the Catholic cathedrals of Austria and Spain. The final defeat of the Jacobite cause followed the surrender of Limerick on 3 October 1691, and the 'Glorious Revolution' was complete.

The Protestants of Ulster had defended Derry and Enniskillen. They had saved Ireland for the British Crown. Yet all this passed for nothing. The English Church was Episcopalian and the 'Protestant Ascendancy' which now established itself in Ireland was thus actually an Episcopalian Anglo-Irish one. Having reduced the rebellious Catholics by the harsh Penal Laws under William which were based on the French Catholic legislation against Protestants, the High Church Party had gained in strength and by the reign of Queen Anne (1702–14) were pressing for complete conformity.

In 1704, the Test Act was passed which required all office holders in Ireland to take the sacrament of the Anglican Church. Although ostensibly to further discourage Catholicism, its real object was to place the Presbyterians on the same plane of impotence. Presbyterian ministers had now no official standing and marriages performed by them were null and void. To the High Churchmen they were actually inferior to Catholic priests, who were considered lawfully ordained in the line of apostolic succession. Presbyterians and other Dissenters could not now serve in the army, the militia, the civil service, the municipal corporations, the teaching profession or the commission of the peace. At Belfast, the entire corporation was expelled, and Londonderry lost ten of its 12 aldermen.

Added to this were severe economic pressures. The Woollen Act of 1699 had forbidden the export of Irish wool, making sheep rearing unprofitable, and absentee English landlords steadily increased their rents. Thus began around 1717 the great migration from Ulster to America.

An earlier emigrant to America was Francis Mackemie, born of Scottish parents near Ramelton, County Donegal. He settled in Eastern Virginia and in 1706 was one of the most prominent members of the first Presbytery founded in America. Mackemie is justly considered to be the founding father of the Presbyterian Church in America, which was well organised to receive the new Ulster immigrants. The stream of emigrant Ulster Presbyterians became a flood, and by the time America declared for Independence, a quarter of a million Ulster men and women had settled there and were estimated to have comprised 15 per cent of the population. Because of their Lowland Scots ancestry, they became known in America as the 'Scotch-Irish' – although 'Scots-Irish' is nowadays the preferred spelling. To both Ulster and America also came many people from the Southern Highlands, mostly members of the Episcopal Church of Scotland and Jacobites. More followed after the Jacobite Rebellions of 1715 and 1745.

These Scots-Irish had a profound impact on their new country of domicile:

> It can be said that the Scotch-Irish made three contributions to colonial America: they settled the frontier, they founded the Kirk, and they built the schools. They, more than any other group, created the first western frontier. To the Ulster Scots must largely go the credit of being the first pioneers west of the Appalachians and of opening the Mississippi Valley.[28]

Two of the best-known of the Scots-Irish pioneers immortalised in frontier history were Jim Bowie and Davy Crockett, who both fell at the Alamo in 1836.

The independent streak of the Scots-Irish, coupled with their hatred of aristocratic landlordism, had far-reaching consequences in that they were to be foremost in the Revolutionary War against Britain. Indeed, the first armed clash occurred in 1771 when Scots-Irish settlers fought British forces on the Alamance River, North Carolina. On 20 May 1775 they were the most prominent signatories of the Mecklenburg Declaration of Independence drawn up in Charlotte, North Carolina. They subsequently supported the Declaration of Independence passed by the Continental Congress on 4 July 1776 and comprised the flower and backbone of Washington's army. A German captain who fought alongside the British redcoats was quite explicit: 'Call this war by whatever name you may, only call it not an American rebellion; it is nothing more or less than a Scotch-Irish Presbyterian rebellion.' The Pennsylvania Line, the famous force of regular troops, was of primarily Ulster descent, and Washington said: 'If defeated everywhere else I will make my last stand for liberty among the Scotch-Irish of my native Virginia.'

The Official Declaration of Independence was handwritten by Charles Thompson from Maghera, printed by John Dunlop from Strabane, given its first public reading by Colonel John Nixon, the son of an Ulsterman, and the Scots-Irish were well represented among the signatories. Ten United States Presidents have been of direct Ulster descent: Andrew Jackson, James Knox Polk, James Buchanan, Andrew Johnson, Ulysses S Grant, Chester Alan Arthur, Grover Cleveland, Benjamin Harrison, William McKinley and Woodrow Wilson.

One direct influence of the radical thinking that was now being formu- lated in the 'New World' was the work of the great Ulster philosopher Francis Hutcheson, son of an Armagh Presbyterian minister, who was born probably at Drumalig, County Down, in 1694. He studied for the church at Glasgow from 1710-1716, but then started a private academy in Dublin. In 1729 he was appointed professor of Moral Philosophy at Glasgow, where he died in 1746. His most important work is *A Sense of Moral Philosophy*. Hutcheson was quite explicit about the right of resistance by the people in the event of a betrayal of trust by a government. He expounded the doc- trine of religious toleration and he deeply admired the tradition of armed militias for the protection of civil liberties. The principles he espoused found their way via American revolutionary thinkers into the Declaration of Independence and are embodied in the American Constitution. Hutcheson's influence on Thomas Jefferson, John Adams and others is explored in M White's *Philosophy of the American Revolution* and G Wills' *Inventing America*. In fact Wills concluded that Hutcheson's influence on Jefferson was stronger than that of John Locke.

The radicalism fostered in America soon found its way back to Ireland, especially among progressive Presbyterians in Belfast, where it proved a potent stimulus to the founding of the Society of United Irishmen, the aim of which was 'to form a brotherhood of affection among Irishmen of every religious persuasion', and whose attempt to create an independent Ireland led to the ill-fated rebellion of 1798.

Although the Scots-Irish, like other ethnic groups, eventually merged into the American nation, the Ulster speech itself was to stay alive in the hill country of Appalachia and beyond, where Scots-Irish traditional music may still be heard. Among the earliest songs were ballads of King William of Orange, so those who sung them became known as Billy-boys of the hill country, or 'hillbillies'. Rooted deep in the traditions of the British Isles peasantry, the fiddle had become an instrument of major importance in the development of Irish, Scottish and Welsh jigs, reels and hornpipes. As with folk custom in general, traditional music themes reinforced the ancient cultural divide between North and West Britain and Ireland, and South and East Britain. Transposed to America, the hoe-down fiddle reached the peak of its development in the Southern states. Musicologist W H Williams has written:

> Ireland's initial impact upon American music came predominantly from Ulster
> . . . Whatever their influence in terms of cabin and barn styles, field layout, town planning, and so on, it seems likely that the greatest and most lasting contribution of the Scotch-Irish was music. And however one may define their particular religious and ethnic identity, musically they should be considered Ulstermen, for they brought with them the mixture of Scottish and Irish tunes which is still characteristic of large parts of Northern Ireland. When the great English folklorist Cecil Sharp went into the Appalachians to rediscover 'English' folk song, he was in fact often dealing with people of Ulster descent. Wherever they settled in large numbers and remained in relative isolation, balladry has been found 'live and in a healthy condition'.[29]

As the authors of *The Story of English* tell us:

> The Scots-Irish brought with them a rich oral culture; aphorisms, proverbs, superstitions and an ability to turn a striking phrase – *mad as a meat axe, dead as a hammer, so drunk he couldn't hit a wall with a handful of beans*. It was the frontiersmen who first spoke of someone with *an axe to grind* or someone who *sat on the fence* when he should perhaps *go the whole hog*. Their rhymes and ditties came from the traditions of Scotland and Ireland. Their ballads, such as *Edward*, tell the stories of their ancestors, and the tunes of the Scottish Lowland ballads of the sixteenth and seventeenth centuries have been an important influence in the making of American country music. Today the ballads of the Scots-Irish . . . are imitated and reproduced from Arkansas to Alberta, by singers like Dolly Parton and Kenny Rogers who have internationalised a style that was once confined to the hills.[30]

The American Civil War of 1861–65 was to produce a galaxy of military leaders on both sides who had Ulster-Scots and Irish lineage. Names like

Ulysses Simpson Grant, Commander-in-Chief of the Union Army; General Philip Henry Sheridan, the cavalry commander who outmanoeuvred Confederate Commander-in-Chief Robert E Lee and forced him to surrender at Appomattox; General George B McClelland, the soldier of greatest reputation in the North for a considerable part of the war; Thomas 'Stonewall' Jackson, the outstanding Confederate General and the only man victorious against him, General James Shields.

Robert E Lee was once asked: 'what race makes the best soldiers?' To which the General answered: 'The Scotch who came to this country by way of Ireland . . . Because they have all the dash of the Irish in taking a position, and all the stubbornness of the Scotch in holding it.'

In the nineteenth century America was to receive yet another flood of humanity from Ireland, in the aftermath of one of the most traumatic events in Irish history – the failure of the staple potato crop and the resultant Great Famine of 1845–49. A million of the starving and disease-ridden population perished and an equal number took part in the massive emigration which followed, many not getting beyond Glasgow and Liverpool. The total demoralisation engendered by the famine profoundly affected the social, economic and ultimately the political history of Ireland. The emotional shock of the tragedy was followed both by a marked resurgence of Roman Catholicism and an upsurge in Nationalist sentiment. The political outcome of the amalgamation of these two forces was the unfortunate abandonment of the old Belfast idea of a common Irish identity in favour of Daniel O'Connell's Catholic nation. As Estyn Evans wrote:

> For the best part of a century the Irish people had been steadily losing their identity in losing their native language and heritage, and they were to find a new identity in the Catholic faith, which became a substitute symbolic language. The old idea that there was a common Irish identity indifferent to religious belief was thus superseded by the concept that Catholicism was the essence of Irishness.[31]

By the middle of the nineteenth century, writers of Romantic fiction and Irish Nationalist cultural propaganda had also begun to promote the notion of an ideal Celtic past and this too became incorporated into an energetic Catholic Gaelic Nationalism. The Northern Protestants however, had long fostered a loyalty to their British inheritance, a development due in large part to the industrial development of Ulster which linked it directly with the industrial interests of mainland Britain. In response to the rise of militant Irish Nationalism which seemed so exclusively Catholic, the Orange Order was able to expand to become the mass movement of Unionism and the voice of organised Protestantism. In Ulster the two communities, who in reality had so much in common, now viewed each other with ever-increasing suspicion and antagonism.

In the decades following the partition of Ireland in 1921, the intellectual and academic élites on both sides of the border displayed little desire to help the populace explore the richness and diversity of their common heritage, and the simplistic dichotomies of Planter/Gael and Irish/'Brit' were allowed to flourish almost without critique. Academic obsession with the 'Celts' continued to permeate scholarship to such an extent as to obviate rational discussion on the subject, especially with regard to Ireland's pre-Celtic past. This tunnel vision, coupled with and mirrored by a similar English Nationalist approach in Britain, stifled any real appreciation of the unique inter-relationships between all the peoples of the two islands. But, as Bob Quinn wrote, in regard to the 'Celtic' ethos with which much of Irish Nationalism was imbued: 'The people must develop the confidence to dismantle the unitary myth that has served its honourable purpose and replace it with the diverse richness that lies beneath.'[32]

A proper awareness of this diversity could do much to overcome the antagonisms which have beset the peoples of Britain and Ireland – and especially the peoples within the North of Ireland – for far too long. And what better place to start than with a proper exploration of the ancient and ever-continuous link between the peoples of Ireland and Scotland, a heritage which can never be the preserve of either Catholic or Protestant, Williamite or Jacobite, Celt or non-Celt, but which by right belongs to them all, and is the most vivid reminder of the essential unity which binds together the peoples of the two islands?

2

Belfast: Walking the Shankill

SARAH NELSON

This is a personal account, with no academic pretensions, about beginnings and endings, concerning my experience and feelings when I arrived in Belfast in 1972 and when I left in 1978.

PART I

I first came from Scotland to Belfast as a raw 21-year-old, to take up a job as an unqualified social worker. I often thought afterwards that Belfast Welfare Department (West) must have found it extremely hard to recruit staff during the turmoil of 1971 if they could accept an application from someone so unprepared for adult life, for Ulster or for social work. Kinder, more tolerant clients offered help and advice: 'Oh, Miss Nelson,' pleaded one young unmarried mother on her doorstep, 'don't you be making the same mistake as me.'

I arrived just after the immense upheavals of internment, when an estimated ten per cent of the city's population had left their homes and social work had been thrust into the front line of emergency aid. The next ten months, before I left to start a Ph.D. thesis, saw a string of momentous events, including a massive escalation of the Provisional IRA bombing campaign; the 'Bloody Sunday' shootings; the birth of the militant Ulster Vanguard and the Ulster Defence Association; the imposition of Direct Rule; a mounting campaign of sectarian killings by Loyalist paramilitaries, and the 'Bloody Friday' IRA bombings.

Oddly, the earliest, and so far as I was concerned, most geographically remote event, Bloody Sunday in Derry, came across as the most shocking and significant at the time because, if you were British, you felt it had been done in your name. It was the revelation of British denial and hypocrisy, the refusal of the authorities to admit how they kept making a mockery of the rule of law, which was to become so familiar and which suddenly knocked off the thick, rose-tinted spectacles. It made you see how and why so many other nations perceive Britain as, above all else, dishonest and perfidious.

My first assignment was to make a pot of custard for 40 people in an old folks' lunch club on the Springfield Road. I was put to work in a cavernous old building (long since demolished) in Townsend Street, which runs directly between Lower Shankill and Lower Falls. We could hardly have been closer to the nerve centre of communal conflict.

The building, which was already condemned, had one of those huge creaking lifts with clanking metal gates and smelt terrible after heavy rain. It had been a mortuary among other things, which gave us some frissons of doubt about the aroma of bad drains. There was a big clothes store in one room and half the smooth-talking crooks in Belfast seemed to home in on it with sob stories. There were extended families of them whose very names evoked in old hands evasive action and groans of recognition. Later we moved to College Street, in the heart of Belfast's commercial centre. Most days there would be one or two big bombs. I lost count of the times we trooped out for bomb scares or I crunched over broken glass as I made for the bus home and heard the familiar rhythmic hammering on hardboard as shattered windows were boarded up. Glaziers were as busy as lawyers then.

Assigned to the fiercely Loyalist Shankill Road, I also worked daily at the heart of a historic working class community just before major redevelopment gradually and inexorably swept away most of its landmarks and its cluttered two-up two-down streets for good. Ever since, my most vivid recollections of its bustling life, pervasive poverty and unassuming hospitality have been those of the senses: bright-painted door jambs crowding in on each other above broken paving stones of faded red, white and blue; cropped-haired children with missing teeth on makeshift lamp-post swings; the piles of old furniture and decayed beams stacked before each Eleventh Night; the sunlight always labouring to filter through layers of dust. Most powerfully evocative is the smell: an ever-present mixture of Jeyes fluid and the sweet, unhealthy scents of damp and dry rot in the mean lodgings jerry-built by factory owners a century earlier.

It was an area where everyone knew each other's business, where many people were related, where strangers like me were slotted into categories bearing labels long since abandoned by officialdom. Puzzled housewives would politely check me out: 'Are you the Welfare, the Assistance or the School Board?' Ever since then, I have been amazed at how poor people appear to tolerate, or feel they have to tolerate, official intrusion into their privacy.

The Shankill was a shock, not because conditions were particularly terrible, nor unemployment especially severe (it was not), but because the average Scottish university student did not think it existed. Of course we'd seen it in TV news-flashes, but we had no real conception of its thousands of inhabitants and none at all beyond the savage images of Burntollet and the burning of Bombay Street. We assumed, from the bits and pieces we gleaned of 'civil rights' that Catholics were subjected to all kinds of oppression for no comprehensible reason and that most Protestants were highly paid middle class or manual workers, living in well-appointed estates.

When you work constantly within a community, especially in a profession such as social work, you quickly have to accept the reality of how people are. You see how complex and diverse a single community can be and how fall-out from internal conflict can be dispersed through the atmosphere. These experiences did not just shape the decision to focus my research on Loyalist politics. They were also to put barriers between people like myself and a number of other researchers and academics in Belfast – both Irish and English – with left-wing views who had little personal experience of Loyalists and sought no further knowledge, seeing them as a unified and reactionary political force. People who did not share these certainties and who were researching within Loyalist communities were either suspected of actively supporting the Loyalist cause, which left them open to malicious rumour and personal risk, or their analysis was considered so flawed that they were not even worth engaging in serious personal discussion or debate. They were non-persons.

One particularly striking thing about the Shankill – and, I am sure, some frontline Catholic communities – at a time of unsurpassed violence during the current Troubles was that although it was meant to be a nerve centre of political and military activity, most people did not feel in control of events; indeed, they felt less and less so: little more than witnesses. Nor did they necessarily take the views that others assumed them to hold. For instance, many local people were clearly shocked, bewildered and personally disturbed as the campaign of sectarian killings gradually unfolded and one hooded body after another was found in alleyways, sometimes having been brutally tortured. Some would reassure themselves with stories being passed around that victim X or Y was definitely an IRA man, while others would state openly that this was no part of what Protestants should be doing. What shook them was no longer being able to recognise which type of Protestants their frontline defenders might be.

Again, when masked and hooded UDA men started strutting around the streets after January 1972 – which supposedly restored wounded pride in areas like the Shankill – many families were overtaken by foreboding rather than relief or triumphalism. They did not know who some of these people were, even on their own streets. They were full of fear when their sons were mixed up in it or might become so, risking injury, death or jail, and felt the young people were slipping even further out of their control.

Most people had very basic human priorities, and accordingly, made human judgments. Unlike people outside the area, they judged known gunmen less on what they did than on the kind of people they already knew them to be. There was a tremendous undercurrent of resentment against the British Army because of the impact upon young girls in the area. At the time, admission to Army discos only cost a few pence and there was no proper check on the age of attenders. Girls of 14 and 15 had become pregnant after quick bouts 'up against the wall', after which the usually married soldiers disappeared and the army stonewalled their pursuit. Sometimes bizarre, almost comic incidents obscured the human distress and exploitation of it all. The 15-year-old daughter of one of my clients had a row of 'scalps' on her mantelpiece – badges from the Royal Scots, the Royal Greenjackets and 'a couple of those Anglicans'.

It is interesting to note that old people seemed the best able to adjust psychologically to the mental and physical upheaval. Many were additionally able to maintain some kind of relationship with Catholics, in places such as lunch clubs and day centres. This was because they had already lived through many outbreaks of communal conflict. Old certainties were re-established, and however depressing this might be, it was part of their lives in Belfast and they drew upon buried resources in order to cope with it.

It seems odd that my most vivid and lasting recollections of the Shankill, from a time of such turmoil and 'keynote' events, are not political ones. What made the most impact upon me were situations which Shankill people shared with countless other communities – my first experience of battered wives and children; a woman who committed suicide soon after threatening to do so; a young girl whose tears dropped silently on to the paper as she signed away her baby for adoption.

In retrospect, it makes sense that political issues never dominated more than one part of people's lives. Nor were political problems necessarily the most intractable. The exception in terms of impact was something that happened to an excellent social worker in our office. She was having a cup of tea in the Abercorn Restaurant on the March day in 1972 when a small IRA bomb caused enormous havoc in a confined space. She had her leg amputated and suffered many internal injuries which kept her in hospital for nearly a year. We had been annoyed when, inexplicably, she had not turned up on the Monday morning, because she was the person who brought the milk for our coffee. I remember this because soon afterwards, when word filtered through in whispers, it seemed such a ludicrously inappropriate thing to feel. There was much subsequent debate about which side was responsible for the Abercorn, and if it had been a mistake. Once, in angry despair, she retorted: 'What does it matter to me?'

The event was shocking, not just because she was a friend and colleague, nor even because it seemed so brutally random and senseless, but because we had been leading a charmed life. We did crazy, simple things as part of our job, like walking about every day in all conditions in the most dangerous areas, and barely thought about it. At one point in 1972 there were four Catholic social workers in the Shankill area. Ballymurphy staff regularly had their cars politely commandeered for 'jobs' and one male worker kept being lifted and interrogated because he looked like Gerry Adams. It seems extraordinary, looking back on it, how people played down the stress and fear and carried on, not only in our profession but in so many others.

There were some fine social workers and assistants in West Belfast, people of strong commitment, some of whom have now left their native land. Catholics and Protestants worked together and I realised later that for some people more everyday effort had to be put into that than into relations with clients. This, however, was not unusual in Ulster. In this confined space were many suppressed tensions and unspoken feelings or resentments, though tensions were least, solidarity highest, among the younger social workers, several of whom were in mixed marriages. Middle class Catholics were now well established at basic grade professional level, barely so as social work assistants or in promoted posts, and I later discovered that some Protestant assistants did not believe Catholic colleagues should be there at all. I was naively dismayed and astonished when a respected principal social worker, who had seemed free of any prejudice at the time, later told me he did not believe there had been any discrimination in Northern Ireland. Now I can recognise him as a common type. Another Protestant, an older, very sensitive woman senior, eventually spoke of her anguish that she had done so little to speak up for the rights of the minority.

Some young receptionists and secretaries stared suspiciously at each other across a yawning gulf. One girl had been burned out of Bombay Street, and each day she angrily returned the verbal abuse of soldiers and told phone callers from England who inquired about Londonderry that the place did not exist. But when a Mass was held for the woman who had been injured in the Abercorn, most people attended, whatever their private feelings about the service.

My experience was that it is very valuable and important for any social or political researcher from Scotland to spend time living and working in Northern Ireland before putting people's behaviour under the lens. I say this not just because it clarifies our two people's complexities and similarities, but because there are some deep-rooted differences in our conception of politics even though Ulster is so close to Scotland geographically and has so many historic ties with it. It takes a long time to identify these differences and even longer to accept them, and many British people never do. It is much less clear to me now whether it was ethical to learn all these lessons by inflicting my inept self upon the recipients and practitioners of social work. Largely because of what both these groups of people taught me, I know I would make a better social worker now, although I recognise that this may seem a convoluted kind of justification. Researchers have not found it easy to admit that their attitudes, too, bore a touch of colonialism. They can only hope for better than they deserve – that their research work will be judged on the basis of its results.

PART II

I left Belfast in 1978, not from lack of friendships or professional achievement, nor lack of 'good crack', but because I had become so depressed with the claustrophobic and continuing political impasse that I could not face living there any more. Most people in the province don't have the luxury of making that choice: it is something that will always set outsiders apart.

Yet I have double standards, being often reluctant to allow local people the freedom of my own decision. It is hard to witness the moving out of so many people of talent, courage and free-ranging minds, not simply to find work but because they have run out of energy to battle on, or cannot squeeze their brains and views into the right shapes, or aren't prepared to see their own children confined in this straitjacket, or even reject their own land in disgust or disillusion. I always have the urge to say: 'If you don't stay, if all that energy and impatience drain away through the door in the wall, what hope will there ever be of lasting change for the better? You must be loyal to the place and the people you come from. How could you turn your back on them?'

Outsiders don't ask the obvious and fairer question, about why individuals should make sacrifices with their own lives. I think you can only display such arrogance when conditions in your own country have not starkly challenged your love for it, and that is the luxury of a minority of people in the world.

The main lesson of Northern Ireland, for me, is that the size of a population bears little relation to the impact of a conflict: in global terms, the suffering hardly registers. About three thousand out of 1.5 million have died in 25 years of unrest. But such figures are meaningless for those who exist there. Ulster is a village. Hardly anyone has not had a friend or relative killed, bereaved, permanently injured, mentally affected, jailed, burned or intimidated from their home, forced to leave Northern Ireland, or driven to violent action. No-one can escape witnessing it. Faces and scenes are stamped indelibly upon your memory.

But the hardest things to bear are not what you might expect. When people you care about are killed, have their legs blown off or have attempts made on their lives, it is certainly shocking, but there is also anger and solidarity or admiration for the stubborn, inspiring way they and their kinfolk react. It is far more destructive, as time passes, to watch so many people distraught because they cannot and may never be able to make sense of it, and because you feel impotent to help or explain.

During the 1970s, a Christian group called Witness for Peace used to display a makeshift public board in the centre of Belfast showing the number of people killed in the Troubles. Each day, the total crept inexorably upwards. Once a year, WFP held a simple, stark service where bereaved people would plant rows of small white crosses in the grass outside Belfast City Hall. They looked like lost souls, staring glassily through us in uncomprehending desolation.

On a late-night train from the Larne ferry to Belfast, I once sat opposite a shaken and exhausted woman who talked compulsively, in a soft West Highland accent. She had travelled all day from Kyle, after receiving a telephone call informing her that her niece had been blown up in Belfast. This clever young woman who she described animatedly, with love and pride, and the young man who had died with her, were the educated children of two respectable Catholic families. What the aunt did not know was that they had been blown to pieces in the act of preparing an IRA bomb. The families' baffled rage and grief made the newspapers, because they refused to allow an IRA funeral or tribute, and had known nothing of the course their children's idealism had led them to take. The aunt kept asking me how such a good girl could have lost her life. I knew that in a few hours she would learn the truth, and that it would be far more shocking and disorientating than the fact of her niece's death.

People who opt openly for political or military action take their chance. They and their families have an ideology and support system to sustain them and explain the sacrifice, however inadequate these may feel at the time. But the everyday impact upon people in militant areas is great beyond words. I remember the forlorn knots of women and children standing along the Shankill, faces pinched by poverty and the January winds, watching for their bus to the jail as they would do year upon year, clutching parcels of comforts for their menfolk which they could not really afford.

Nor is it always easy to come to terms with the fate met by activists. Staunch Republicans Miriam and Jim Daly, well-known lecturers at Queen's University, Belfast, held their principles with utter conviction. They had many critics and made many enemies: they sometimes made accusations against others which put those people at genuine risk. You spoke with them across a great gulf, often frustrated, enraged or bemused, bouncing off the wall of their obstinate sincerity. The last time I spoke to Miriam – a friendly next-door neighbour in the hall of residence at an academic conference – she expounded in impassioned detail on how Irishness was passed through the female line. Soon afterwards, she was assassinated by a UDA squad, who kept her tied up for hours in expectation of death as they waited in vain for her husband to come home.

No-one could have wished such a death on anybody. Those who knew her and could imagine her courage could not fail to be haunted by the mental sadism of her killing, nor to be struck by the irony of it.

For Miriam Daly's thoughts and vitriol had been directed with such search-light intensity upon Britain, and not upon the Loyalists who finally picked her out. Despite her political views, I never heard her pass an un-charitable comment on the Loyalist people: sometimes it almost seemed as if they were incidental. Of course, they are not. In Milltown Cemetery, the Irish National Liberation Army gave her a memorial and openly named her as a 'volunteer'. She would have been greatly pleased by these gestures.

Because the scale of violence and upheaval in Northern Ireland is so small and intermittent in international terms, it may seem feeble to admit that it can leave permanent scars, or that you deal with some memories by running away from them. But I think that has been many people's experi-ence. 'Trigger' events can tear off the bandages and in an instant shoot you back 20 years. It feels absurd to be so panic-stricken and mentally disturbed by an innocent celebration such as the fireworks display at the end of each annual Edinburgh Festival. There is such a diversity of noise. It is just the same combination we heard over and over again, with such casual familiarity, in the early 1970s.

However, physical violence and its after-effects are not even the main problems involved in facing up to this conflict. Far worse horrors and pri-vations can be survived, mentally and physically, if there is some hope of justice and a better life for significant numbers of oppressed people.

Twenty years ago there was a sense of hope, amidst the bombs, that this often devastating upheaval might give birth to some kind of radical and permanent political change. By 1978, only a few years later, when trendy restaurants were almost turning Belfast's university area into bright, cos-mopolitan normality and 'acceptable levels of violence' allowed many people to put nerve-wracking obsessions on the back burner, there seemed only the prospect of more of the same. Direct rule *ad infinitum,* involvement which so often brought out the worst in the British authorities, gross breaches of civil liberties, hypocritical denials of same, patronising arro-gance, reactive policy. What was there but a destructive political stalemate and the apparent prospect of unending military conflict?

When your mouth dries up with fear as you are trapped in a bus amid close gunfire, or when the Dublin train, as always, slows to a crawl in the open fields between Newry and Dundalk, you think: is it worth being killed or maimed for any of this? If you really cannot believe that it is worth it, then one day you just leave. Feelings like this will come across as arro-gant, politically shallow or self-indulgent to the minority of the passion-ately committed on both sides of the sectarian divide. Not least because on the whole, and however much their detractors deny it, it is they and their families who have suffered the most; and because none of us can categori-cally say we would not have become alienated and embittered ourselves, nor convinced of the necessity for violent action, had we been subject to anything like the same social conditions experienced by these, the most marginalised sections of society.

But you can respect such commitment and the political courage and imagination of thousands of Ulster people and still ask what greater goal in this particular conflict has really justified such suffering and misery. It is very hard to see the answer, even if you spend 20 years searching for it in either Loyalist or Provisional Republican ideology. Nor has either side yet managed to convince a majority even of its own community that the human goal is inspirational or noble enough to justify 70 or 700 years of violent struggle.

It is even more depressing to realise, through speaking to militant activists on both sides, how little thought has gone into the working out of their goals, how poorly the human obstacles have been understood, how rarely they have had the self-belief even to consider taking and exercising political power for themselves. Perhaps it is naive to believe that people who demand so many sacrifices from themselves, their families and communities as well as from their enemies, will at least do so with some coherent, realistic and achievable plan in mind. But it is a belief which many people there need to cling to, if any sense is to be made of the struggle.

If you have a choice between staying or leaving, I think much of the impetus to spend the rest of your life elsewhere comes from a sense of claustrophobia and gradual suffocation, the belief that the dreary spires of Fermanagh and Tyrone will endure, however many empires fall in the world beyond. If you cross from Scotland by plane, you look down at the fields of Ayrshire, a tiny strip of water and identical fields in Antrim. Yet in that space, the world has changed and the knowledge comes with a sinking heart. It is a powerful feeling of people's minds being turned inwards obsessively upon one another in a small stranded place, where voices are saying the same predictable things from one decade to the next. Yet it is easy to forget that Ulster has many parallels throughout the world, and indeed prepares you little enough for the intensity of visiting a land like Israel.

The province comprises so many outwardly respectable people, unshakeable in their Christian bigotry, meticulous in keeping up appearances, obstinate in their refusal to recognise any connection between their own beliefs and the actions of militants on the streets or in the jails. It is a place where those who fight impartially for civil liberties without double standards of sectarian or class bias, are rare. It is a place where native socialists battle for a lifetime and wear themselves out looking for acceptance, decent support and small piecemeal achievement; where children are still segregated not just by religion, but by class, 'ability' and gender; where authority demands so much blind respect in family, school, church, club and lodge and where people who question find merely that they shock.

The situation can be overwhelming for natives and outsiders alike, for

all those who fail the test of stamina and commitment. That seems a demor-
alising message to give to those who battle on. It ignores real changes won
by those who refuse to stop pushing with their hands at such great inert
blocks of stone, not least the determined people who have finally realised
their dream of schools for children of both religions and none. All you can
say is that it is an explanation, not a justification made with any sense of
pride, and that people who have shifted boulders should never have had
to take on the whole effort by themselves, with so little support from powerful forces beyond their own shores. For one of the great unfairnesses of
Ulster is that local people take the rap for other people's conduct and lack
of political courage. Such has been the constant British 'nanny' propaganda
about holding the ring between warring tribes, about 'the people of
Northern Ireland having to sort this out for themselves' before a lasting settlement is possible, that simple truths have been obscured from many
people throughout the international community. In reality, the people of
this small province have very little power to effect major or lasting change
by their own efforts, because they and their land are so profoundly dependent, both politically and economically, upon Britain and wider international systems.

To shift the logjam, change the balance of power between communities,
make major economic injections that ensure a consistently larger cake to
share, enforce basic civil liberties laws: all this would need a radical and
far-reaching package of political initiatives by Britain, in agreement with
the Irish Republic, and probably backed by international sanctions and
guarantees. The political will and motivation to do that may well be absent
for at least another 25 years, if not a great deal longer.

Putting the lid on the pot, taking initiatives round the edges, however
worthwhile they may be, has a heavy cost even if it avoids the gamble that
violence might escalate for a while beyond the 'acceptable' level. For it sus-
tains and freezes not just political, social and economic injustices, but attitudes as well. It is these attitudes which depress or suffocate many natives
and outsiders alike, to such an extent that they end up so often venting their
impatience and frustration on the people around them, instead of on those
with the main power and influence. Many of the issues people agonise and
battle over are the same as they were 300 years ago, because in terms of the
reality and balance of political or economic power, so little has changed
since then.

It feels important to be honest – with oneself, for the first time, and with
others – about the 'down' side of living and working in Northern Ireland.
But it means the result gives an unfair and one-sided picture of the reality
of experience. It was often rewarding and exciting to live in Ulster, but it
was also a privilege because of at least two lessons you learned from its
people. It is difficult to think of two more fundamental or crucial lessons
for anyone to learn.

The first is that human beings are very complex and cannot be divided simplistically into good and bad, guilty and innocent, psychopathic and normal. The most apparently inflexible people are capable of profound personal change. Such a view is very disturbing to many people, wherever they live, and they refuse to acccept it. But surely such acceptance is essential if societies are to behave in a civilised way towards anyone they see as stigmatised, deviant or different from themselves.

Northern Ireland turns your most basic assumptions upside down. You meet a few psychopaths; many sane, idealistic and courageous people who kill each other; respectable, law-abiding people of savage and racist views; bigots of great personal kindness; impeccable liberals who lack conscience and humanity. The most unlikely people go through dramatic personal and political transformation. Afterwards, you never again make quick character judgements, and that feels like beginning to grow up.

The second lesson I learned in the province is that bitter conflicts produce extremes of heroism and brutality. They bring out the worst and the best in those who are caught up in them. You may never be able to emulate inspiring people but you will always remember the example they set. In particular, the extraordinary courage and energy of some people who not merely survived long prison sentences with unquenchable spirit, but sustained and revived many people around them. Afterwards, you do think twice before lying down for dead at the first hurdle.

3

Sporting Symbols, Sporting Identities: Soccer and Intergroup Conflict in Scotland and Northern Ireland

GERRY P T FINN

In Northern Ireland (and Ireland in general), sport is often proclaimed as being above politics and communal conflict. It has been demonstrated[1] that this claim needs substantial revision, but many still hope that sporting contact will help bring the two different ethno-political communities[2] together. By contrast, football in Scotland, especially matches involving Celtic and Rangers, is believed by some to keep people apart, or by others to provide a cathartic outlet, which restricts intergroup conflict to the football ground, and allows Catholic and Protestant Scots to come together outside.[3] This essay will explore the interplay between soccer and intergroup conflict in Ireland, primarily Northern Ireland, and in Scotland.

The English view of sport as a means of cultural socialisation was countered in Ireland by the establishment of the Gaelic Athletic Association (GAA). The founder of the GAA, Michael Cusack, had initially been a strong supporter of cricket, rugby and athletics. He had hoped that sport could unite the various communities in Ireland. Cusack worked for a more democratic athletics. Meetings that incorporated traditional Irish sports would lead to an even greater involvement of the mass of the Irish people. Cusack, a curious sort of radical, rapidly became disillusioned by the socially exclusive, imperialist nature of Anglicised sports. The London-based Amateur Athletics Association (AAA) refused to allow meetings under its auspices to include Irish events. Any athletes that took part in these faced suspension by the AAA. Cusack discovered that the vast majority of sporting clubs and their members, mostly Protestant and Unionist, were unsympathetic to widening their membership and their activities. An important exception was the Caledonian Society of Ireland. Organised by expatriate Scots, some of its members saw Scots and Irish as sharing a common Celtic identity and heritage with identifiable similarities in traditional Irish and Scottish sports.[4] Faced by the dominant Anglo-centrism of sport in Ireland, Cusack eventually concluded that it was necessary to establish an Irish governing body that would control specifically Irish sports. In 1884, in the face of opposition from English-oriented athletic bodies, the GAA was set up. Again Cusack received some support from within the Caledonian Society for the establishment of this Celtic sporting body.

Ironically, the formation of the GAA was a back-handed compliment to the English sporting world. Cusack's beliefs were almost the mirror image of those that comprised the ideology of athleticism among his English opponents.[5] The ideology of the GAA as it evolved was similar to that associated with the development of sport in England: but now sport in Ireland was to be brought into play for Irish goals. Irish athletics and games would widen the appeal of sport and ensure that Ireland's own sporting traditions would not disappear. Participation in Irish sports would also divert Irish youth away from English or 'Saxon' sports and re-orient them to the glories of their own Irish heritage. Gaelic athletic events would assist the Gaelic cultural revival that was necessary to de-Anglicise Ireland, strengthen Irishness and the sense of an Irish identity, and so increase the likelihood of Irish self-government.

There was also an element of protectionism in Cusack's thinking. Irish athletes were seen to be at a disadvantage when competing with the English in fundamentally English sports. Sporting defeats at the hands and feet of the English reinforced English dominance over Ireland. Irish and English ideological perceptions certainly agreed on the propaganda values of sporting victory and defeat; but for those establishing the GAA, to be forewarned was to be forearmed. Irish sport would diminish British dominance: the GAA would help create an Irish identity for Ireland. Just as the AAA had banned athletes who wished to participate in their meetings from Irish sports, the GAA banned its athletes from joining in English athletic events. Other bans were to follow.[6] British games were not to be allowed on Gaelic sports grounds. Cricket and rugby were condemned, particularly the latter. Rugby was already popular in Ireland, but the GAA viewed it as quintessentially English, the sport of the British garrison in Ireland. The cultural imperialism of English sport was to be stopped.

Soccer was also condemned, but less often and less vigorously. The enforcement and scope of the bans varied: sometimes the ban was applied fearlessly. In 1938 the GAA removed as its patron none less than Douglas Hyde, the first Irish President and founder of the Gaelic League. His offence was that, acting as State President, he had attended an international soccer match between Ireland and Poland.

The ban in its various manifestations was, and remains, a source of some controversy. Yet it was the ban that ensured that a distinctive Irish sport did evolve, because it forced athletes to declare themselves for Irish or English sports. As a result, the ban could have ended the development of Gaelic sports and the GAA. Instead it was a gamble that paid off. Gaelic sports in Ireland went on to achieve the popularity achieved by soccer in England.[7] The ban had an impact on the development of soccer in Ireland: it helped ensure that an initially Protestant sport remained a Northern Irish redoubt for around a century. Formally the ban on foreign sports was not lifted until 1971. By then much had happened in the world of association football in Ireland.

Irish soccer demonstrates a strong Scottish connection, being the result of missionary work in the Belfast area by Scottish clubs. The secretary of the Scottish Football Association had first attempted, but failed, to arrange an exhibition match in Belfast in 1877. A year later Queen's Park and the Caledonians met in the first game on Irish soil at the grounds of the Ulster Cricket Club. The exhibition match was a success. Other clubs sprang up as a result, most being based on existing organisations. Association football clubs were born out of rugby and cricket clubs, others were linked with some of the bigger and more prestigious schools. The YMCA involved itself in soccer as well as rugby. A number of clubs had Scottish opposition for their first game. Clubs and district selects from Scotland were common touring visitors for a number of years thereafter. Many clubs relied heavily on Scottish players, and Scottish influence on the game was marked. When Queen's Island won the Irish Cup in 1882, ten of the team were Scots. The trophy was handed over to E J Harland, founder of Harland & Wolff, who was president of the club. Queen's Island, from which the club took its name, had been created by the construction of channels for shipping in Belfast harbour basin. The island became the location for the Harland & Wolff ship-building yard in which the Scots were employed. In Scotland, Scottish pride was aroused by the success of what was claimed to be really a Scottish club.[8]

Footballers were qualified to play for Ireland if they had been born there or had been resident there for seven years, and a number of Scots who fulfilled this latter requirement represented Ireland. As a fledgling footballing nation, Ireland still had much to learn, but the Scottish presence in the Irish team had little positive effect. The first international match was lost against England 0–13 in 1882, and Irish results over the next few years continued to make dismal reading. Until their first ever victory, a 4–1 win over Wales in 1887, the most they had ever managed was a drawn game against the same opposition. Previously there had been fourteen defeats, with a total of ten goals scored and 95 conceded. Nor was the 1887 victory to prove to be a turning point: it would be another four years before their imposing 7–2 defeat of Wales. That marked a genuine improvement: Ireland continued to lose more games than they won, but heavy defeats were fewer.

Such performances show that Cusack and the GAA were justified in their concerns about Irish competition in non-Irish sports: Irish footballers did make their country seem inferior, and Irish supporters were concerned by the defeats. In 1885 when Ireland lost 8–2 at home to Wales, the Irish goal-keeper was so disturbed by the barracking of the home fans that he walked off the field in the middle of the second half. Persuaded to return, he was again verbally abused by the still unimpressed fans.[9] This was one player the fans wished had been ineligible for Irish selection. The residency require-ment for Irish representative honours also measured eligibility to partici-pate in Irish cup matches. In 1885 the residential period required to qualify non-Irish players as Irish was reduced from seven years to three months.

Teams representing British military regiments based in Ireland took advantage and entered the competition. At that time some Scottish clubs competed against English clubs for the FA cup. Some Irish clubs followed that example. The participation of non-English clubs in the FA cup and English regimental teams in the Irish cup led some to suggest that an 'Irish' club in Scotland, Hibernian, might be persuaded to enter the Irish cup. There is no evidence that Hibs harboured any ambitions in this direction. The suggestion seems to have been based on the usual misunderstanding of the nationality of Hibs players. Formed by Catholic Irish-Scots in Edinburgh, the team was ineligible because the players were Scots-born. However, a Scots connection was responsible for the decision to reduce the residency period to only three months. The reduction was made to accom-modate the Belfast Scottish Association's wish to have its team, the Caledonians, included in the Irish cup. The Scottish influence on Irish foot-ball bore definite results off the field, even if it proved of little help in inter-national matches.[10]

Players from outwith the North of Ireland were chosen for the Irish international team for the first time in 1885; two Protestant footballers at Trinity College, Dublin, represented Ireland. Teams in the South were much fewer than in the North, perhaps because the Scottish missionary effort had focused predominantly on the North-East. Belfast was where the Irish Football Association was formed in 1880 and the city was seen to be Ireland's soccer centre. The Association's roots were among the Protestants of the North, although clubs did evolve in the South, also based in the Protestant Irish population. Indeed, it has even been claimed that Belfast Celtic was 'the first club willing to select Catholics', but the accuracy of this statement is uncertain. What is clear is that Irish soccer teams, regardless of their geographical location were essentially Protestant: Irish soccer was seen to be a Protestant game.[11]

So the arrival of a new club in 1891 produced a big change in Irish soccer. This club modelled itself on Glasgow Celtic, took its name and sought its patronage. This was readily granted, along with a generous donation to help establish the new club. Belfast Celtic's base was in the predominantly Nationalist Catholic Falls Road. Yet Celtic emerged from an already existing cricket club and obtained a temporary ground with the help of the local Gaelic football club. Following four very successful years as a junior club, the Irish FA made Celtic a senior club, sooner than the club had expected or desired.[12]

Crowd violence was a feature of the early days of football, in Ireland as much as in Scotland or England. The history of Belfast Celtic was, however, to be plagued by intercommunal violence and strife. Matches against teams with a strong Protestant and Unionist image, Glentoran and especially Linfield, were frequently marred by disturbances. Attacks on Celtic players interrupted, and were finally to end, the club's otherwise increasingly successful course. The club and its players also felt that they were discriminated against when it came to international honours or the choice of grounds for internationals or Irish cup finals or semi-finals. Predominantly Protestant clubs in the Dublin area made similar complaints and made accusations of 'Northern prejudice'. Differences between North and South and Protestant and Catholic intensified alongside the political struggles over the future of Ireland. War in 1914 led to the suspension of the Irish League and the formation of a Belfast & District League in the North, with Dublin clubs joining a Leinster league. Celtic reverted to amateur status, rejoining other Belfast clubs in 1918. The war and the Easter Rising ensured that the two leagues remained until 1919.[13]

Then the Irish league was reconstituted. With political sentiments running very high, games between teams from Dublin or Belfast Celtic and those from the Unionist North became tense occasions. All the old complaints about prejudice became even stronger. Soon there were again two different regional leagues and Belfast Celtic had withdrawn – some accounts suggesting that the club was suspended – from Irish football altogether.[14] During a match against Glentoran, Fred Barrett, a great favourite of the Celtic fans, had been sent off. That decision had led to a full-scale riot, during which guns were fired. Celtic went out of Irish football, but remained involved in boxing, cycling and other sports. As Ireland was partitioned, the geographically separated leagues formed the basis for soccer in a newly divided Ireland. Both Football Leagues and their linked Football Associations claimed ownership of the description Irish; both still claimed authority over the whole island. The southern organisation obtained support from many Nationalist-inclined Northern Irish clubs, but not Belfast Celtic. Celtic had by then dispensed with its own football team, and it even refused to allow its ground to be used for tournaments organised by the southern body. Paradoxically, GAA clubs did allow these soccer tournaments to be played on their grounds despite the ban on 'foreign sports'. And when Belfast Celtic did return to the football field, after a four-year absence, it was to play in the Belfast-based Irish League, under the overall authority of the Belfast-based Irish Football Association. Celtic's return to Northern Irish football in 1924 gave the Northern game a credibility it would otherwise have lacked; in addition, it gave Nationalist Belfast a senior Northern Irish team with which it could identify once more.

Belfast Celtic, like its Glasgow counterpart, had an open recruitment policy. Unlike GAA clubs, members of the Crown forces were not excluded. The Protestant Fred Barrett, whose sending-off led to a riot and Celtic's absence from soccer for four years, had even had his release bought from his regiment so that he could play for Celtic. Nor did the major clubs identified with the Protestant, Unionist cause then discriminate against Catholics. Linfield, Celtic's principal rivals, did not pursue an anti-Catholic policy. From its early days it had Catholic players, even a Catholic trainer.[15] Wexford-born Irish Catholic Davy Walsh, who played for Linfield in the 1940's, stated that he 'was treated well by everyone', and took pride in having played for 'a great club with a great tradition'. The open policy of the clubs meant that some players had spells with both Belfast Celtic and Linfield. Tommy Breen was only one of these players. An Irish international goalkeeper with Celtic, Breen was transferred to Manchester United and then back again. Breen lived close to Celtic Park, in the heartland of Celtic's most devoted and most Nationalist supporters. After a contractual disagreement with Celtic in the 1940s, Breen left in disgust and 'defected' to Linfield, then the club's greatest rivals. The defection was accepted by both sets of fans. However, sometimes Breen had to accept ribbings from his Celtic supporting neighbours: 'He had the grim prospect of leading the Blues out at Celtic Park before his Falls Road neighbours, and coming out of mass on Sunday morning from St Paul's he would meet the banter with unfailing good humour.'[16]

Players with one club could have relatives associated with the other. Jack Jones had been a very famous Linfield captain. His young cousin Jimmy Jones scored three goals in a trial match, but Linfield surprisingly failed to sign him. Instead he went to Celtic where he became a big favourite with the supporters. On Boxing Day 1948, 25,000 people packed into Windsor Park for a crucial home league match for Linfield against Belfast Celtic. The political situation in Northern Ireland was tense because of de Valera's support for the new Anti-Partition League and the bitter response this provoked from Unionists. Attention at the match was on Jimmy Jones, who was in prolific goal-scoring form. It was a hard, competitive match. Following an accidental clash with Jones just before half-time, a Linfield player had to be taken off the field, and during the interval, Linfield's secretary announced over the public address system that the player had suffered a broken leg. The match resumed amidst mounting tension. Two players were ordered off for fighting. A penalty award allowed Celtic to take the lead ten minutes from time, only for Linfield to equalise with three minutes to go.

When the referee blew for time-up, some Linfield fans invaded the ground and attacked Belfast Celtic players. Jones was singled out for a brutal beating in which he sustained a broken leg and severe bruising. Other Celtic players were also hurt: one was unable to play for two months because of his injuries. Linfield directors published a statement deploring the incident and many Linfield fans expressed their own disgust in the letter columns of local newspapers. Appalled at the events, Celtic directors issued a strongly-worded protest that included criticism of the lack of protection that had been offered to Celtic players by those in authority. In secret, they also decided to withdraw from football, though this announcement was delayed until almost the end of the season.[17]

Communal strife had forced Belfast Celtic to withdraw from Irish football for four years in the 1920s. So when former player Charlie Tully returned in 1952 to Belfast to captain Glasgow Celtic against a reconstituted version of Belfast Celtic some hoped that history might repeat itself. Banners appeared asking 'Will ye no come back again?' but most knew the answer to that question. Belfast Celtic's 1948 decision was final and an admission that the city's ethnic conflict was too strong to allow a team representing the minority community to continue. Tully, whose mesmerising wing-play had made him the toast of his new club's fans, had been transferred to Glasgow Celtic some eighteen months before the Windsor Park riot; after the departure of Belfast Celtic some of the club's supporters transferred their allegiance to Glasgow Celtic as well. Supporting Glasgow Celtic in Scottish football did not properly fill the vacuum created by the disbandment of Belfast Celtic in Northern Irish football. Belfast Celtic, as its decision to remain within Northern based Irish football in 1924 demonstrated, was certainly associated with Irish nationalism, but it also reflected a Northern Irish sense of place and identity. The Northern Irish majority community's sense of identity is even more complicated[18] and also displays some of that complexity in the football arena. The majority showed genuine pleasure when, following some real efforts at persuasion, Belfast Celtic returned to soccer under the authority of the Northern based footballing bodies. That decision meant the continuation of ethnic conflict in Northern Irish football but it also accepted the dominance of Northern Irish football and its organisations. In addition, Celtic's continuation in football in the partitioned North confirmed the ideological value attributed to sport by both English athleticism and the GAA, by demonstrating the recognition by the minority community in the North that its immediate future remained within the new Northern Ireland statelet.

Belfast Celtic's final decision was, however, a recognition that there was no future for the minority community in Belfast football, but that did not mean the end of ethnic conflict in Northern Irish soccer. Instead it appears to have marked the beginning of an intensification of the Unionist, Protestant image of Linfield. Seen by many as the 'wee Rangers', and having a close relationship with the Glasgow team, Linfield had always been seen to be the main standard-bearer for the majority community.[19] When, sometime in the 1950s, Linfield reversed its earlier policy on the selection of Catholics and became exclusively Protestant, the club took sole possession of an aggressively anti-Catholic image in Northern Irish football. Consequently, some former Belfast Celtic fans started to support Glentoran, which still picked Catholics without antagonising its Protestant and Unionist supporters. Glentoran was not released from its own Unionist and Protestant imagery, but the complex interplay of social identities within Northern Irish soccer became even more complicated. Sometimes predominantly Unionist supporters of substantially Unionist clubs would affect a minority identity to provoke Linfield's 'true blue' support.[20] Apart from Linfield, most other Belfast teams could attract some genuine minority support in the city. Distillery's location made it one alternative for former Belfast Celtic supporters and it became briefly a focus for the Nationalist community.

In the late 1960s Northern Irish Catholics sought full civil rights with the majority population. The attempt by some Unionist politicians to modernise Northern Ireland failed; too little, too late for the minority, it was too much, too soon for the majority. The resulting intergroup conflict became a battle over the status of Northern Ireland, and football did not remain untouched by it. Distillery's matches became a venue for intergroup violence and in 1972 the club moved away from West Belfast. In Londonderry, Derry City was forced to leave the Northern Irish league. Its Brandywell stadium lies in the largely Nationalist Bogside, the locus for the creation of 'Free Derry'. Apart from crowd trouble at some Linfield matches, the club had managed to attract support from both communities but, as the conflict in Northern Ireland grew, other clubs, especially those perceived to be Unionist, suffered from the political situation. Similar worries affected Derry and its supporters when they played away from home. Eventually Derry had to agree to play its matches some forty miles away in Coleraine. The overall political situation and the added costs and loss of revenue forced an increasingly debt-ridden Derry City to withdraw from Northern Irish football in 1972.[21]

The continuing communal conflict then seems to have led Glentoran to exclude Catholic players for a period in the late 1970s. The Reverend Armstrong, a Presbyterian minister, a dedicated Glentoran fan and the club's courageous and persuasive chaplain, prevailed on the club and its support to revert to its original open recruitment policy.[22] Other changes in Belfast were more permanent. Population movements in Belfast and an upturn in Cliftonville's fortunes in the late 1970's coincided to bring that club a substantial Nationalist following. Again matches generated serious crowd trouble. As a result Cliftonville has been forced to play its matches against Unionist opposition away from home. Controversy surrounds these decisions. Clubs in Nationalist areas believe that decisions that force them to journey into inhospitable, sometimes dangerous locations, display bias against them, and give an unfair playing advantage to Glentoran and Linfield.[23]

To avoid these conflicts, when a reconstituted Derry City returned to football in 1985, the club's directors reversed Belfast Celtic's decision of sixty years earlier by applying to join the southern-based Football League of Ireland. The club was accepted and has been successful, winning trophies and attracting the largest support in the League. Despite the club's open recruitment policy, including the appointment of former Linfield manager, Ray Coyle, to manage the club, Derry is now believed to have less support among the local Protestant population than was the case when it played in the Irish Football League, based in Northern Ireland. Playing outside of the North means that Derry avoids the ethnic conflict there, though its supporters' buses are often attacked as they travel through the North to away matches in the Republic. Many Unionists now firmly ascribe a Nationalist identity to Derry City.[24] However, if football was to make its return to Derry, it could only be achieved by City playing outside of Northern Ireland: security concerns had ensured that discussions with the Irish League had come to naught.

Football's continuing potential to attract inter-communal violence in Northern Ireland was dramatically demonstrated in 1990 when the West Belfast Intermediate team, Donegal Celtic, was drawn at home against Linfield in the Irish Cup. The game was switched to Windsor Park by the IFA following security advice from the Royal Ulster Constabulary. Celtic, who had hopes of eventually becoming a senior team in the Irish League, tried to have the decision overturned in the law-courts. The RUC's argument that security could only be ensured by playing the match at Linfield's ground was crucial. The outcome, however, was not unlike the events of Boxing Day 1948. Donegal Celtic players were assaulted, one being Brendan Tully, a relative of Belfast and Glasgow Celtic's Charlie Tully. As well as violence between both sets of supporters, there was this time, unlike 1948, a running battle between the Celtic supporters and the RUC, which involved plastic bullets being fired and rioting in Nationalist areas of Belfast. In the 1991 Irish Cup Donegal Celtic was drawn at home to Ards, a team that is not usually identified with Unionism. Again the RUC and IFA decided that the match should be switched to Celtic's opponents' ground. Celtic then withdrew from the competition and applied at the end of the season to join the League of Ireland. Unlike Derry, Donegal Celtic was unsuccessful: the League feared that travel into the heart of Belfast was much too risky a proposition for clubs and supporters from the Republic.[25]

The events surrounding Donegal Celtic led to considerable minority comment about the level of discrimination Catholics experienced in Northern Irish soccer. The IFA and Linfield were especially criticised. Pressure on Linfield mounted when the manager stated in January 1992 that he did not believe that he would sign a Catholic. The Irish National Caucus in America built up a strong campaign against discrimination in Northern Irish football. They challenged Northern Ireland's participation in the 1994 World Cup to be held in the USA and worked to dissuade multi-nationals from continuing their sponsorship of football in Northern Ireland. Soon Coca-Cola announced that its sponsorship of the IFA was to be discontinued. Thorn-E.M.I. then withdrew its sponsorship of Linfield, officially for economic reasons, though few believed this to be true. Linfield took action later that year to demonstrate that it had firmly dispensed with its policy of excluding Catholic players: the club began to recruit Catholic players, who now total three, including two from the Republic of Ireland. Yet, welcome as this is, more time is required to judge the full consequences of Linfield's actions in returning to an open recruitment policy.[26]

These blemishes on Linfield's history show how social identities and prejudices are reflected in football, and how they can vary over time. That is also shown by the increased difficulties clubs from the minority community have faced when attempting to remain in Northern Irish football. Nonetheless, the long running and highly emotional debate between two bodies, each claiming to be the *true* Football Association for *Irish* people revealed, at least in part, some sense of Irishness that is, or arguably was, found amongst Northern Ireland's Unionist population. The Northern body still retains its title as the Irish FA but it was during the 1960s, as inter-group tension grew, that the IFA's national team accepted the title 'Northern Ireland'. Since then, other identities have been reflected in Northern Irish soccer.[27]

Some commentators have believed there to be a greater willingness in the IFA than in the other British Associations to contemplate the entry of only one *British* team representing all four associations in World and European Championships. A readiness to discuss submerging the identity of Northern Irish soccer in a British team might reflect an increased determination not to surrender a British identity and to reject any trace of a specifically Irish component. Others have recognised a different tendency, especially among the Northern Ireland supporters when their team plays against England. There is increased barracking of the opposition and a greater display of green and white – the colours worn by Northern Ireland – rather than the Unionist red, white and blue, also the colours of England. These trends have been linked with Unionist moves towards the creation of a more autonomous political identity for Northern Ireland, and their perceptions of an actual or potential betrayal of the Unionist cause. Recent events however have also confirmed that the unity of Protestant and

Catholic support behind the Northern Ireland football team was fragile and not a sign of any genuine convergence.

Glasgow Celtic footballers representing Northern Ireland have been subjected to abusive treatment by the crowd. Anton Rogan and Allan McKnight were the first players to be selected from the club for over a quarter of a century. Previous Glasgow Celtic players had been well received but were selected before the present conflict had begun: one Celtic player, Bertie Peacock, a great favourite with the Celtic fans, though often rumoured to be an Orangeman, had gone on to become the Northern Ireland team manager from 1962–67. In recent times suspicions of bias in Northern Irish team selections have also re-emerged. Some surprise has been expressed at the reluctance to choose eligible players from Derry City, now playing in the Irish Republic's soccer competitions. And former internationalist Felix Healey (coincidentally now with Derry City) has publicly commented that earlier in his career he damaged his future international prospects when he crossed himself before a home international match at Windsor Park.[28]

Social identities are complex phenomena;[29] arguments over them and about them can be complicated and emotive. Unionists in Northern Ireland have a particular affection for an Ulster identity, claimed to be an Ulster-Scots or Scotch-Irish identity, linked to a Scottish line of descent.[30] Football tournaments are often described as Ulster tournaments, even though participating clubs only come from the six counties that constitute Northern Ireland and not the historic nine counties of Ulster. Nationalist opinion usually disputes the validity of the title. So it is intriguing to discover that the Ulster GAA, representing the traditional nine-county Ulster province, opposed the national executive's decision to cancel GAA sporting events that clashed directly with live television coverage of the Republic's national soccer team during the 1990 Italian World Cup. The Ulster GAA argued for the continuation of their programme of events because Ulster's national soccer team was Northern Ireland, not the Republic of Ireland.[31]

Despite the claim of the Ulster GAA, the evidence is that an overwhelming number of the North's Nationalist community, impressed by the success of the Republic's team and depressed by the politics of Northern football (and Northern Ireland itself), now identify with the soccer team of the Republic. Anti-English sentiment and perceptions of betrayal paradoxically lead a few Unionists to support the Republic against England at soccer. And although the Unionists remain largely antagonistic to the Republic, they are almost equally split in their preferences for an all-British or an all Irish team. The removal of the GAA ban on foreign sports shows that Nationalists no longer see soccer or other sports as an alien threat within: soccer can represent an Irish identity. However, the success of the Republic's national team managed by an Englishman, Jack Charlton, has led to an outbreak of soccer fever in the Republic. The GAA may face a new threat in the future. Gaelic sports have very limited international links; their real locus is within Ireland. So continued success in global sport could lead to soccer becoming the game that best represents an Irish identity on the international sporting stage.

Unlike in the Republic of Ireland, soccer (more usually simply called football) has been the dominant Scottish sport for some considerable time. Some sense of a Scottish nationhood is probably most overtly displayed at Scottish international football matches. The contrast between this apparently intense commitment to Scotland and to a Scottish identity and the repeated failures of the Scottish National Party to make headway is stark. After Jim Sillars, the former deputy convener of the SNP, lost his parliamentary seat in the 1992 General Election, he complained about this disjunction in behaviour and dismissed the Scots as 'Ninety Minute Patriots'. Historically, Scottish football has been used to express anti-English sentiment and to display a Scottish identity,[32] but that is different from displaying the will to break the Union with England. Instead, for most of its history, the main concern of Scottish football was its alliance with the other British Football Associations.

A weak version of the GAA's concern about sporting imperialism can be sustained when the history of the British 'Home' Associations is examined. The British Associations constituted a small network of studied insularity and self-proclaimed superiority in the face of organised football elsewhere in the world.[33] The IFA wish to retain authority over all Ireland did express a sort of all-Irish identity, reinforced by its willingness to select for its national team players born anywhere in the island of Ireland, but it also revealed a belief in the superiority of Britain, the British Associations – and the British association. IFA's stance was Irish, but it reflected a forlorn hope that there could be a return to the *status quo ante*, in which being Irish was the same as being British.

The contradictions in Scottish football and society were much less serious and much less obvious. For most of its history the Scottish Football Association simply played junior partner to England in the British Associations. The football it administered was Scottish, but Scottish within a sporting structure that reflected the hegemonic Unionist, British political context; a sporting structure that mirrored the strange ideological nationalism of the British state. The British or 'Home' Associations and their championship represented a Nationalist paradox within an imperial enigma. Matches between England and Scotland allowed an expression of Nationalist identities and 'Nationalist' sentiments within an insular (literally) Unionist perspective that reinforced the Imperialist ideology from which it was born:[34] 'national' teams within Britain competed to become the *British* 'nation's' champion team. Although Scottish 'Nationalist' sentiment was at its highest when Scotland played against England in the

British Championships, the paradox was that the very event celebrated the peculiarity that is British nationalism. Throughout most of the existence of the British Championship it is arguable that the Scots were not even ninety minute patriots. That may have been changing in the last years of the Home Championship's existence or during its brief replacement with the Rous Trophy in the late 1980s. Yet for most of the history of the event, participation in the British Championships celebrated an identity of being Scottish Britons; to be Scottish was to be British.

That identity was not an aberration. Unionism was, and in evolved forms remains, very strong in Scotland. Scottish Conservatism remained strong while it emphasised its Unionism: the Scottish Conservative and Unionist Party won 50.1% of the Scottish vote in 1955, becoming the only political party in Scotland in the twentieth century to gain a simple majority of the general election vote. Unionism arose out of opposition to Irish Home Rule. Unionist opponents of Scottish Home Rule did not fail to link the two campaigns together. They argued that Scottish Home Rule was desired by Irish Catholics and extreme leftists who believed it would enhance their influence;[35] and sometimes these two groups were presented merely as different aspects of the same unified political bloc.

The SFA played a role in the British Associations which represented a conventional Scottish Unionism, recognising the fundamental nature of the British State. But on the football field a much stronger, more exclusive and more aggressive variant of that Unionist identity was represented in Scottish club football by Glasgow Rangers, the country's best supported club. So the political context of Scottish society and soccer ensured that there were sporting parallels with Northern Ireland. Divisions in society were again reflected in football and that ensured that the largest ethnic minority, Scots of Catholic Irish descent, had to establish their own football clubs.[36]

Soccer in Ireland was very largely a Scottish creation. Many clubs relied largely on Scottish players. Yet Scots in Ireland, who faced no discrimination or disadvantage, still felt the need to create their own sports clubs and have their own football teams. Generally, wherever the Scots travelled abroad, they established a range of Scottish societies and exhibited a strong tendency to take their own sporting activities with them. In North America numerous Scottish football clubs were formed. That was true also in England: in London exclusively Scottish football clubs existed in the 1880s. Even in Scotland itself, football teams took proudly Scottish names. Caledonian references were plentiful, thistles abounded; the national identification was often made very clear.

National sentiment was expressed in and through Scottish football, but usually in a form that recognised the dominance of Britain. The SFA did act to protect a specifically Scottish identity from being eroded by English football. To save the status of the Scottish Cup, the premier Scottish trophy, in the late 1880s, the SFA no longer allowed Scottish clubs to participate in the English Cup. But a narrow, exclusive sense of a Scottish identity was also demonstrated. Initially the SFA was reluctant to accept teams from the Catholic Irish-Scottish community and later the SFA showed an unwillingness to recognise their players as Scots by selecting them for the international team. Some Scottish journalists even urged that Ireland select these Scottish-born players because they were really Irishmen and not true Scots. This misunderstanding of the status of the Irish-Scots and their clubs has persisted throughout the history of the Scottish game.

Just as soccer in Ireland was associated with the Protestant community, in Scotland it had similar origins. Teams emerged out of already existing social organisations, including Protestant religious organisations. Queen's Park, the very first Scottish team, had YMCA associations. The 3rd Edinburgh Rifle Volunteers was the very first football team in Edinburgh. The Volunteer company had been founded by John Hope, 'the quiet bureaucrat behind the anti-popery movements in Scotland of the last half of the nineteenth century'[37] as part of his total temperance and no-Popery campaigns. The football club, which was only open to members of the Volunteers, was provided as another attraction to keep good Protestant lads safe from temptation. In Moffat, the local club was started by the local minister, the Reverend Churchill, a Cambridge University graduate, both a product and a proponent of athleticism.

Catholic Irish-Scots were largely excluded from early Scottish football on the basis of their ethnicity, religion and social class. If they were to participate in soccer, the sport that was sweeping Scotland, then they had to form their own clubs. The first significant clubs, Hibernian in Edinburgh and Harp in Dundee, were linked to the Catholic equivalent of the YMCA, the Catholic Young Men's Society, and both, particularly Hibs, were part of the Catholic anti-alcohol campaign. But the motivations behind the formation of these clubs were complex. Certainly there was a sense of protection to be gained from having clubs that were within the Irish-Scottish community, especially as many of the clubs of the majority were not exactly welcoming to members from the minority. But the Irish-Scots also saw soccer as a means of making contact with the wider community, believing that through sporting exchanges social prejudices could be broken down. The clubs represented a community that intended to participate in and contribute to Scottish society. Success by Irish-Scottish clubs would win the respect of the Protestant Scottish majority.

The creation of Glasgow Celtic encapsulated all these beliefs. In addition, a main purpose was to obtain gate-money that could be put to charitable use. Yet another economic depression in Glasgow had meant that again there were many hungry poor in the city. The Irish-Scots were, along with other relatively recent migrants to the city, inevitably badly hit. Celtic's profit would allow the Catholic Irish-Scots to demonstrate that their community was not, as many alleged, a drain on Scottish society's resources, but one that could look after its own, and help the majority too. Celtic was a demonstration of community self-help and a celebration of the community's sense of pride. Its formation was also intended to help the community defend its own. Most Scottish charities had a religious dimension. Protestant charities expected recipients to participate in some way in Protestant religious services. Some used their charitable work as the basis for vigorous proselytism among destitute and starving Catholics; the young were special targets. These actions were especially offensive to the Irish-Scots minority, but the foundation of their own strong charities could ensure that these tactics became irrelevant.

So Celtic demonstrated the resilience and resourcefulness of the community that had given it birth: the club demonstrated that Glasgow's Irish-Scottish community was determined to play its full part in Scottish life. Unlike Ireland, where soccer was an alien game, those of Irish descent in Scotland were joining in and embracing Scottish life while retaining a pride in their ancestry. The club's very name, Celtic, was then in use to refer to a common heritage for both Ireland and Scotland. Michael Davitt, a prominent advocate of a joint Celtic heritage and Scotland's most popular Irishman, was patron of the club along with the English Catholic Archbishop of Glasgow. Davitt, also a patron of the GAA, had already suggested that the GAA establish a pan-Celtic Olympics, to which Scottish athletes and sportsmen would be invited.[38] Davitt was one of the foremost advocates of land reform, trade unions and labour politics in Scotland. So successful was he in making this case that the Protestant heartland of Skye wanted Davitt to represent them in parliament. It was Davitt who opened Celtic's new stadium in 1892. He laid a square of Ulster turf from Donegal in the centre circle to symbolise the community's past roots but spoke to them of their future Scottish destiny. Davitt was convinced that Celtic's successes would make the Irish-Scots community even more acceptable to the wider Scottish community; so were the others associated with the club. The belief had some resonances with the ideology of athleticism and the counter-ideology of the GAA. Celtic footballing success would prove that the Irish-Scots were at least the equal of the majority. Unlike adherents of the GAA, the Irish-Scots did not attempt to create their own alternative forms of evaluation: they would prove themselves on grounds of the majority's choosing.

Dundee Harp, Edinburgh Hibernian and Glasgow Celtic all went on to become successful clubs in their own way. Unfortunately the success of the Irish-Scottish clubs was not welcomed by all. The resentment at Irish sporting success became more acute as the conflict in Ireland became even more dominant in British, and particularly Scottish, politics. Clubs from the minority community were judged to be alien clubs and their successes were resented. The club histories show that considerable opposition focused on their pride in their Irish ancestry and their desire to retain symbols of that heritage. When ownership of the clubs has passed into the hands of the Scots majority, steps have been taken to remove or diminish their Irish dimension. Dundee Hibernian, formed after the demise of Dundee Harp, lost its green team colours and was re-named Dundee United in the 1920s. A few years later, Edinburgh Hibernian lost its Harp symbol from the ground and reputedly came close to losing its name and colours.

Recently Hibs supporters have complained about the loss of the Harp from the team's jersey. The opposition to the Harp in the club's boardroom was summed up as follows: 'I have never been able to understand those who profess to support Hibernian and then break out in a massive rash of bigotry anytime anything to do with the club's origins is mentioned.' One contributor perhaps summed the matter up: the old design had 'incorporated Hibs' Irish origins, their modern-day Scottishness . . .'[39] This duality has been singularly misinterpreted through the years. Glasgow Celtic has experienced years of criticism for honouring its Irish connections by flying the Irish tricolour. Yet nowhere was that duality, that sense of an Irish past and a Scottish present, better captured than when Celtic won the European Cup in Lisbon in 1967. On the boundary parapet wall stood a Celtic fan encouraging the club's supporters to cheer their team on. He held aloft the green, white and orange Irish tricolour, and he wore the Scottish kilt.[40] Celtic, a club with Irish roots, won the European Cup for Scotland.

Norman Tebbit created a furore when he recently proposed his 'cricket test' of British loyalty. In an attack on black Britons, Tebbit argued that true Britons would support the English cricket team, not the West Indians, nor national teams from the Indian sub-continent. For a long time some Scots have been applying their own 'soccer test' of true Scottishness. True Scots would not support clubs of Irish-Scottish origins: truly Scottish clubs would not honour associations with another country. In a peculiar twist, true Scots can barrack genuine Scots doing their best for the country's national side, if these Scottish players are selected from Glasgow Celtic. Consequently some Celtic supporters feel unwelcome when supporting Scotland and judge that Catholic Irish-Scots remain an unacceptable Scottish presence in the eyes of a noisy number of other Scots. Older Celtic supporters remain Scottish supporters but some among the younger section now claim to support Ireland.[41] There is a real irony here. Many in Scotland, Celtic protagonists and antagonists alike, believe that the club has a substantial following in Ireland, but Irish interest in Celtic is modest indeed.

Some support for Celtic can be found in Ulster on both sides of the border. Despite the influence of the GAA in Donegal, there is a tradition of support for Celtic and an interest in Scottish football because of the county's historical connections with Scotland. Many Donegal men played both soccer and Gaelic football. One of these was Paddy Bonner, Celtic and Ireland goalkeeper, who has, however, found little interest in or knowledge of Scottish football elsewhere in the Republic. That hindered his selection for the Republic's national team. Bonner claims that in the South of Ireland, 'People talk about Liverpool, Manchester United, Everton, Arsenal and Spurs, never about Celtic.' Bonner argues that Jack Charlton only aroused any interest in Celtic in the Republic when he included three of the club's players in the Irish team in the late 1980s. So it was 1989 before a Rangers and Celtic match was first televised live. English football still remains the big attraction.

One example shows the relative importance well. In 1989 the whole Scottish Cup Final, between Rangers and Celtic, was shown for the first time on RTE, but it was not broadcast live. Instead, it was shown end-on to the English Cup Final, which was televised as the live match. The appointment of Liam Brady, former Republic international and favourite, as Celtic manager in 1991 ensured that some limited interest in Celtic remained in the South. But interest in Celtic there is determined by contemporary associations, not the past. In the Republic Celtic is seen to be a Scottish club with very distant Irish links. Irish identification with Celtic is weak: the club is unimportant to any sense of an Irish identity.

Glasgow Celtic does have some resonance with an Irish identity in Northern Ireland. Part of that is to do with the Belfast Celtic connection; some of it is to do with the historic links between Ulster and Scotland. But most important is the interplay of ethnic identities which surrounds the traditional rivalry between Glasgow Celtic and Glasgow Rangers. Rangers has considerable support among the Unionist population. Even adolescent adaptations of traditional Unionist identities, such as those manifest in the more militant Loyalism of the 'Tartan Gangs', retain support for Rangers as a symbolic gesture.[42] Yet it is an error to explore the importance of Rangers in terms of the posturing of supporters or of those who claim (or are claimed) to be supporters. Football supporters, or sections of fans, can associate a club with an image regardless of the club's own actions or policies.[43] The case of Rangers is very different: it was not the supporters, but Rangers' own policies that created that image.

Anti-Catholic and anti-Nationalist prejudice has occurred in Northern Irish football, but direct discrimination has been much less evident. None of the Northern Irish soccer clubs has consistently adopted anti-Catholic recruitment policies. Supporters of some clubs have done their best to foster an anti-Catholic image, but none of these clubs has either given a lead to this bigotry by discriminating against Catholics or pandered to it by instituting a discriminatory policy on a permanent basis. Linfield, which did adopt an anti-Catholic recruitment policy for quite a period of time, is now strenuously and very publicly reversing its practice. Anti-Catholicism has not been the traditional policy of any Northern Irish club. Yet, in the

supposedly less divided Scottish society, Glasgow Rangers has traditionally discriminated against Catholics, allowing some Northern Irish
Unionists a footballing outlet for their prejudices: they have been able to
support an anti-Catholic Unionist club in Scottish football.

Rangers' tradition of anti-Catholicism has a long history.[44] Suspicion of
Catholic players was evident early in the club's history. Catholic players
were not to be trusted. As early as 1890 a Protestant player was accused of
being a Catholic who had allowed Celtic to win. After an investigation by
Rangers, only his proven Presbyterianism saved him from a guilty verdict.
The belief in the untrustworthiness of Catholics runs through much of the
history of the club. In the early 1900s Catholic players were asked to leave
the club once their religious affiliations were determined. The club's tradition relies upon an ideology based on a conspiracy theory,[45] which identi-
fies Catholic Irish-Scots as an untrustworthy, subversive minority.
Glasgow Rangers has signed players of many nationalities and many religions and none. Recruitment principles may have appeared to be Scottish
and Protestant; in truth they were anti-Catholic.

Club officials have been active in Scottish freemasonry, sections of
which have been involved in anti-Catholic discriminatory practices. The
first two chairmen, James Henderson and John Ure Primrose, belonged to
the same masonic lodge, Lodge Plantation 581. At a public charitable event
held by this lodge in 1890, Primrose, then the club's very active patron,
publicly associated Rangers with the efforts of Scottish freemasonry. The
Unionist tradition of the club is also long-lived. Sir John Primrose took over
as the second club chairman in mid-1912. A few months later he was on the
platform with Sir Edward Carson in Glasgow in 1912, as the Ulster
Unionists launched their determined campaign against the Irish Home
Rule Bill, and Primrose also played a prominent part in the 1913 and 1914
campaigns. Primrose had first become club patron in 1888, just two years
after he had broken with the Liberal Party over Irish Home Rule. He
remained a very active Unionist for the rest of his political life, frequently
occupying anti-Home Rule platforms with fellow Unionists and their
Orange allies.

His successors as chairmen included ex-Baillies Joseph Buchanan,
another Conservative and staunch Unionist, and Duncan Graham, who
had been a Liberal Imperialist but moved to a much more explicitly
Unionist position following the 1916 Irish rising. His successor, James
Bowie, in an address to the Orange Order, praised its principles and traditions,[46] while Sir John Cargill, club president during most of this time, was
a prominent Unionist. Following a power struggle, Bowie was replaced by
W R Simpson, son-in-law of the first chairman, with J.F. Wilson as vice
chairman in 1947. When Simpson died two years later, J F Wilson became
chairman with W G Bennett joining the board. Bennett was the chairman
of the Scottish Unionist Party, and during his tenure, Ibrox Stadium was

used for a massive Scottish Conservative and Unionist Party rally which heard an attack on the Republic of Ireland from Sir Winston Churchill. Within a year of becoming a Rangers board member, Bennett was elected Unionist MP for Kelvingrove. Wilson also stood for parliament as a Unionist, but he was unsuccessful. In local politics Wilson was much more successful. He served for many years on Glasgow City Council and was prominent in the leadership of the council's anti-Socialist bloc, the Moderates. Wilson also met with electoral success in other organisations, being elected Grand Master of a Glasgow south-side Orange Lodge in the 1930s. Inevitably Wilson had very strong anti-Catholic beliefs; indeed so strong were they that Wilson for a while gained the support of the anti-Catholic, anti-Irish, anti-Semitic and eventually full-blown Fascist, Alexander Ratcliffe,[47] founder of the Scottish Protestant League (SPL).

In 1933 the two began an acrimonious dispute that led to Wilson being opposed by the SPL in the local elections, with the result that he lost his seat and the dispute became even more bitter. Wilson and Ratcliffe issued challenges and counter-challenges to debate publicly the relative strengths of their Protestant and anti-Catholic credentials. Rowdy and undisciplined public meetings took place. Disputes about these meetings led to more public meetings, sometimes held by one in the absence of the other. Savage attacks were exchanged in the letter columns of local newspapers. Ratcliffe attacked Wilson for, among other things, donating small sums of money to the St Vincent de Paul Society in his council constituency. Ironically this Catholic charity was involved in the formation of Celtic. He made alliances with other militant Protestants and Unionists, all of whom were united in their intense antagonism towards Ratcliffe. Wilson became the national treasurer of another anti-Catholic body, the Scottish Protestant Vigilance Society (SPVS) led by the Reverend Frederick Watson. This organisation campaigned against Catholic schools, Catholic marriage laws and Irish immigration, and warned of the dangers of the Irish enemy within. The Society, strongly Unionist in both Scottish and Irish politics, was well known in Northern Ireland, where it campaigned against what remained of Ratcliffe's own organisation there. Prominent members of the SPVS, including Wilson, were identified in militant Protestant Irish publications. The campaign against Ratcliffe in Northern Ireland was very successful and soon his support among Ulster Unionists was negligible.[48]

Wilson's prominence in ultra-Protestant and Unionist politics may appear surprising to those aware of his strong support for Celtic in 1952, when the SFA forbade the flying of the Irish flag at Celtic Park because, they argued, the flag had no connections with either Scotland or football.[49] Celtic directors and supporters saw this as a very serious attack on the club's Irish dimension; flying the Irish flag breached no rule of the SFA constitution. So determined was the club to resist this attempt to diminish its Irish connection, that at one point Celtic threatened to withdraw from football. Representing Rangers, Wilson supported Celtic throughout the dispute, stating that the Irish flag caused his club no offence. Positive and negative motives can be imputed to Wilson's actions. Probably somewhere in the cocktail of motives behind Wilson's support of Celtic's right to fly the Irish flag was his own personal animosity towards Ratcliffe.

Ratcliffe seems to have been one of the first to criticise the presence of the Irish tricolour at Celtic Park. In late 1933, around the time of his dispute with Wilson, Ratcliffe had claimed that the IFA had, after a game between Scotland and Northern Ireland at Celtic Park, complained that Celtic flew the Irish Free State tricolour and that Celtic had refused to remove it. Even Ratcliffe, unlike some in the SFA in 1952, accepted that no law demanded that Celtic remove the flag, but he advocated a two-part strategy to ensure its removal:

> all that needs to be done is that Protestants stay away from matches there . . . And when Rangers are due to meet the Celtic in Celtic Park *they should refuse to play* until the Free State Flag comes down . . . as the 'Free State' is anti-British, surely the footballers in Glasgow who profess to be loyalists can do something to put an end to the flying of an anti-British Flag over a football field [original emphasis].[50]

Ratcliffe's comments say much about Rangers' known political affiliations; the club's refusal to act shows it accepted the realpolitik of Scottish football. Wilson's support for Celtic in 1952 reveals the continuation of that acceptance; the strength of that support shows the emotional scars left from his battle with Ratcliffe.

Wilson remained chairman until his death in 1963, his son J F Wilson jnr becoming vice-chairman to his father's successor, John Lawrence. The new chairman publicly defended the club's refusal to sign Catholic players but was himself appalled when the Catholicism of fellow director David Hope's long-dead wife became an issue in 1973. The matter was successfully used in the board-room battle to prevent Hope from replacing Lawrence as the new chairman that year,[51] and it was Hope's successful opponents, including Rae Simpson, grandson of the first chairman and W S Simpson's son, who ran the club from then until the mid 1980s, when the Lawrence business empire eventually obtained full control. In 1986 Graham Souness arrived as manager, apparently determined to remove the club's anti-Catholic signing policy. His initial attempts came to naught. Glasgow-born Catholic and Republic of Ireland internationalist Ray Houghton was reported to have been scared off after receiving letters from Rangers supporters threatening to kill him. Two and a half years later David Murray, who had no connections with the families and individuals who had determined the club's policies but was then a friend of Souness, purchased Rangers.[52]

Less than a year later, in a blaze of publicity in July 1989, Rangers knowingly signed its first prominent Catholic player this century. Maurice Johnston's arrival at Ibrox from French club Nantes sparked off protests among Rangers fans and also met with suspicion and strong disapproval from Celtic and its fans. Johnston, a former Celtic player, had been a great favourite of the Celtic fans, but he had left the club in some disfavour in 1987. In May 1989, when he had signed for Celtic again, he had proclaimed his relief and pleasure at this, his second chance with the club he really loved. To Celtic's evident displeasure and irritation, Johnston suddenly discovered alleged contractual difficulties with Nantes, which led to his withdrawal from the transfer. Throughout this time he pledged undying allegiance to Celtic, so his eventual move to Rangers met with accusations of treachery. Rumours flew about the reality of the intended transfer to Celtic. Recently it has been confirmed that, while Johnston was publicly declaring his dedication to Celtic in May, he was indeed involved in simultaneous discussions with both clubs and that his signing was designed by Souness to put one over on Celtic.[53]

Nonetheless, many Rangers fans were outraged that the club had signed a Catholic: the fury was magnified in Northern Ireland. Boycotts were planned and season tickets returned. Johnston's agent was Bill McMurdo, a well-known Unionist and participant in Belfast Orange Walks, who spoke of the importance of Rangers dropping outdated practices and putting the best possible team on the park. In some enigmatic comments, McMurdo also emphasised Johnston's father's staunch Protestantism and long allegiance to Rangers.[54] A few months after arriving at Ibrox Park, Johnston, who was not a practising Catholic, was reported singing that well known Orange standard, 'The Sash', as well as attending events at a masonic lodge.[55] The impact of the now-departed Johnston's signing on Rangers is still to be evaluated, but considerable foresight may have been displayed by one commentator who pondered whether Johnston's signing simply interrupted, rather than ended, Rangers' anti-Catholic tradition.[56]

Although the answer to that question remains uncertain,[57] it is now clear that the present Rangers owner and chairman, David Murray, a well known Conservative, holds dear some elements of the club's tradition. Immediately before the 1992 British General Election, David Murray was among a number of prominent Scots who signed a 'Save the Union' letter, this time in the specific context of opposition to the 'disintegration of the United Kingdom' that they argued would be the result of Scottish devolution. Another signatory to the letter, published in a major Scottish newspaper, was Walter Smith, the Rangers manager and director.[58] Others in the Rangers management team have the same political sentiments. The present Rangers vice-chairman is Donald Findlay QC, formerly the Conservative parliamentary candidate for Cunninghame North. The seat, which contained a larger than usual Orange vote, had long been held by the Tories, but had been lost to Labour in 1987. The new Labour MP was Brian Wilson, author of the official Celtic centenary history. However, Findlay stood down before the 1992 General Election was called, judging that he had insufficient time to devote to fighting the seat. Recently he has publicly expressed his own political views to a wide audience, appearing on television to defend the British Royal Family, which he observed was held in very high regard by some sections of the Glasgow community.

The modernisation of Rangers may be more restricted than might be hoped, or argued.[59] The role of Catholics in the club remains uncertain, but the associations with Unionism appear irrevocable in the immediate future. The electoral decline of the Scottish Conservative Party has led some to argue for the reinstatement of the old Unionist label and the elimination of Conservatism as a title in Scotland. Journalist Allan Massie, who had signed the same 'Save the Union' letter as Murray and Smith, argued in September that year that 'The name 'Unionist' could bring back the Rangers vote in Glasgow'.[60] Letters published in reply to Massie's suggestion alluded to this backwards look to Unionist opposition to Irish Home Rule. None saw the suggestion as an especially forward-looking move. Clearly Massie still sees Rangers as a rallying-point for, and a symbol of, a Scottish Unionist identity.[61]

It is the recent activities of the club's own officials that have made possible a future vision based on a return to the past. Even Souness, the club's icon of change, judged by some as a figure outwith the Ibrox political tradition, did not threaten that wider Rangers culture. In 1992 Souness, who saw himself as British more than Scottish, sent a congratulatory telegram to the victorious Conservative Prime Minister, John Major, who had, in the general election of 1992, made the maintenance of the Union an important political issue even in England. Souness, who had resigned as the Rangers manager in 1991, may even have been changed by his own time with the club. In some instances sport may, as the proponents of the ideology of athleticism believed, socialise individuals into another way of seeing things. That explains an otherwise perplexing image of Souness, the cosmopolitan footballer and moderniser of Rangers. Before a match with Celtic he eschewed any talk of football tactics. Instead he placed a photograph of the Queen before the Rangers players and told them that they were about to go out and play on her behalf.[62] And presumably the strange anti-Irish ranting of the then Rangers and England captain, Terry Butcher, during the Italian World Cup in 1990, demonstrates just how affected he also had become by his immersion in the Rangers Unionist and anti-Irish tradition.[63]

As the club's most significant personnel publicly uphold Unionism, it cannot be surprising that Rangers remains the footballing standard-bearer for Unionist values in Scotland and Northern Ireland or that its on-field exploits become confused with Unionism's off-field political needs. Rangers represents a Unionist identity for the very simple reason that for over a century prominent Rangers figures have publicly identified themselves with Unionism. Moreover, Unionist Rangers has been the only club to express in a clear and consistent manner the anti-Catholic dimensions that have often accompanied that political credo because, unlike Northern Ireland's clubs, the club's own on-field tradition demonstrated an anti-Catholic recruitment policy. It has been a Scottish soccer club, not one from Northern Ireland, the centre of the intergroup conflict between Catholic Nationalist and Protestant Unionist, that has best symbolised a narrow and exclusive, anti-Catholic, Unionist identity in both Scotland and Northern Ireland.

Only time and the club's own further actions will reveal the reality of the appearance of change that envelops Rangers. The practices of Rangers have provided some social acceptability for the principle of anti-Catholic discrimination and legitimised a narrow and exclusive Scottish identity; but a genuinely transformed, open Rangers would not hinder, and might even assist, the search for a modern, open Scottish identity, suitable for the twenty-first century. Optimists may even allow themselves the quiet hope that such a new Scottish identity could have some positive impact on Northern Ireland, where many, especially amongst the Unionist population, do still look to Scotland for a lead.

4

Ulster Attitudes to Scottishness: the Eighteenth Century and After

LINDE LUNNEY

By the late eighteenth century, there had been three or four or more generations of inhabitants of east Ulster descended from the Scottish settlers of a hundred years earlier. The country was fairly peaceful, the wars in Europe were at a safe distance, the linen trade was bringing prosperity, and the ideas generated by the European Enlightenment were having an impact in Ireland as elsewhere. This article will examine the cultural links between Ulster and Scotland in this period, particularly the shared enthusiasms for vernacular verse composition and for the poetry of Burns. I shall argue that factors such as these combined to produce in a number of individuals in the North of Ireland an unprecedented interest in their Scots heritage. I shall also analyse the development of attitudes in Ulster to various traits perceived as Scottish, whether these were to be found in Scotland or Ulster.

The interest shown in Scottish traits evident in a coterie of poets, most of whom lived in County Antrim around the turn of the eighteenth century, can clearly be seen as novel when it is contrasted with what could be described as a communal memory loss, which seems more generally to characterize those of Scots descent in Ulster.

The Ordnance Survey Memoirs for the parish of Carnmoney in Co. Antrim, compiled in 1838–9, contain the observation that 'there is scarcely a tradition in the parish . . . it is rather surprising that scarce a farmer can tell how even his father or grandfather came into possession of the farm on which he dwells.'[1] John A Oliver has made some important points about the parallel and equally surprising lack of impact that the movement of people from Scotland to Ulster had on Scottish consciousness:

The migration – not just the organized Plantation under King James, but also the Hamilton and Montgomery settlement of 1601-10, the New Scots Army of the 1640s and the flight of the harassed Covenanters in later years – was by any standard a sizable event, causing possibly fifty thousand to a hundred thousand men to leave their homes, their friends and neighbours in Scotland (out of a total Scottish population of half a million to possibly a million). It is a matter of continuing surprise to me that such a migration should have left no trace whatsoever [in Scotland] in the form of letters, stories, poems, street ballads, or other folk material. And yet I am assured by Scottish authorities that that is the fact of the matter.[2]

It is equally surprising to me that Oliver, writing in the late twentieth century, is one of the first scholars to comment on this gap in the record. The corresponding silence on the subject of the migration in Ulster folk tradition has similarly attracted little scholarly attention. Ulster's most assiduous antiquaries and genealogists over the past 200 years have recorded hardly any material relating to Scotland and the migration. The poet and scholar Sir Samuel Ferguson (1810–1886), born, like Oliver, in an Ulster-Scots area, is one of the few to make reference to the absence in Ulster of this kind of folk tradition. In 1836 he wrote: 'It is remarkable that the recollection of the mother country is scarcely if at all cherished; yet there is a perfect similarity of habits and disposition.'[3]

In the paper quoted above, John A Oliver calls for further investigation of the interface between Scotland and Ulster, to try to understand the 'human values' of the people affected by the migration, and their descendants. A large number of documents survive from the last half of the eighteenth century, and these letters, poetry and contemporary description make it possible to investigate the nature of the national or cultural identity experienced in the region; material from earlier periods is both scantier and less concerned with such topics.

It should be remembered that the first one or two generations of settlers would have been too busy coping with the practical problems, even the dangers, as well as the opportunities of their new lives, to have had much leisure to study the past or to analyse their relationships to their ancestral home, their new land and those who shared it with them. That luxury had perhaps to wait for the development of a more settled and affluent society, which had been achieved by the mid or late 1700s. Certain psychological hypotheses can be put forward to explain the behaviour and attitudes of the migrants: these are discussed here solely in the hope of stimulating further discussion since there is little chance that they can be either proved or disproved.

It can be suggested, for instance, that Scotland (using this term for the moment to signify the collective lives and emotions of those who remained in the country of that name) chose to forget those who left, regarding them as having in some sense rejected what Scotland had to

offer. It is not impossible that those who did leave felt at some uncon-
scious and unexplored level of their souls that they had indeed rejected
their motherland, even though the decision to migrate had been made for
the best possible material, and perhaps, spiritual reasons. Psychologists
point out that partial or complete amnesia can sometimes be an individual's way of dealing with guilt or trauma.

If this tentative reconstruction of seventeenth century motivation is even
partially valid, it is perhaps permissible to go a stage further and suggest
that the first settlers and their direct descendants might have been doubly
burdened with guilt. Not only could they see themselves as having rejected
their motherland, but the land they had taken up in Ireland had previously
been the birthright of others. The native Irish were much more like some of
the Scottish settlers in culture and language than the American Indians
were to contemporary settlers in America. As John Gamble wrote in 1810:
'It would appear incredible how pertinaciously they retain the customs and
usages of their ancestors, were it not considered that they were settled
among a people they detested.'[4]

What is rather surprising is that curiosity about Scottish ancestors seems
to have been somewhat uncommon throughout the period (and even
today), although the Ulster Scots inhabitants of east Antrim in the last
century were so markedly 'proud of their own descents' that this trait was
commented upon by the writer of the Ordnance Survey Memoirs for the
parish of Templecorran.[5] Samuel Davidson (1806–1898), born in Co.
Antrim and later a professor of Biblical criticism in Belfast and Manchester,
is, despite his academic training, typically vague in describing his family
background: 'I understood that my forefathers had come from the West of
Scotland not long before, and have an impression that my grandfather did
so.'[6] Even those with an interest in family history today are in general not
much interested in what happened to their ancestors before the proverbial
'seven brothers came up the Bann in an open boat'. Such origin myths
represent the dawn of history for many Ulster families. This concentration
on the generations back to a particular event has analogies, of course, with
the efforts of those people in England and America who like to trace their
lineage back to the Norman Conquest or to the landing of the Pilgrim
Fathers, but it should be noted that the equivalent Ulster events occurred
much more recently than the Conquest and involved only a very short
journey from a country still visible. The American settlers, by contrast,
made a journey to the other side of the then known world.

One possible hypothesis to explain the apparent lack of interest in the
physical re-location of their ancestors is that geographical awareness and
knowledge in the seventeenth and early eighteenth centuries, and perhaps
later, may have been in some ways different from those which we currently
assume to be the accepted way of viewing the world. It is very difficult for
us to think back to a mentality with little knowledge of places and place

names beyond parish boundaries and with no acquaintance whatsoever with maps and the way maps impose a structure on perceptions of space. Perhaps our ancestors had no concept of boundaries between countries, even of the 'otherness' of a new place, as we perceive them today.

Ulster people of the eighteenth century may not have been very curious about the Scotland of their forefathers, but daily life did provide many opportunities for contact with contemporary Scotland, and it is possible to trace increasing knowledge of Scotland during a period in which the first signs of the explosion of information in which people live nowadays can be detected. Any residual sympathies would have been strengthened by such contacts; an examination of some of the more important links between the two countries will indicate the kinds of people who might have experienced an enhanced interest in Scotland and therefore perhaps in their own Scottish traits.

The short sea passage between the North of Ireland and Scotland, and the relative stages of development of the two neighbouring economies, made trading between them easy and sufficiently lucrative. Such contacts served to maintain mutual commercial interests, perhaps initiated in the early years of the settlement, and also and most significantly, provided frequent crossings for passengers. In 1784, for instance, the port of Irvine in Ayrshire handled 496 sailings for Ireland, only one ship sailing to any other destination.[7] In the period 1771–1785, 'Irish trade utilized approximately one third of Scotland's overseas shipping capacity.'[8] It must have been relatively uncomplicated to travel to Scotland from any of Ulster's ports, even Ballycastle, and probably quite difficult to obtain passage to any other destination. This would have served to further strengthen the importance of the Scottish connection in the minds of Ulster people, especially those in the important mercantile classes.

Some of the passengers who travelled regularly between Ireland and Scotland were Presbyterian young men attending Scottish universities, particularly Glasgow. The only Irish university, Trinity College, Dublin, was officially closed to them on religious grounds and they therefore looked to Scotland; it was, after all, the fountainhead of their own religious tenets, even if not all of them were destined for the Church. Between 1750 and 1799 there are known to have been 791 Irish at the colleges of Glasgow, St Andrews and Aberdeen – quite a significant proportion compared with totals of 245 from the Colonies and abroad, 333 English and 7,221 Scots.[9] It is probable that most of these 'Irish' were from the North of Ireland, their experiences further deepening mutual knowledge and shared experience, and developing a network of acquaintance which underpinned, in the late eighteenth century, what Louis Cullen has called 'a pan-Scottish world on both sides of the North Channel.'[10]

Books by Scottish authors were widely available in Ulster and are frequently mentioned or quoted from by Ulster authors. James Orr,

(1770–1815), a weaver of Ballycarry, Co. Antrim, seems to have read James Thomson, Robert Heron, Robert Burns, Robert Fergusson, Macpherson's *Ossian*, John Home's *Douglas*, William Robertson's *History of Scotland*, David Hume and one or other of the Erskines who wrote in the eighteenth century. Schoolteacher Samuel Thomson, (1766-1816), of Carngranny, Antrim, mentions Allan Ramsay, Fergusson, Burns, James Beattie, Lord Craig, Robert Blair, John Logan, Michael Bruce, William Wilkie, James Thomson and John Lapraik. Similar wide acquaintance with Scottish literature can be traced in the few surviving booklists of local reading societies, as for instance in 1868 in Ballyclare, where Wilson, Hugh Miller, Sir Walter Scott, *Chambers' Journal*, Hogg, Burns, Jeffrey and others were all available. We should remember, too, the amount of Scottish material orally transmitted or circulated in broadsheets, ballad sheets, chapbooks or even in manuscript.

Scottish society was thus very well known to literate Ulster people of the late eighteenth century, and they expressed their admiration of its achievements, particularly in education. The industrious and self-improving miners of Leadhills, Lanarkshire, became almost a cliché in the many articles written in Belfast on educational developments. There are also some striking celebrations of the kind of political beliefs which were felt to have developed in parallel in Scotland and around Belfast. Henry Joy McCracken, leader of the United Irishmen, was the joint author of enthusiastic verses on the subject:

> The Scotch and Irish friendly are,
> Their wishes are the same,
> The English nation envy us,
> And over us would reign.
> Our historians and our poets
> They always did maintain ,
> That the origins of Scottish men and Irish were the same.[11]

Another song popular with Belfast's United Irishmen contains the lines:

> Come here my frien's an' gie's your han',
> Although we're frae a neighbouring lan',
> We for the cause of truth will stan'
> And fight till we die in the morning.[12]

The light sprinkling of Scots spellings in this song leads to a consideration of what was possibly the most important shared trait between Scotland and Ulster, then and later. Contemporary descriptions of Ulster frequently mention the Scottishness of many people's speech. A Scot, visiting in 1853, who met a woman on a farm near Londonderry, 'was so struck with this that I asked her if she was herself really a Scotchwoman, but she assured me that her family had lived in the country for some generations.'[13] In 1834, Samuel Ferguson, writing in the *Dublin University Magazine*, remarked that 'Scotch language, Scotch looks, Scotch habits, will strike [a visitor to Ulster] wherever he turns.'[14] The same article contains a description of other traits which linked Ulster with Scotland:

> There is a perfect similarity of habit and disposition between Ulster and Scotland. In nothing does this appear so strongly as in the popular taste for poetry. Robert Burns' own parish was not more deeply imbued with the love of song than the central district of the county of Antrim. We could enumerate at least half a dozen rustic poets in a district not more than 15 miles in length by 10 in breadth.[15]

In the late eighteenth century this part of Antrim, North Antrim, the Lagan valley, north and mid-Down and, to a lesser extent, Londonderry and Armagh, 'pertinaciously retain[ed] the customs and usages of their ancestors'.[16] In 1812 John Gamble noted that 'the lower classes here, like the Scotch, are brought up in a habitual reverence for literature, and to have written a printed *buke* is high praise.'[17] There is some interesting evidence of how those who did produce literature felt about their avocation. Thomas Beggs, of Glenwherry, Antrim, employed in a linen bleaching works, desired to devote his 'whole existence to poetry. No other pursuit in life is for a moment to be compared to it.'[18] Another poet, the weaver Edward Sloan of Conlig, Down, ingenuously asked 'when was there one who possessed the least spark of the divine fire of poetry who did not long for a share of fame? It is enough that I wish for a place among the bards of my native land.'[19]

The publication in 1786 of Robert Burns' poems and their rapidly increasing international celebrity naturally stimulated much poetical and allied activity in Ulster. Burns' chosen subject-matter and style also served to focus people's attention upon their own language, community, and Scots/Ulster heritage. The poet's persona and personality, as they came to be familiar in east Ulster, quickly brought about a kind of popularity never before experienced by anyone and seldom accorded since then to a poet. Contemporary sources are full of enthusiastic references to his poems and there are so many descriptions of visits to Burns by Ulster men that it seems he must have done little after 1787 but drink the health of his visiting Ulster fans!

> Among these enthusiastic admirers were two from the parish of Ramoan [North Antrim], named Anderson and McCormack. The old harbour at Ballycastle was then in pretty good working order and was visited occasionally by small trading vessels from Largs, Ayrshire. In one of these, the two voyagers made their way to Ayr in 1787 . . . although very much engaged in his own affairs, he received his humble admirers most kindly and even gratefully for their visit from such a distance. Having entertained them hospitably, and delighted them by his conversation, he left them safely on the returning boat.[20]

Similar experiences are chronicled by others, especially by members of
a circle of literary-minded friends, some of whose letters and papers
survive in the letter book of Samuel Thomson of Carngranny, Antrim. The
collection is preserved in the Library of Trinity College, Dublin. Thomson,
a schoolmaster and poet, whose *Poems Chiefly in the Scottish Dialect* (1794),
were printed in a format matching Burns' volume, seems to have been in
contact with Burns from at least March, 1791, when a Dumfries correspondent wrote to Thomson with an apology:

> My much esteemed friend Mr Burns is deprived of the pleasure of personally
> acknowledging receipt of your very polite epistle by the illfated misfortune of
> having his arm broke a few days ago ... he meant to send you Fergusson's Works.
> I know he would like it if you could send him a pound of Snuff known by the
> name of Blackguard. Lundy [Foot] in Dublin is the famous manufacturer of it.[21]

In 1792 Thomson published *An Epistle to Mr Robert Burns*, adding that
'the author sent a copy of it to Mr Burns some time ago, who was not only
pleased with the compliments it contains, but expressed his admiration of
his talents and genius, and requested Mr Thomson to accept a present of
books as a token of esteem from his Scotch friend.'[22]

The acquaintance thus begun led to Samuel Thomson visiting Scotland
in February–March 1794, and to the composition of a lengthy description
in Jonsonian blank verse of his experiences and emotions:

> Twas then, abandoning the 'din of business',
> That I resolved to see the 'Land of Cakes'
> To feast my eyes upon those fairy scenes,
> So oft by Caledonian poets sung
> But thou, sweet Burns, the Scottish Shakespeare
> Of modern days, I chiefly longed to see.[23]

It took Thomson and his companion two days to walk from Portpatrick
to Dumfries; on the third day,

> Soon as I knew his Bardship lived convenient
> I for him sent, nor could I wait till morning
> I sent – he came! – But O ye heavenly powers
> What strange emotions ran o'er all my soul
> When I beheld the Ayrshire poet's face.
> And is it he? I looked and look'd again,
> And scarce could credit give my wandering eyes.
> He spoke – I listen'd with a pleasing awe,
> Attention hung on everything he said.
> O yes Hibernians, I beheld the Bard,
> Old Scotia's jewel and the Muses' darling,
> Whose matchless lays, despite of wasting time,
> Shall to the last of earthly generations
> Remain old Nature's boast and Scotia's [?][24]

On his return to Ireland, Thomson suggested to John Rabb, printer of the *Northern Star*, a radical Belfast newspaper, that he should contact Burns. Rabb replied on 4 March, 1794:

> I'll very gladly open a correspondence with Mr Burns and send him the Star, which I have a prospect of getting forwarded by Lennon [?] of Dundee [?]. I would like to devote a wee corner of the newspaper to the Muse constantly, but while this blessed war lasts, the Papers will all be filled with foreign news, that is to say such stuff as the London folk please to give us. I'll watch a slack and gratify our readers with some of what you have sent me . . . The first day you're in Belfast *Garrison!* will you call and tell me how Burns lives now? what the Scotch people are about, etc., etc.[25]

Another of Thomson's correspondents, the young naval purser Luke Mullan, formerly a neighbour in Carngranny, resembles Rabb in his impatience with contemporary politics and strong preference for literary subjects. In one letter he writes:

> By all means send me the 'Ayrshire Rose'. The leaf you sent smells so sweet I must have the whole . . . I have seen the new edition of the Poet's in Edinburgh. The Mutiny [at the Nore] is all happily settled. They have granted us all we desired and pardon'd us for asking it. For a more particular detail I refer you to any newspaper.[26]

Mullan visited Burns also and his graphic and interesting account contrasts markedly with his terse handling of the Mutiny:

> We were at the time in the Sun Tavern and at the instant saw the Edinburgh coach stop at the door and Mr Burns alight *limping* from a fall he had got in Edinburgh. The great man limped into the room – Menzies said he hop'd he would excuse the freedom he had taken of sending for him, and added that the only business we had with him was to have the honour of drinking with the only Scottish poet now alive. We were drinking porter – Mr Burns laid hold, and after drinking our healths *heartily* said, 'There are many Scots poets besides me. However, I thank you for the compliment.' I ventured to say, 'They are so distant from you, Mr Burns, that you cannot say they are beside you at all.' Burns laugh'd heartily, and shook me by the hand and I never felt so pleased at having said anything like a good thing in my life before.[27]

Burns' life history, his character, infidelity to his wife, his bons mots, anecdotes concerning the composition of his poems, schemes to obtain samples or even facsimiles of his handwriting, occur frequently in Thomson's correspondence. There is a particularly charming story from Mullan:

There is a young man on board that has seen him [Burns] many a time, and had the superlative honour of sleeping with him one night in the same bed. I was eager to glean anything ever so trifling of so great a man – he inform'd me that there was not a word passed between them except that when they lay down Burns said, 'You strip very fast' and in the morning asked him, 'how do you like me for a bedfellow?' Behold the vanity of collecting the sayings of great men![28]

Volume I of the *Ulster Journal of Archaeology* records an interesting folk-tale which has parallels even in our own less naive times, when you can meet people who claim, for instance, that they 'jammed' with Eric Clapton in a pub in Portrush:

Some 4 or 5 years ago, an old gentleman told me that when he was a boy, he knew an aged farmer who professed to have met Burns repeatedly in different parts of the north east of Co. Antrim, at country jollifications especially when the poet, he said, would sometimes sing his own songs for the company. According to this tradition, he would seem to have been [in Ulster] 'fou for weeks thegither.'[29]

There seems to be no record of such a visit by Burns. Possibly the story arose from some kind of communal wishful thinking, or perhaps some Scots rogue was capitalizing on Burns' phenomenal popularity in Co. Antrim! Even after 'the shock of hearing of the death of Burns', Ulster poets and literati continued to pay homage at his cottage and at his grave.[30]

In 1825, Thomas Scott produced an 'Extemporaneous Effusion on Seeing the Cottage in which Burns was born', and David Herbison wrote 'Lines Composed at the Grave of Burns' sometime around 1848. The poet John Fullerton, writing around 1867, seems almost to conflate Robert Burns and the whole experience of Scotland: 'I twice visited Scotland, once in my youth and again at the end of thirty years. I looked on the monument of Burns and the scene of his nativity.'[31]

It is not hard to understand why Burns made such a profound impression on his Ulster contemporaries. His successful use of a dialect very close to their own, his perceived social status and educational attainments, his attractive personality and his political views all combined to make him seem like one of their own. At the same time, his poetry was clearly deserving of, and received, international acclaim and it quickly became almost as much part of the local culture as the Bible or the metrical psalms. Indeed, there is one striking instance in the Thomson correspondence when a Burns tag is used in a context in which one would expect a Biblical quotation. In a letter which arrived on June 1 1815, the day Thomson died, J Getty of Cullybackey wrote to his friend:

I am truly and heartily sorry to hear that you are so low. I trust however that you may still remain a little longer with us but if it is otherwise determined God grant you a saving interest in our Lord Jesus Christ and that you and I may meet in [a] happier and better world, where to use the expression of Burns, worth of the heart is alone distinction of the man.[32]

Even after the myth of the Ayrshire ploughman and the personality cult had faded somewhat, Burns' poetry retained its appeal for people in the North of Ireland. In 1858, Abraham Hume wrote that in 'the Scotch districts Burns' poems were better known than in many parts of North Britain itself.'[33] A year later, Belfast celebrated Burns' centenary with a banquet and speeches. The novelist Benedict Kiely, born in Tyrone in 1919, says that

Burns became a popular folk author in Ulster, Catholic and Protestant, as he never was nor never could have been in any other part of Ireland. He still remained so in my boyhood, and I recall the local ragged rhymester saying to me with a seriousness at which it was not possible to laugh, 'Burns was the best of us.'[34]

The Ulster poets of the eighteenth century, even more than those of the twentieth, acknowledged Burns as 'a man and a brither.' Thomson's papers and poems, and the verse of his colleagues, is full of evidence of how they regarded the poet's craft as a freemasonry, but despite their eulogies, they were far from being awestruck by Burns' attainments. They imitated some of his subjects and diction, partly in flattery, partly in hopes to excel him in what was clearly to them almost a communal enterprise: a printed version of the popular Ulster evening entertainments known as 'singings' or 'singing schools'. It was at these events that several of the Co. Antrim poets had their first and inevitably addicting experience of the exhilaration of success in competitive verse composition, and of the resulting applause. These were occasions where 'any person who could manage to manufacture an extempore verse was at liberty to repeat the lines, while the members of the company were obliged to repeat them.'[35]

Not all those in the audience were applauding, however. The *Belfast Newsletter* of 8 June 1792, printed a long and intemperate letter from one 'Civilis', which indicates that not everyone in Ulster shared the tastes in literature and language of those associated with Burns. He attacks

the disgusting gibberish of Scottish versification with which our eyes, our ears, our feelings, have been so much wounded. It is strange that, when so noble a language as the English can be had, any writer whatever in these countries should yet have recourse to a dialect absolutely barbarous, especially as the best authors among the Scots themselves have long since abandoned it for the elegant and expressive English. I do not think I am easily wrought upon by prejudice, but I acknowledge myself to be one of those who have an invincible

aversion to the Scotch language and the Scotch accent; and I may say the same
with regard to the Irish. Happily for the republic of letters, they are both falling
fast into disuse and oblivion while the beautiful, the energetic, the admirable
English language . . . should be made the universal medium of communication
throughout the British empire.

He goes on to admit reluctantly that Scottish verse might appeal to 'the
bucolic inhabitants of Galloway or some of our own countrymen round
the shores of Newtown-lough or the back parts of Island-magee', but
regrets that 'authors should so prostitute their talents and obstruct their
own reputation by writing in such a contemptible tongue.' Civilis' linguistic impartiality and objectivity is surpassed only by his knowledge of
natural history. His letter continues with a commendation of a Scottish
writer's 'Ode to a Cuckoo' in pure English, but he complains that the
author has erred in describing the bird's seasonal migrations:

He could not be so far ignorant of the real history of the bird as not to know
that it performs no such peregrinations over the earth; but like other species of
creatures, when it leaves us, remains in a torpid state in some place of con-
cealment until revived by the return of spring.[36]

The letter is so extreme it might almost be a joke, but the views
expressed would certainly have been familiar at that time. In the eighteenth and nineteenth centuries, Ulster still preserved what one observer
described as the

usual division into English, Irish and Scotch. The dialect and customs of these
distinct races are as . . . different from each other as their respective creeds. The
members of the established church are denominated Englishmen, they speak
with an accent less provincial than the Dissenters or Roman Catholics, the
Scotch and Irish, and forming a kind of medium between these two discordant
bodies of people in religious opinions, language and habits, are usually treated
with respect and kindness by both.[37]

What passed in Ulster as the 'genuine form of the English language' was
of higher status throughout the period under discussion and has remained
so right up to the present day.[38] The rural poets generally, though not universally, quit Scots to write in English on serious subjects such as death;
when they do use English, they are sufficiently linguistically aware to
avoid rhymes which could betray a Scots pronunciation, such as between
'laughed' and 'soft'. Newspapers were full of advertisements for schools
which stressed the importance of the high status language. In 1787 Eliza
Tucker stated that her establishment in Hillsborough, Co. Down, would
teach young ladies to read with an English accent, and in 1796 another

teacher was still better qualified to correct provincialisms in her young ladies: 'her place of residence [in England] was the court end of the town in London.'[39]

Scots forms and archaic or dialectal English forms alike were attacked by teachers and orthoepists, though the Scots forms were more noticeable and therefore more vulnerable to attack. Some of those who wanted to eradicate provincialism were opposed to liberalism in politics, and seem even to have viewed them as intertwined errors; they favoured instead 'an unerring fixed standard . . . in our living language to surround our constitution with a brazen wall'.[40] Still others – perhaps the majority in the late eighteenth century – were motivated by a desire to modernize their speech as well as other aspects of their society: 'Whatever then the prevailing mode adopted by the first of adepts in the English language, ought as far as possible to be propagated among those whose . . . willingness to lay aside established error can scarcely be doubted.'[41]

In 1860, the local orthoepist David Patterson remarked that since Belfast people were 'in communication and intercourse with every part of the world' and 'increasingly in the world's notice . . . it behoves us to mind our Ps and Qs.' It is worth noting that Patterson recognised and valued Belfast's 'continually increasing importance', but was unable to resist the pull of the centre in his demand for conformity to the standard of the 'metropolis of the English language'.[42] (He was also sufficiently obtuse to print as the motto to his preface the Burnsian tag, complete with non-standard forms, about the 'chiel amang ye takin' notes'!)

An interest in language and linguistics is present in most intelligent people. Individuals' attitudes to their own language simultaneously shape and reflect many allied assumptions and aspirations in their society, on matters as diverse as nationality, educational theories, religion and child-rearing. As the nineteenth century went on, Ulster people, particularly Scots speakers, found themselves in a quandary which would be familiar to whole societies today. On the one hand, they felt an attachment to their native Scots forms and the Scots poetry that reflected the culture in which they had been reared; on the other, they wished to see themselves as progressive, modern and improving. This tension is exactly paralleled by the contemporary conflict in which the Romantic interest in rural life and in dialect pulled against the status accorded by society to the industrial and non-provincial.

There were a few in Ulster who displayed a robust provincial pride, proud of the achievements of local poets and printers and intellectual life generally. 'It has long been the fashion to recommend books to public notice by stating them to have been printed in London. The public will probably be better pleased to hear that the above small piece of elegant printing [was] PRINTED IN BELFAST.'[43] Others recommended that local poets should be encouraged and that all evidence of talent should be fostered, quite often drawing metaphors from the contemporary enthusiasm for the exploitation of mineral resources.

In a long essay delivered as a paper to a literary society in Belfast in 1840, Henry R Montgomery pleaded for a native literature 'rife with reflections on the distinctive manners, customs, opinions and peculiar characteristics of the people to whom it belongs', and he expressed concern about the harm done to local life by 'the servile adoption of the manners and feelings and sentiments of others.'[44] A few of those who wrote in Scots, chiefly in the preceding generation, seem to be exploring and celebrating their own identity in just the way Montgomery recommended: 'Should the reader of the following effusion suppose that in some parts the author has imitated the Scottish dialect, he would wish to correct this idea by alledging that he has written in *his own* style – in the language of his native glen.'[45]

In 1844, Robert Huddleston of Moneyrea, Co. Down, wrote in still more trenchant style to defend his use of

> Ulster-Irish (which some in their unmeaning eccentricity may term Scotch, to tear even the credit of language from its native home) . . . Neither has he travelled to London for the prevailing and genteel idiom of the sister-land . . . but with the language which Nature brought him to his door and handed to him at the first dawn of prattle and bade him wear through life; he sings with pride the funny drolls, the loves and pleasures of his native land.[46]

Optimism like Montgomery's, and confidence like Huddleston's, are not strongly represented in Victorian and twentieth century Ulster. The middle ground between rural/conservative values and the values of a progressive centralizing society, like all middle grounds, is hard to hold. Those who try to assert local pride run the risk of being described as provincial, and those who seek to foster local identity need to be lucky as well as enthusiastic – economic prosperity in this context can sometimes be a mixed blessing.

Increasingly through the nineteenth and into the twentieth century, circumstances have combined to weaken Ulster's earlier ties with Scotland. Ironically, decisions unwittingly taken by central government have been crucial. The system of National Education, introduced in 1831 for the whole of Ireland, seems intended, through its reading materials and ethos, to focus the child's attention on only two aspects of his identity – as an Irish person and as a citizen of a magnificent far-flung empire. There was little or no recognition of a Scottish element in the culture of the northern part of the island, probably because the materials were prepared either in Dublin or in England. Again, as part of an all-Ireland plan, and to answer the needs of that wider community, Queen's College, Belfast, was founded in 1849 and has provided third-level education for generations of Ulster students within an Irish and British context, who would earlier have been influenced by the Scottish system and ethos.

Perhaps most significantly of all, the political history of Ulster in the last 150 years has diverted people's attention from a concern with their cultural roots: they have been forced to decide between the Irish or the wider British context for their economic and social aspirations and political ideals. The links with Scotland are now acknowledged only by Protestants, and generally at a somewhat superficial level – sentimentality regarding Burns, pipe bands and scenery, and the preference for Scottish universities over those in England evinced by young people who choose not to attend Queen's University in Belfast. There is little real knowledge of Scotland and too many competing interests nowadays to permit the re-awakening of old affections.

Language remains the strongest link and is felt to be so by most natives of the province, Catholic as well as Protestant. Both Ulster and Scotland however, see their heritage in language diversity as under unprecedented threat from the twentieth century's inventions – radio, film, television, even the telephone and mass tourism. Is it a sign that a language variety is regarded as central and vital to a given community, or is it a sign of the final triumph of the standard language, when schoolteachers begin to urge their pupils to collect and record local dialect?

It is scarcely surprising that links between two communities separated by a sea channel will weaken with time. It *is* surprising that the migrants and their descendants seem to have forgotten their ancestral homes, family connections and Scottish traditions so quickly that the sudden flowering of interest in Scotland in the late eighteenth century comes more as something new than as merely a revival. The existing connections were suddenly reinforced by the emergence in Scotland of an important rôle model – Robert Burns. The intellectual life of Ulster was enriched by the poems of those who admired him, and this helped to sustain the short-lived maturity of cultural identity and sense of place evident in certain literati, a development perhaps paralleled by the political aspirations of those who supported the United Irishmen. The resulting prominence given to Ulster-Scots in local publications produced an adverse reaction among those in the province who looked to England and its language as models for the whole of Ireland.

This language controversy, as so often, was merely one aspect of a deeper and still more problematic uncertainty and disagreement about cultural or national identity. Protestants in present-day Ulster characteristically tend to make negative responses to questions about national identity – 'not Irish and not English'. Once again, they seem to have forgotten the positive contribution made by their Scottish inheritance, unlike the eighteenth century's Hugh Porter, who recognised that he was

> not Scotch nor English either,
> But part o' baith mix'd up thegither.[47]

5

'A Mere Irish Faction': The Orange Institution in Nineteenth Century Scotland

ELAINE MCFARLAND

The intellectual and cultural cross-fertilisation between Scotland and Ulster was a commonplace by the late eighteenth century. Until this point, the process had a basically 'progressive' stamp. The Scottish universities, at which Ulster Presbyterians received their higher education, powerfully aided the diffusion of Enlightenment ideas in the Province.[1] The United Irishmen, no less, paid tribute to them as, 'those seminaries who have supplied the world with statesmen, orators, historians and philosophers.'[2] In turn, Scottish radicals like Thomas Muir looked to the vigorous tradition of middle class politics in Belfast and the North East for inspiration and guidance.[3]

And yet it was not political radicalism, and certainly not its associated 'brotherhood of affection' between Protestant and Roman Catholic, which was to prove the most enduring product of the interchange between the two societies in the 1790s. Instead, this role can be claimed by a movement of the 'lower orders', and one which appeared as an anachronism even at its birth, when set against the general eighteenth century tide of rationalism and religious toleration. The movement was that most famous bulwark of popular, pugnacious Protestantism – the Loyal Orange Institution. Its energetic growth soon perplexed and disgusted liberally-inclined Ulstermen like William Drennan and his circle, just as it was to confound generations of commentators on both sides of the North Channel.[4]

This essay considers the importation of Orangeism into Scotland, and analyses its most formative period of development in the nineteenth century. In a sense the movement has met with striking success here, displacing the native covenanting tradition in all its complexity, as the typical image of 'militant Protestantism' in the minds of most Scots: 'No

Surrender' has a far greater resonance today than 'Christ's Crown and Covenant'. At the same time, Orangeism's great ideological power and high public profile were arguably never fully mobilised in Scotland, where the Orangemen were to remain marginalised as a social and political force. The explanation for this relative failure tells us a great deal about Scottish Orangeism's characteristic internal problems, but is also testimony to the practical disjunctures between the societies of Scotland and Ulster, which persisted despite their ethnic and ideological affinity.

The Orange Institution was a spontaneous populist phenomenon rooted in agrarian conflicts between Protestant and Catholic peasants in the border counties of Ulster.[5] An unfavourable land-population ratio and tenure system had resulted in chronic land hunger. This found expression in a bizarre variety of secret societies, of which Orangeism was destined to be the most successful. The decisive conflict came on 21 September 1795 at the Diamond hamlet in County Armagh. A 'battle', or more correctly, a brawl, took place in which Protestants, greatly outnumbered, drove off a force of Roman Catholics. In the euphoric aftermath the first Orange Lodge was founded, based loosely on freemasonry and the models of earlier Protestant defensive associations. Lodges quickly expanded in Armagh, Antrim and the Lagan Valley, at this stage with little help from the gentry. This group's involvement was shortly to increase, but to the dismay of conspiracy theorists, throughout much of the Order's subsequent history the issue of upper class control was to prove a divisive one, with the actual extent of control historically variable.[6]

Despite the highly localised conditions which surrounded its foundation, Orangeism spread rapidly outside its Ulster heartland. This was hardly surprising since emigration was a central fact of Ulster's social history from the late eighteenth century. Nor was it unexpected, given its close geographical and cultural proximity, that Scotland became one of the Order's earliest outposts. The first lodge was established in Maybole, Ayrshire, some time in 1799, probably by a company of the Ayrshire and Wigtownshire Militia, returning from service in the 1798 Rebellion in Ireland with an Orange warrant of authority from the Irish Grand Lodge.[7]

No official records survive for this early period, but it seems likely that, as in England, Protestant Irish migrants were even more common than ex-servicemen in Orange ranks.[8] Murray, in his history of the Scottish weavers, notes 'a prodigious influx' of Irish into Scotland in 1799, following a heavy flow throughout the decade.[9] This reflected both political unrest following the upheaval of the '98 Rebellion and the undermining of the independence and prosperity of weavers and other skilled craftsmen as a new, more intensively capitalist, mode of production emerged in the North East of Ireland.[10] The Ulster counties, where Protestants were numerically strongest, indeed provided the majority of new settlers.[11]

Not all of these were, of course, potential Orange recruits. Some may have even brought with them the tradition of Presbyterian radicalism, but a close correlation does exist between the pattern of early Irish migration and the diffusion of Orangeism in Scotland.[12] The Irish settled in the south western counties of Wigtown and Kirkcudbright where the rural labour market was buoyant, and in Ayrshire, Renfrewshire and Glasgow where weavers were still in demand. In Maybole, for example, heavy immigration began precisely in the 1795–1800 period.[13] Similarly, the first lodges were also rooted in the agricultural South West and the Ayrshire weaving centres. By the early decades of the century they had spread to expanding textile areas such as Paisley and Pollokshaws. The first Orange walk had already been held in Glasgow in 1821 and contemporaries were in little doubt concerning Ulster Protestant involvement in the foundation of the lodges there.[14]

For all its new blood, Orangeism had a slow and uncertain start in Scotland. Its origins were clearly less dramatic than in Ulster, with no equivalent of the Battle of the Diamond and its accompanying mythology. The Orange Institution in Scotland seems to have crept in without raising much significant comment. Its initial progress was unremarkable, but by the 1820s the lodges were already beginning to broaden beyond their original functions as benefit and convivial societies, and now displayed that same spirit of faction fighting and 'combative sectarianism' which marked their Ulster brethren.[15]

Various factors helped account for the relative weakness of the early movement in Scotland. In the first place, the general cultural context was less favourable than in Ulster. There was indeed a powerful, emotional strand of No Popery, rooted in the Scottish Reformation, but the more specific *Orange* tradition, which drew on the Glorious Revolution and the subsequent Williamite military campaigns, was much less relevant than in Ireland, where it had potent symbolic value for the embattled settler community. Lacking this basic point of reference, Orangeism found it difficult to anchor itself into the older, undifferentiated form of militant Protestantism, and to translate indigenous anti-Catholicism into lodge membership.[16]

Secondly, as an organisation with a large membership of working class migrants, the first lodges seem to have been extremely sensitive to the rigours of the economic situation in early nineteenth century Scotland. Labour scarcity and high real wages began increasingly to be reversed in the 1820s. In this climate, members were less able or willing to pay dues, and lodges were hence liable to fold.[17]

Thirdly, it is vital to underline the independent attitude maintained towards sectarian disturbances by magistrates and the judiciary in Scotland. This was less common in Ulster, where protection from legal proceedings was often regarded as a fringe benefit of Orange membership.[18]

Behind this lay the basic fact that it was only the plebeian rank and file of the Irish lodges which had been transplanted to Scotland. Protestant migrants were not drawn from the gentry and aristocracy, and there is no evidence of the Scottish lodges recruiting local representatives of these groups.

The lack of upper class members who might have offered legal protection was not for the want of trying. Notably in the early 1830s, Orange officials such as the poet and journalist William Motherwell joined the Order with high political ambitions, wishing to make the lodges the nucleus of a new ultra-Tory grouping to counter reform initiatives in Scotland. The actual result was a hostile Parliamentary Commission on Orangeism and bitter recrimination from Orange leaders.[19] Attempts at manipulating the Order for political ends ran against decisive obstacles. Particularly telling was the refusal of Tory magnates to identify with Orangeism, in view of its vulgar populism and its status as an 'alien importation'. This latter view was indeed gaining more general currency in literate Scottish opinion by the 1830s, and is neatly crystallised in the comments of Motherwell's despairing biographer McConechy. To McConechy's own mind, Orangeism was really 'a particular form of one of those murderous factions into which Irish society was divided.' It had not occurred to Motherwell that:

> whatever the merits real or imaginary of the Orange Confederation might be, its introduction to Scotland could be attended with no benefit whatever and that if it was intended to achieve benefits of a permanent kind, it was only on the soil which had generated and nourished it that this could have happened. As an antagonist to Popery and Jacobinism it was certainly not wanted in Presbyterian Scotland, and a little reflection might have satisfied . . . that the civil and religious rights of the people of this country were not to be upheld through the instrumentality of a Hibernian political fraternity which had outlived the necessity which gave it birth . . . it had too many of the characteristics of a sectarian club to be agreeable to sober minded Scotsmen.[20]

Faced with this damning rejection from above, the Orangemen were further thrown back on their own resources in the 1830s and 40s. In this they showed a certain resilience and popular momentum. Following on earlier disappointments and the demise of its more politically-minded leaders, the Orange Institution in Scotland now positively regrouped. The plebeian lodges continued to function and even expand, and a new Scottish Grand Lodge, significantly under the titular patronage of an Irish peer, was formed in 1835. As well as administrative reorganisation, these two decades also saw an upsurge of more 'energetic' activity. The industrial areas of Ayrshire and Lanarkshire now became distinguished by growing sectarian tensions and open faction fights.[21]

This new impulse was maintained in the 1850s and 60s, with heightened violence, especially in the Lanarkshire coalfields.[22] It was also reflected in a quite impressive growth in following. Compared with the total membership of 660 listed for the year 1848, single Orange demonstrations in Airdrie, Paisley or Glasgow could now turn out this figure with ease. Yet this Orange advance was still within definite constraints. There is no indication, for example, that the native working class were attracted to Orangeism as a mechanism to give voice to their own antipathy to Irish Roman Catholics. Instead, Ulster Protestants remained the backbone of the lodges. Responding to the pull of industrialisation in the West of Scotland, they had continued to settle in increasing numbers, bringing with them their familiar tradition of ritualistic physical confrontation with Catholics.[23]

Again, contemporaries were acutely conscious of these developments. The *Glasgow Courier* viewed an outbreak of sectarian rioting in Paisley in 1859 as: '. . . a necessity imposed by the introduction of a new element in the population, given the opening up of extensive mineral fields in the neighbourhood.'[24] The Sheriff of Ayrshire, reflecting on the disturbances in his county in the 1860s, gave the same explanation:

> Of late years numbers of Irishmen amounting to a very considerable part of the population, have become resident in the parishes of Dalry and Kilbirnie, where they are employed in the coal pits and ironstone mines . . . There are amongst them a certain number of Orangemen. And an Orange lodge is established in each of the towns of Dalry and Kilbirnie.[25]

In short, while assisting expansion and firing the Orangemen's fighting spirit, the Ulster influx was doing little to mitigate the early Order's negative reputation in Scotland. The Orange Institution was viewed not as a legitimate vehicle for safeguarding Protestantism, but as a fighting society whose '. . . party displays, however well intentioned, are not for this latitude. They are imports as unwelcome as many of the Irish themselves.'[26] Against this background, a further, even more dramatic acceleration in Orange fortunes from around the mid-1860s surprised the Orangemen as well as sceptical onlookers.

The years 1865 to 1900 mark the real expansion and consolidation of Orangeism's mass membership in Scotland, an advance paralleled by the Order in Ulster. Grand Master George McLeod's claim in 1875 that he stood 'at the head of 60,000 members in Scotland . . .' and likewise the *Glasgow News* estimate of no less than 90,000 Orangemen in Scotland in 1878 can be treated with caution.[27] Nevertheless, the figures which could now be turned out at the Order's great ceremonial occasions were impressive: well-marshalled 12th of July parades indeed began to replace violent confrontation as the major form of Orange public activity. Twelfth attendances did tend to fluctuate greatly from year to year, but as growth was generally sustained in the 1870s and 80s, it is likely the Order approached the new century with a membership of at least 30,000. This figure can be put in some perspective if one notes that two of the most powerful trade unions in Scotland, the Amalgamated Society of Engineers and the Society of Boilermakers and Iron Shipbuilders, each had around 8,000.[28]

Two questions arise from this spurt of growth: what were the causes, and how far did it represent a real break with the uncertain progress of the early lodges? Institutional reorganisation, with the healing of an organisational schism in the late 1870s, was one useful adjunct to expansion. Certainly, this smoothed the complex logistics required for elaborate Twelfth processions. Yet, while official Orange history particularly highlights this factor, other sustained developments were also at work in Scotland at the levels of politics, ideology and economics.

First, from the mid 1860s onwards, the Order was confronted by a series of energising political issues, which taken together help explain the cyclical pattern of Orangeism's public displays. Initially came the crisis from 1866–68 over the disestablishment of the Church of Ireland. This was followed by the successive disestablishment crises which shook the Church of Scotland in the 1870s and 80s. By 1879, Orangemen were faced also with the prospect of a restored Roman Catholic episcopal hierarchy in Scotland. Finally, an even more decisive and galvanising challenge came with Liberal attempts to push through Irish Home Rule in the Bills of 1886 and 1892.

A second, more broad-based and passive pre-condition for Orange expansion was an improving ideological climate. The lack of a significant Scottish vein of 'Orange' Protestant patriotism, which had hampered the fledgling Order, was eventually less circumscribing. The lodges had now managed to survive over half a century, and had established a familiar, if negative, public profile in their country of adoption. The Orangemen, from mid-century until the late 1870s, were also able to operate against the background of a febrile wave of No Popery in Scotland, which assumed a variety of forms from missionary societies to an anti-Popish press.[29] The direct causal role of this receptive environment should not be exaggerated. For besides chronological and geographical objections, personal and organisational links between Orangeism and the more indigenous forms of anti-Catholicism remained weak. One of the latter's most prominent outposts, the West of Scotland Protestant Association, wished explicitly to distance itself from Orangeism, which it identified with 'political faction'. Meanwhile, Orange leaders like George McLeod were openly contemptuous of the rival body, '. . . what are they worth, who can rely on their Protestantism?'[30]

In fact, a much more active factor in the Order's sustained 'take off' can be traced to continued Irish labour migration. An initial impressionistic connection might be made between the increased volume of Catholic Irish settlement and Orange expansion, but this does not bear close empirical scrutiny. The Order's largest numerical advance took place from the 1860s, precisely at the point when the number of immigrants of Roman Catholic Irish birth and descent was beginning to stabilise and even decline.[31] Conversely, in the 1840s, when rapid Orange expansion might have been expected to follow on increased Catholic numbers, the evidence presented above suggested sporadic violent outbursts, but a weak institutional basis for the Order, with fewer than a thousand members.

If a connection cannot be forced in this case, a more direct link is probable between the Order's progress and the further development of a thriving Ulster Protestant community in Scotland. The continuity with the first half of the century was noted by hostile contemporaries, but the Orange historian Cloughley was also well aware of the impetus still gained from Ulster migration. Of the 1860s, he commented: 'Many young Ulstermen crossed the Channel to find employment in Scotland. True to their principles they joined up with the Order in Scotland. The membership increased considerably, ever since the loyal Ulster immigrants and their descendants have rendered yeoman service to the Institution.'[32]

Actual quantification of this migration and subsequent settlement is constrained by the lack of religious data in the census, but Hutchison has calculated that between 1876 and 1881, 83 per cent of Irish immigrants to Scotland came from Ulster, and of these, 58 per cent hailed from the four predominantly Protestant counties.[33] Similarly, the exact extent of Ulster involvement in the late nineteenth century lodges is impossible to specify. Official documentary evidence is scanty. Orangemen leaving their own lodge in Ulster would be presented with a transfer certificate, which would be offered to the appropriate local lodge on arrival in Scotland, but these have not been systematically retained and collated. However, the number of prominent office-bearers of Ulster origins at Grand Lodge level is striking.[34]

The Ulster connection also adds a persuasive element to the motivation for Orange membership, namely that the lodges could provide a familiar rallying point in a new country at a time of inevitable social and economic stress. The lodge network retained a vital benevolent function, paralleling the provisions of the many late nineteenth century friendly societies. It also provided colour and pageantry, at minimal cost, in many otherwise bleak working class communities. It is notable that the Order in Greenock in the 1860s and 70s organised pilgrimages back to Ulster for the Twelfth celebrations there, a tradition which continues in Scotland today.[35]

Reviewing the peaceful mass parades of the 1870s onwards, the Orange Grand Masters McLeod and his successor C I Paton still had cause for anxiety and disappointment. Like the leaders of the 1830s, they had ambitions to make the Order 'the Mainspring of Conservatism' and 'a Power in the Land'. In reality, the absolute numerical advance of Orangeism was not sufficient to reverse its relatively marginal position in Scottish society. Political influence never developed sufficiently to meet the Order's aspirations, links with the major Scottish churches were weak, and its image with the wider Scottish public remained problematic.

There were other more basic limitations to Orange progress. At no point did the Order really manage to extend its geographical stronghold beyond the West of Scotland. Its rank and file remained firmly drawn from the industrial working class, with a large unskilled or 'lumpen' element in some areas such as Greenock, where casual labour predominated.[36] Meanwhile, despite attempts to woo an upper class membership like that in Ulster, by the foundation of a 'gentlemen's lodge', Beaconsfield's Purple Guards, the Scottish Grand Lodge was still largely drawn from lower middle class shopkeepers and professionals.[37]

Even the quantitative advance of Orangeism in Scotland is less impressive when viewed comparatively. Whereas there were around 30,000 Orangemen at the turn of the century, Ulster, with one third of Scotland's population, had some 1,500 to 2,000 local lodges with a 100,000 members.[38] Even when set against other major importations of the Order, Scotland's position is rather unfavourable. In Canada, where the Order had been introduced by Ulster settlers in the 1820s, there were estimated to be a 100,000 members by 1870, out of a population of four million. Membership spread with the opening up of the country westwards, and by World War One it had increased by a further 50,000.[39]

As in the case of the early lodges, the unfortunate position of the mature Orange Institution in Scotland cannot be reduced to a single causal factor. Instead, it is helpful to reconsider the key internal characteristics of Scottish Orangeism and to examine how these interacted with specific features of Scottish society and politics. The most significant contribution was made by what can conveniently be summarised as 'the Ulster factor'. For here we discover that although boosting the order's growth, the Ulster membership could still prove a double-edged sword when trying to establish Orangeism as a respectable and organic 'Scottish' institution.

A distinction must immediately be drawn between the indigenous Scots' reaction to Ulster Protestant migration and their hostile perception of the Orange Order as an 'alien', 'Irish' transplantation. The Orange historian Sibbet noted approvingly the '. . . wonderful intimacy which had existed since the early Plantation days between Scotland and Ulster.'[40] Doubtless, tensions did exist between the migrants and the host society: it has been suggested that in Lanarkshire, for example, Ulster Protestants were considered 'a community within a community'.[41] Yet it seems clear that Ulster's Protestant population were much more easily accepted than Roman Catholic migrants, and that they achieved a greater degree of integration. The Church of Scotland report which excoriated the Catholic

Irish in Scotland, typically commented that there was no complaint, '. . . of the presence of an Orange population in Scotland, they are of the same race as ourselves and are readily assimilated into the Scottish population.'[42]

Despite becoming popularly associated, as the above quote shows, with the generally well-received Ulster population, the Orange Institution continued to arouse a much more suspicious reaction from all classes of indigenous Scots, who condemned its roots in 'Irish issues and quarrels'. Often this was compounded by their recognition of two further unwelcome Orange characteristics, ironically similar to native perceptions of the Catholic Irish. The first was the Order's combative nature and territoriality, which had been vital to its functioning in Ulster, and the second was the impression that 'the Orangeman is anywhere seldom a teetotaller'.[43] In practice, these elements were inter-related and were often jointly cited whenever one was called into account.

Clearly, here was an important continuation of the contemptuous neutrality of the 1820s and 30s, towards what was viewed as the import of alien party feeling into Scotland. Even the *Glasgow News*, which had proudly proclaimed in its first edition that 'Glasgow is the head and heart of Protestantism in Scotland', commented in its editorial on the Twelfth celebrations of 1874:

> We never seem to escape from the possibility of the turmoil which occurred at the Boyne being resuscitated and sounding in our ears . . . We can understand people differing from each in their religious sentiments: but their disputes . . . ought to be settled by words and not by blows. The absurdity of these wretched quarrels between Protestant and Catholic is evident to all out of the immediate range of their influence . . . The quarrel is one of the most foolish and groundless the world has ever seen.[44]

It is equally significant that the Orangemen themselves viewed these problems as priorities. A pioneering Orange public gathering in Paisley, in the form of an alcohol-free 'soirée', was hailed as a bold innovation in 1856, not so much because of opposition from the local Catholic community but because of 'almost universal Protestant prejudice'. The display, it was felt, had far to go to prove the Orangemen were 'not mere party zealots but among the best, most loyal and trustworthy of Protestants'.[45] The platform speakers could not resist imparting advice to their audience, especially since most were 'natives of the Sister kingdom and therefore . . . in a great measure strangers to Scotland'. The Rev. James Stewart stressed that: 'in the battle of religious controversy . . . the two [Ulster and Scotland] are brethren and shoulder to shoulder they will stand or fall. Study therefore,' he suggested, 'the peace of the people among whom you dwell, for in their peace you shall have peace.'[46]

His clerical colleague, the Rev. Fraser, was more pessimistic on the Order's Scottish prospects:

> In this country Orangemen are usually shunned as returned convicts, many intelligent and conscientious men avoid them as they would a mad dog. If I found my notion of an Orangeman from prevalent opinions, I would describe him thus:- An Orangeman is a senseless bigot who sports Orange lilies in Summer and is especially fond of fighting and marches on the 12th July, and who delights to sing *Boyne Water* and *Croppies Lie Down*; and to drink strange toasts about 'the Glorious, Pious and Immortal Memory' . . . Unfortunately, . . . when an idea fastens itself in the mind of a Scotsman it is as difficult to get out as the burr of a Scots thistle, when it has wrapped itself up in the fringe of his plaid.[47]

The latter observation may have contained an element of truth, since in 1870, William Johnston of Ballykilbeg, a prominent Ulster Orange figure and guest chairman of an Orange soirée in Greenock, was still making the familiar complaint:

> In Scotland you are misunderstood and misrepresented, you are spoken of as though you were a mere Irish faction, a foreign import brought to disturb the peace of the country. You are no such thing (hear, hear). If you were rightly understood and your principles looked at you would soon be found to be the true apostolic descendants of John Knox. If other people have forgot the contest waged in Scotland for an open Bible, the Orangemen have not forgotten it.[48]

Johnston's concern to mitigate Orangeism's 'foreignness' was also shared by the Scottish Grand Lodge in the 1870s and 80s. This was voiced in attempts to emphasise the anti-Papal element in Scottish history, and to link the Scottish experience to events in the Glorious Revolution and Irish history. Particular candidates for the treatment were the Scottish Covenanters, and the most fervent exponent of this version of Scottish history was Grand Master Paton, who himself boasted a prominent Covenanter forbear. His bombastic claims on the 1879 Twelfth platform were typical:

> It was for no insignificant question that the Covenanters struggled, they contended and they suffered, but for the right to worship according to their own conscience and to the Commandments given in His Word . . . If they had failed the British Isles would have been mere vassal Kingdoms of the Pope. The struggle ending in the battle of the Boyne, however, secured it to them, who had been persecuted by Claverhouse and his troopers in the wild moors in which they sought refuge, as truly as it was the crowning victory of the brave defenders of Iniskillen and Londonderry.[49]

The pervasively negative image of Scottish Orangeism in the late nineteenth century certainly makes the absence of an upper class following credible. It also suggests that the apathy to the Order of the average Scottish worker was not simply the product of some innate set of 'liberal values'. If the Order was seen as some intrinsically 'Ulster' phenomenon with undertones of disorder and drunkenness, lodge membership would hold little attraction for the indigenous Scot, often employed in a skilled trade, where the exclusion of Roman Catholics was an established fact. Nor would an annual ritualistic assertion of 'Protestant Ascendancy' on the 12th of July have much practical relevance in most Scottish workplaces and communities.

If, indeed, the native worker was inclined towards ceremony and arcane knowledge, the Masonic Order was a more familiar and realistic alternative. Freemasonry was more widespread in Scotland than Orangeism, with nearly 70,000 members in 1879.[50] It also had distinguished patrons among the royal family, aristocracy, municipal leaders and major employers of labour.[51] The organisation could even claim deep historical roots in Scotland, springing from the masons who had built Kilwinning Abbey in the twelfth century.[52] All this the Orange Grand Lodge could only look upon with baleful envy.

To understand fully the Orange Institution's marginalisation, we must also consider its relations with other key agencies in Scotland. The case of the Scottish churches, for example, represents probably the Order's least successful adaptation to Scottish conditions.[53] Here, Orangeism's negative reputation was effectively compounded by factors rooted historically in Scottish society, and beyond Orange control.

In contrast, Orangeism in Ulster enjoyed healthy ecclesiastical links as the nineteenth century progressed. Episcopalian clergymen were drawn into a closer relationship with the Order from the 1820s onwards in the face of an anticipated attack on tithes and state endowment. This set the typical early pattern for the lodges, particularly in Antrim, Down and north Londonderry, consisting of landlord, rector and curate, servants and agricultural labourers. As Protestant denominational rigidities weakened in the later years of the century, and Presbyterians shifted from their radical past into a staunch anti-Home Rule position, some of their ministers and congregations now also eagerly embraced Orangeism, additionally attracted by its official stand on Temperance and Sabbath observance.[54]

The Scottish Orangemen were less fortunate. The Institution had its clerical enthusiasts, but often these were eccentric mavericks like Rev. Robert Gault or Robert Thompson of Ladywell parish, Glasgow. The behaviour of the latter, an ardent self-publicist, was embarrassing even to the Orangemen.[55] While other ministers might appear on 12th of July platforms, they seem to have viewed this as part of their general missionary activity and very few mainstream clergymen were actually motivated to join the Order. Indeed, those who did were often, like Gault, themselves from Ulster, and thus familiar with Orangeism in its most congenial setting.

To some extent this distance again reflected elements in the Order's own ideological and social make-up. One factor working against a closer relationship with the churches was the Orangemen's rather arrogant claims to be 'pure Protestantism in action', and consequently superior to mere competing denominational interests. Drawing on the experience of the episcopalian Church of Ireland, the Order's very vocal insistence on a strong link between Church and State further alienated denominations such as the Free Church and the United Presbyterians, who had split from the Church of Scotland on precisely this type of issue. These claims were irritating in themselves, but when coupled with what many clergymen considered the squalid reality of the Scottish Orange lodges, they were particularly alienating.

Yet these points provide only part of the explanation for the lack of rapport with the Scottish churches. Similar problems after all had been faced and surmounted in Ulster. More critical was the disjuncture between the ecclesiastical situations in Orangeism's country of origin and its country of adoption. This was symbolised in the identification of the Order as a creature of the Irish episcopalian establishment and therefore, as McConechy had noted in the 1830s, 'certainly not wanted in Presbyterian Scotland.'[56]

Ulster Orange migrants, who had been communicants of the Church of Ireland, lacked a comfortable ecclesiastical roost in Scotland. Their own church had a strong Hanoverian and Constitutionalist background, and its churchmanship was often highly evangelical and 'Protestant'. As a former national church, it drew heavily on the aristocracy and gentry, but also assumed responsibility for the rural poor, and increasingly, the industrial working class.[57]

The Scottish Episcopalian Church into which these Orangemen would have been received was a very different body in terms of history, worship and class composition. It had been a mainstay of the Jacobite rebellions in Scotland, and it was not until 1792 that the penal laws to which it was subject were finally repealed. It took a considerable time before the Church could properly expand. Even in the 1840s and 50s, when many churches were built, there were only 40 or 50 clergymen in the whole south western diocese, which included Glasgow.[58] Besides, although there were some predominantly working class congregations in the north east, the west and Edinburgh, the real strength of Episcopalianism's nineteenth century advance lay in the anglicising gentry. Compared with its Irish counterpart though, the Church seems to have had a less imperative concern for poor relief or sense of duty towards less privileged sections of society.

At this level of development, then, the Scottish Episcopalian Church was as yet unprepared for the influx of thousands of migrant workers from Ulster. The rector of St Andrew's by the Green in Glasgow, for example, claimed there were 10,000 Episcopalians in the city by the late 1830s, but complained that 4,000 of them were 'Irish and destitute'.[59] More commonly, it seems, this group was received not in the mainstream of the Church, but by missions largely catering for the poor. Several of these opened in Glasgow, such as St Luke's, founded in Springburn in the 1870s, expressly for 'the English and Irish of the artisan class'.[60]

Alongside the logistic problems of finding a hospitable congregation, the strongly 'High Church' nature of Scottish Episcopalian worship was also a deterrent to the Orangeman arriving in Scotland. After attending Communion while on a visit to Scotland, Johnston of Ballykilbeg recorded in his diary: 'Took the sacrament with considerable hesitation, as I am of the opinion that it may not be right to participate in the pro-popish Scottish Episcopal Church'.[61] In fact in Scotland, most of the principles of the Oxford Movement were in operation long before the days of the English Tractarians and 'Puseyites'. These included the divine origin of the Church, apostolic succession and even, as concerned Johnston, the real presence of Christ in the eucharistic ceremony. Most commonly even in Glasgow and Edinburgh, it was the old 'Scottish rite', strongly liturgical in character, which was employed in services. Such 'ritualism' would of course be abhorrent to an Orangeman reared in the Irish Episcopal tradition of stern preaching and plain services.

Problems of transition also confronted Ulster Orange settlers who were Presbyterians, usually communicants of the Presbyterian Church in Ireland. These were doctrinal and partly political. Although the General Assembly of this Church had condemned the principle of disestablishment, and from the 1860s began to display determined Tory sentiments, it had allied itself with the Free Church of Scotland at the time of the 1843 Disruption. This then became its sister church in Scotland and the receiving body for its communicants. Thus, while most Orangemen would have preferred being taken under the wing of the Church of Scotland, they were directed towards membership of its rival. Not only was the Free Kirk a bulwark of Liberalism in Scotland, but its position on the autonomy and independence of Christian society lay at odds with the Orange insistence on the virtue of state endowed 'national' religion. Indeed, even if the Orangemen were willing to swallow their distaste and enter the Free Kirk, they may have faced difficulties caused by the often strict admission to membership among the dissenting bodies. For given widespread anti-Orange prejudices, the more douce congregations may have been less than willing to welcome these over-enthusiastic defenders of Protestantism.

So great was their frustration over these dislocations that the Orange leadership was moved to set up its own churches, such as the 'Independent

Congregation' established at Rutherglen in 1881, under another Ulster-born minister, T W Patrick.[62] Clearly, the nagging anxiety here was that their members would stay away from church attendance altogether, thus confirming the Scottish public in its worst suspicions of the Order.[63]

The Scottish Orangemen seem to have enjoyed a more positive presence in the political than in the ecclesiastical sphere.[64] Under the impetus of Disestablishment and Home Rule issues, links were developed with the Conservative Party from the mid-1860s onwards, and the result was something resembling an 'unofficial liaison' in Glasgow areas such as Bridgeton, Tollcross and Shettleston. The Orange contribution at ward level was rewarded in extravagant rhetoric from local Tory leaders like W C Maughan and J N Cuthbertson, and culminated in the presence of Orange leaders on the welcoming dais for Lord Salisbury's visit to Glasgow in 1884, and their presentation of a very long loyal address.[65]

Yet the Order's political relationships were to prove uneven and often tense. Orangemen did have a high public profile on the streets of key localities at election time, but this was not generally translated into representation on the Conservative Party's directing committees and councils. Admittedly, by the 1890s the party grew less abashed by Orange links, partly because a new generation of Conservatives could now identify with Orangeism as an effective popular bulwark for the preservation of the Unionist establishment in Ireland. Even so, the Orange presence in constituency bodies remained heavily localised in areas where they could best do their duty in turning out the working class vote. The reality was that the higher public visibility the Conservatives were now prepared to grant their Orange connections took place against the background of the party's general expansion and growth of confidence. The Orangemen were thus only one of a series of useful 'interest groups'.

Brief comparison with Ulster also underlines the limitations of Scottish Orangeism's political progress. In the former case, the anti-Home Rule campaign and the Toryism which sustained it had the Orange Order as its central binding component. Its enormous weight on the political establishment received formal acknowledgement in the Order's right to have 10–20 per cent of all delegates on the governing council of the Ulster Unionist Party.[66]

Obviously, in explaining the Order's more circumscribed political role in Scotland, its familiar internal characteristics again come into play. The simple fact of its more modest numerical progress here meant that it was never an indispensable electoral asset, although it could be a useful adjunct in some 'working mens' divisions'. An outright Orange alliance was also positively problematic at times in the 1880s, when the Conservatives were trying to woo right wing Liberals and even Irish Nationalist voters.[67]

Even when these alternatives were no longer relevant, Orangeism's unsavoury reputation could still be a deterrent. This was keenly felt by the Conservatives' new electoral partners from 1886, the breakaway Liberal

Unionists. Drawn largely from those business and professional sections of the Scottish bourgeoisie opposed to Home Rule, they shared the long-standing prejudices of their class against the 'ignorant' and populist overtones of the Orange Institution in Scotland. Typical was the diplomatic refusal of the Partick Liberal Unionist candidate Mr Parker Smith to visit the church of a local Orange partisan in Whiteinch.[68]

The Orangemen's own beliefs also contributed to the friction in their political relationships. Their support for the Conservatives was never unquestioning, but instead remained firmly conditional on the party displaying commitment to 'Protestant Principles'. Despite his wish to increase the Order's standing in the Conservative Party's estimation, Grand Master Paton was adamant that in the final analysis Orangeism was a *religious* organisation, and one which had been called only reluctantly into the political arena because its deadly foe, Popery, was essentially a political beast. By reason of its very superiority in this respect, he believed the Order could never be simple fodder for party manipulation:

> It is no political participation which is the bond of our union. The principles which bind us belong to a higher and nobler sphere. Political parties are always fluctuating and changing, their watchwords and battle cries are soon forgotten, but our principles are not changeable and our course of action must be the same until victory crowns our efforts, and till the cry arises 'Babylon is fallen, fallen . . . '[69]

Ultimately, as in the ecclesiastical case, broader external features of Scottish society had a further role in the Order's limitations. Two key points stand out here. First, for a significant period in the nineteenth century, the political force which the Orange Order felt it appropriate to support, the Conservative Party, was itself marginalised in most of Scotland. Even when anti-Home Rulers did decisively desert the Liberal standard after 1886, it was not to the Tories they turned, as in Ulster, but, as noted above, to their own newly-formed Liberal Unionist Party. The Tories were dependent on the electoral co-operation of this party for their success in Scotland until the closing years of the century.[70]

As for the Scottish working class and the petty bourgeoisie, the Liberals remained the party of the majority even after the split of 1886. Although links with the Liberals began to break down in the following decade as the party's ambiguous attitude towards its working class support became increasingly recognised, it was the need for independently-based working class representation which increasingly asserted itself in Scotland, eventually finding expression in the Independent Labour Party (ILP). In other words, the opportunities remained restricted for that full-blown working class Toryism, so evident in Ulster, which might have given Orangeism greater access to the mainstream of Scottish life.

Secondly, the imperfect political progress of Scottish Orangeism may, as Gallagher has suggested for 'inter-ethnic conflict' generally, reflect the location of most political decision-making outside the country, and the resultant limits placed on any Scottish-based movement.[71] Even when Orangemen did throw their weight behind pet parliamentary candidates, they had little subsequent control over them once they were at a safe distance in London. At Westminster, these figures were bound by national party demands, which far outweighed pledges made on Orange platforms to support the investigation of working conditions and alleged abuses in convent laundries and the struggle against 'ritualism' in the Church of England, or other causes dear to Orange hearts. Glasgow MPs, said the Orangemen, were 'dumb dogs' when in Parliament.[72] Ulster Orangemen may have had similar feelings, but their political representatives, MPs like Johnston of Ballykilbeg, were more likely to be Orangemen themselves and less liable to temporise over Protestantism in danger. In the worst event, they at least had the consolation of local and municipal elections at which sectarian questions could be legitimately raised. This was not a luxury extended to their brethren in Scotland, where local contests more commonly revolved around the basic issues of rates and drains.[73]

To conclude, the advance of Orangeism in nineteenth century Scotland is best understood against the background of labour migration from the Ulster counties.[74] While Ulster Protestants were vital to the development of Orangeism's mass membership, local perceptions of the Order as importing Irish 'party quarrels' showed a striking longevity and helped prevent its integration into the mainstream of Scottish life. Throughout most of the century, the Grand Lodge struggled anxiously against this; in the short term their efforts proved unsuccessful. The Order was, after all, an Irish importation, many of its members and office-bearers were from Ulster, its folklore was built around events in Irish history and it continued to be engaged with Irish political affairs. Even into the 1920s and 30s, suggests Walker, '. . . the most salient characteristic of the Orange Order in Scotland was its importance as a focus for the Protestant Irish in Scotland'.[75]

However, the long term prospect here was a brighter one. As Scotland became a less favoured destination for Ulster migrants and the number of first generation settlers declined, this inevitably mitigated the 'alien' quality of the Order.[76] The relative quiescence of Irish issues in British politics until the 1960s and the modern Orange leadership's determination to remain aloof from the Ulster crisis when it did develop, also assisted. As Bruce has argued, most contemporary Scots, like their nineteenth century forebears, have interpreted Irish conflict not as Roman Catholic aggression but '. . . what happens if you mix religion and politics'.[77] A more militant stand by the Scottish Order would doubtless have raised the old charge of importing sectarian conflict.

Historically, the legacy of ecclesiastical and political dislocations between Ulster and Scotland proved much more difficult to surmount. Even the hostile climate of an increasingly secularised society in Scotland from the end of the First World War was not sufficient to bring Orangeism and the Scottish churches closer together; on the contrary, the Church of Scotland's eventual enthusiasm for ecumenism, itself a by-product of secularisation, concentrated Orange fury.[78]

Similarly, the Order's political fortunes continued to fluctuate. In a further outburst of conditional loyalty, a period of closer links with the Conservatives and Unionists was brought to a close once the party was judged to have deviated from the defence of 'Protestant issues' with their support for the Anglo-Irish Treaty in 1921. The traditional Orange Conservative vote does seem to have remained a presence in key working class constituencies in the inter-war years, but as Ireland receded from the political agenda, space began to be created for a much wider spectrum of political viewpoints within the Orange rank and file, including support for the Labour cause.[79] Multiple political loyalties in turn made impractical the united pro-Tory political front of the previous century and debilitated the Order as a coherent electoral force.

The constraints of its Scottish setting thus outlived Orangeism's nineteenth century stage of development. Faced with this reality, the Order in its present incarnation has been repeatedly forced back on two traditional areas of strength: the organisation of public processions in the 'marching season' and the social and recreational potential of local lodges. Yet, arguably, in modern Scotland it is these, rather than impressive links into the religious and political establishment which are at a premium in the depressed working class communities from which Orangeism still draws the bulk of its members. If this is the case, then the continued presence of the Orange Order in Scottish society seems assured.

6

The Scots Ower the Sheuch

BILLY KAY

> I love my native land no doubt,
> attached to her through thick and thin,
> yet though I'm Irish all without,
> I'm every item Scotch within.

Samuel Thomson, a poet of the eighteenth century, sums up the strong dual nationality felt by the Ulster Scots. Many people of Scots descent furth of Scotland feel a nostalgic tie to the 'old country', but in Ulster the roots go a lot deeper and have been nourished over the centuries by the proximity and consequent cultural interchange between Scotland and the North of Ireland.

One of the principal reasons for the Scots' success as empire builders and colonisers elsewhere in the world has in fact lain in their ability to identify with the local culture, and within a generation or two, assimilate totally into it. The result of this however is that apart from the occasional tartan binge celebrating St Andrew or Rabbie, there is little tangible trace of Scottishness left in any of the many homelands of the Scottish diaspora. They may be Presbyterians, but in language and culture they are unmistakably American, Australian or Canadian. Cape Breton is a rare exception, where even the French Acadiens and Micmac Indians are imbued with aspects of Highland culture, especially the traditional fiddle music and stepdancing. Those will survive, even if the Gaelic language does not survive there far into the next century.

I would argue, therefore, that the only major recognisable Scottish cultural community outside Scotland is the one in Ulster. It runs in a huge arch from the Ards peninsula of County Down, up through Antrim and north Derry, to taper out in the Laggan region of Donegal. In religion, music, literary tradition and especially language, it is thoroughly Lowland and Scots speaking. Its heartland covers a major swathe of Ulster and influences every other part of the province, both in the Republic and Northern Ireland. And it has been ignored. Whether through chronic Scottish introspection, inability to come to terms with the tensions in the sense of identity here at home, or embarrassment and fear over the present Troubles, we have not given the Ulster Scots the intellectual analysis which the importance of their community deserves. Worse than that, we have begun to accept and reinforce the media stereotype of the Ulster Scot as a boorish, bitter Orange Neanderthal. That stereotype is every bit as false and hurtful to the Protestants of Ulster today as were the simian caricatures of Paddy the Irishman in British magazines to Scottish Catholics at the turn of the present century. By serious analysis of the culture and history, perhaps we can set about destroying the caricatures in order to understand the complex humanity of those people.

Personally speaking, I have experienced the same warmth, hospitality and caring in the Catholic Gaeltacht of Gweedore as in the Protestant areas of Down and Antrim. I have always found their common humanity and shared culture of more significance that what separates them politically.

There is a strong case for defining the land that stretches from the west of Northern Ireland to Scotland as one cultural area. Ulster Gaelic is closer to Scots Gaelic than the Irish spoken further south in Ireland. Irish people from the south visiting Donegal for the first time, remark upon the Scottishness of the speech in both Irish and English, and in the very style of music played by the brilliant traditional fiddlers of Donegal. This has been reinforced, of course, by the patterns of seasonal migration of agricultural then industrial workers from Ireland to Scotland. But many Irish-speaking tattie howkers never needed to travel far to pick up the marked Scots strand in their English speech. They simply had to cross over to the fertile east of their own country to pick up the same employment and the same language in the solidly Scots planted area of the Laggan: 'Goin' up till the Laggan tae lift the Scotch' was the way the workers described the linguistic acquisition available with the work. One west Donegal harvester addressed a traveller in his home area thus: 'It's the Irish we speak among wursels, but we hae eneuch Scotch to speak till yer honer.'

Because of the huge permanent migrations from the west of Ireland to the west of Scotland, there is a profound Irish influence in Scottish culture today, showing that the exchange has never been one-sided. Like most Scots, I was comparatively ignorant about the Scots nature of the eastern counties of Ulster until the early 1970s when, at Edinburgh University, I became friends with a young lady from Antrim and fellow contributor to this book, Linde Connolly Lunney. Having spoken nothing but English to one another, it came as quite a revelation when Linde showed me an essay on her local dialect. It was the same as my Ayrshire Scots, and planted in me an interest in discovering more about this branch of overseas Scots.

Given the speed with which Scottish colonists have divested themselves of their native tongues elsewhere in the world in more recent times – a process which has its roots in the colonised mentality of Scots here at home – the most remarkable feature of the Ulster communities is their retention of Scots in their everyday speech. Many of the areas have not had a fresh influx of Scots settlers for more than 300 years, and have been exposed to the Anglicising 'improvers' as much as any place in Scotland. Yet their Scots is rich, expressive and thrang with words you rarely come across in Scotland: ferntickles (freckles), gowpinfu (two handfuls), forenenst (opposite), wale (select) and couter (ploughhead) are a few of the words I recorded folk using, all set in a dialect as rich as anything in my native county. The fishing port of Portavogie on the Ards peninsula is one of the strongholds of Ulster-Scots speech. There I had the unusual experience of hearing a fellow Scot, a lad from Glasgow, describe how he had picked up Scots words like thrawn (stubborn), wheen (lots of) and rape (rope) since he moved to Ireland.

The Ulster-Scots dialects have long been distinctive and worthy of comment. Writing in the nineteenth century, the Rev. John Graham described his parishioners in Maghera, Co. Londonderry thus: 'The Dissenters speak broad Scotch, and are in the habit of using terms and expressions long since obsolete, even in Scotland, and which are only to be found in the glossary annexed to the bishop of Dunkeld's [Gavin Douglas] translation of Virgil.'

A vigorous tradition of Ulster vernacular poetry, fed by Scottish and Ayrshire influences, pre-dates the impact of Burns, and as early as 1730 Francis Boyle from Co. Down was writing in an idiom close to that later perfected by Scotland's national bard. Here is part of his poem describing his 'Auld Gelding':

> Thy bonny face wi star an snip,
> Thy sleekit hide, thy weel-turn't hip.
> Thy tail or mane, I winnae clip,
> Or poll thee bare
> Like them that gang aboard a ship
> For Glasgow Fair.
>
> When snaws lie lang an frost is keen,
> an neither grass nor foliage seen
> I gather whins that's young an green
> An them prepare,
> An feed thee wi them morn an een
> To sleek thy hair.

A spark already kindled became a conflagration when, in 1787, the same year as the first Edinburgh edition, the works of Burns were published in Belfast. Samuel Thomson of Carngranny, Co. Antrim, wrote:

> Tho Allan Ramsay blythly ranted
> An, tun'd his reed wi merry glee;
> Yet faith that *something* aye he wanted,
> That makes my Burns sae dear to me.

In 'The Irish Cottier's Death and Burial', James Orr of Ballycarry uses Burns' 'The Cottar's Saturday Night' as a model, but rarely falls into the artificial posturing of the stilted passages in Burns' poem. Orr's is better for its simple naturalism:

> Wi patient watchfulness, lasses an lads,
> Carefu an kin', surroun his clean caff bed,
> Ane to his lips the coolin cordial hauds,
> An ane behin supports his achin head;
> Some bin' the arm that lately has been bled,
> An some burn bricks his feet mair warm tae mak;
> If e'er he doze, hou noiselessly they tread!
> An stap the lights tae mak the bield be black,
> An aft the bedside lea, an slip saftly back.

The Scots tradition in literature is still engrained in the character of east Ulster writing today, with poets such as John Clifford, Oonagh McClean and the comic performance verse of Alec McAllister providing an unbroken link with the revival of the eighteenth century. Alec lives in Larne, but his roots are in the predominantly Scottish Highland Catholic area of the Glens of Antrim nearby. Here he is reflecting upon 'Love':

> Were ye ever in love? well it's funny to feel
> You are no to say bad, and you're no very weel
> Ye hae wild funny feelins up roon by your chest
> An your heid be's all wandered, like turkeys in mist.
> If you never were you need nae care
> For I was yince an I want nae mair.

Alec's vernacular verse is authentic because it is still rooted in the living speech of his locality. That locality also sent many migrant workers over to Scotland, both Catholic and Protestant, while thousands of Scottish tourists holidayed in north Antrim until the present Troubles began. All of this strengthened the linguistic links, and Scottish popular songs and rhymes were adapted and given Ulster settings. In Greyabbey, 'Wha saw the tattie howkers' became:

> Wha saw the Grey'ba lasses, wha saw them gang awa
> Wha saw the Grey'ba lasses, gangan doon the hard breid raw
> Some o thaim had buits an stockins, some o thaim had nane ava
> Some o thaim had big bare backsides, gangan doon the hard
>   breid raw.

On a different literary plane, the novels of the late Sam Hanna Bell are also graced with a native felicity in the use of Scots vernacular, with *December Bride* beautifully evocative of the tensions in a Presbyterian farming community when the sexual taboos are broken. Born in Glasgow, Bell moved back to the Co. Down home of his maternal grandmother when he was a child, and lived there for the rest of his life. I still recall Sam's face lighting up when he told me the story – illustrative of local linguistic identities – of a Ballymena man discussing the birth of a neighbouring Englishman's son. 'Whit are ye gaun tae cry him?' asked the Ballymena man. 'Well, we were thinking of calling him Nathan,' replied the Englishman. 'Get awa oot o that,' said the Ballymena man, 'ye'll hae tae cry him somethin!'

North Down and east Antrim are of course the areas closest to Scotland. They were not included in the official Plantation of Ulster, for the reason that there were already solid Scottish communities established there. In 1611 the first Presbyterian minister in Ulster ministered to an established flock in Ballycarry, and in 1683 a visitor noted that the parish had 'not a single aboriginal Irishman and only two Episcopalians.' Another current Ulster myth is that the Presbyterian inheritance is one of stifling, life-denying conservatism. The reality is that historically, Presbyterianism in Ireland has been a leading force for intellectual questioning and radical political reform. That very precocious Scottish desire for basic mass literacy, spurred on by the necessity to read the word of God, resulted in the Ulster Scots communities having by far the highest literacy figures in Ireland.

In the later eighteenth century the educated handloom weavers, like their brothers in the west of Scotland, were imbued with the ideals of freedom and democracy imported by the American and French revolutions and expressed in the works of Thomas Paine. Their radicalism was heightened by the discrimination they suffered in Ireland, where they had to pay tithes to the established church, the Episcopalian Church of Ireland. They were joined by clergymen who deeply resented the humiliating penal laws tholed by people of their persuasion; Presbyterian marriage had no validity and their rights of religious burial were denied. In Belfast, the growing Presbyterian merchant class could take no part in the government of their city, let alone of their country.

Presbyterian frustration and radicalism in Belfast led to the founding of the Society of United Irishmen, a movement which urged Presbyterians and Catholics to unite and overthrow the Anglican Protestant Ascendancy in a reformed, independent, republican Ireland. Poets like Orr and Campbell of Ballynure, ministers like the Rev. Adam Hill and romantic leaders such as Wolfe Tone and Henry Joy McCracken, all took arms against the government. The United Irishmen also spawned a similar organisation called the United Scotsmen in the weaving districts of

Scotland. McCracken would have been delighted to see his brethren across the Channel join the struggle.

In the ill-planned insurrection of 1798, many were killed in battle, hanged for treason or else fled to America. Using tactics similar to the Redcoats' brutal pacification of the Highlands following Culloden, the townlands which were United Irish strongholds were terrorised and beaten to submission by the fervid Orange troops of the yeomanry. Orangeism began and took root in the more English-planted county of Armagh, where Catholic and Protestant were evenly balanced and sectarianism was endemic. In the solid Presbyterian Ulster Scots areas, such ideas were alien, and because of the association with the depredations of the yeomanry, would remain alien for a long time to come. For many, however, the memory of the sight of their people fighting musket fire with farm implements made them think carefully about engaging in political agitation again.

Understandably, they retreated into the laager. Gradually, as all the discrimination against the Presbyterians was removed in the nineteenth century, they began to identify with the state and eventually see themselves as an entrenched bastion of a Protestant ascendancy which had excluded them a few generations earlier. Another important reason for the decline of Presbyterian radicalism was the death or forced exile of many of the community's leaders. The westward escape to America was the natural one to follow as waves of Ulster emigrants had already planted 'Scottish-Irish' enclaves right down the eastern seaboard of the States. Their 'settler radicalism' was in the vanguard of the American Revolution. One of the United Irishmen, Campbell of Ballynure, escaped on a ship to New York after the Battle of Antrim. In his poem, 'The Exile', he describes walking the alien streets and the surprise that awaited him.

> Ilk face he saw was a stranger's face and his last bawbee
>   was gone,
> The night was snell and the rain fell fast, as he heartless
>   wandered on;
> He stopped at the door o a public hoose to rest his weary feet,
> And he hurkled close to the sheltering post frae the bitter
>   cauld and weet.
> He heard the crack o the folk inside, he kent the braid
>   Ulster tongue,
> But his senses are numbed and he barely hears the song that
>   the singer sung;
> What mak's him start! Why beams his eye, and why do his
>   heart strings swell?
> The sang he hears! The sang they sing, is a sang that he made
>   himsel.
> Then Campbell eagerly opens the door and boldly enters then,
> And he grat wi joy at the welcome he got frae the kindly
>   Antrim men.

Many see the defeat of the United Irishmen as the death knell of Presbyterian radicalism in Ulster, and it would be convenient for the stereotype if it was. But there, at the height of the anti-Home Rule activity in Ulster in 1912, when Carson and Craig were recalling the spirit of resistance of the persecuted forefathers of the Ulster Scot and exhorting true Ulstermen to sign their Covenant, another Covenant was being organised by the Rev. Armour in Ballymoney, in the heart of Scotch Antrim. It was *for* Irish Home Rule, and was signed by more than 400 local Presbyterians. That radical strand may be harder to find today, but tell me anywhere in Conservative-thirled Britain it is not harder to find today? Certainly, by the end of the nineteenth century, the majority of adherents to the Presbyterian church held little truck with their radical republican forebears. They had also begun to adopt racial stereotypes in describing the differences between themselves and their Roman Catholic countrymen. In an article entitled 'The Place and Work of the Presbyterian Church in Ireland', written in 1890, the Rev. R J Lynd cites 'indolence, thriftlessness and intemperance' as characteristics of the native Irish. The Presbyterians, on the other hand, had 'set an example of persistent and successful industry' which had been 'a blessing to the land'. Lazy Presbyterians who enjoyed a dram did not figure in the Rev. Lynd's world picture. They were all God's chosen children: 'It is God who has planted our Presbyterian Church in Ireland, and made this country our Fatherland . . . We are here to do what none but ourselves can. Others may be called to equally important work, but none can exactly fill the square which has been chiselled for us.'

From this, you can see that some of the warped ideas of an Ulster *Herrenvolk* have their origin in certain sections of the community's spiritual leadership. A Protestant supremacist attitude can emerge with ease out of such ideology.

In recent years a culturally radical movement by Ulster intellectuals has attempted to deflect attention from the separate Irish and British claims for the province and focus on a shared Ulster culture. In *The Identity of Ulster*, Ian Adamson vigorously asserts that it is the Scottishness of Ulster which has given all of its people a uniquely Ulster identity. In so doing, he is attempting to break down the twin monoliths of selective historical perspectives which divide the communities along sectarian lines. Certainly, the simplification of history into a Catholic and Protestant version is inherently false. In the Catholic/Nationalist version, for example, the Catholics of the Glens of Antrim are Irish, and belong to the ancient Celtic civilisation of the nation; the Protestants of the rest of Antrim are interlopers who drove the native Irish off their lands. In fact, the only area where the native Irish were driven out by force of arms was in the Glens by the Catholic Highlanders of the MacDonnell Lords of the Isles. The Glens were a Scottish Gaelic stronghold until comparatively recently and still maintain strong links with Islay and Kintyre, proving in fact that blood ties and a common history can overcome religious differences.

The culture of the Glens of Antrim was beautifully articulated in my radio series *The Scots of Ulster* by Jack McCann: 'If there is such a thing as a ghost in Cushendall,' said Jack, 'he's standing on the strand there on Christmas morning, caman in hand, gazing longingly to the coast of Kintyre in the hope that someone will come and play shinty with him!'

The people of the Glens are as Scottish as the Scots-speaking Lowlanders; it is their Catholicism which welcomes them into the 'Irish' fold and excludes the others. The father of modern Irish nationalism, Daniel O'Connell, gave the stamp of approval to this limiting vision of Irish nationhood when he described Protestants as 'foreign to us since they are of a different religion.' Fortunately, on a personal level, the two communities have lived well together in the country areas of Antrim better than in the counties of the official Plantation west of the Bann. There, in the frontier territory of Fermanagh and Tyrone, yet another example of the diversity within the term 'Ulster Scot' held sway: the border-riding families of Elliott, Armstrong and Johnston. They were encouraged to leave the suddenly friendly Scottish/English frontier in the early seventeenth century to go and hold the outposts of the Plantation in a border which is not peaceful to this day. A land war has been raging since the present round of Troubles began. Farmers held their lands by muskets in the 1640s. They carry shotguns in their tractors in the 1990s. The war of attrition practised by the IRA has had its effect, though, and there has been a gradual selling up and retreat into 'safer' areas such as Antrim and Down. Some have actually 'returned' to Galloway and Ayrshire.

What they find if they settle in Wigtownshire is a place with a strong Ulster-sounding dialect. In neighbouring Stewartry, the locals speak of going 'over the Cree and into the Irish' and refer to the inhabitants of Wigtownshire as 'sowl boys'. As to which side of the 'sheuch' influenced the other first, it is impossible to tell. This recent migration is smaller than previous ones but it nevertheless fits into the ancient pattern of migration between the two countries. It also could gain momentum if there were dramatic changes for the worse in Northern Ireland. One weary old gentleman I interviewed, living close to the Border on land held by his family since the early seventeenth century, confessed that Scotland would be the choice of the majority of his tradition, should the need arise: 'That's where I would go. And do you know, I've visited Scotland and I've stood on the boat and I've said to the boys that was standing on the boat beside me: "What made us leave this country? I feel I'm going home."'

This historic 'special relationship' is valued by both traditions in Ulster, and is respected also by the men of violence. It has had surprising ramifications down the centuries, even at times of extreme political tension. Since the present Troubles began, for instance, the IRA has left Scotland out of its bombing campaigns in Britain, a parallel with the situation at the start of the 1641 Rebellion against the Planters, when: '. . . the Rebels made open proclamations, upon pain of death, that no Scotchman should be stirred in body, goods or lands, and that they should to this purpose write over the lyntels of their doors that they were Scotchmen, and so destruction might pass over their families.'

The historian Graham Walker echoed my own experience in Ulster when he commented that 'as a Scot, both sides presume you are on their side.' What you certainly get is a fellow feeling that as a Scot you will understand what is going on in Ulster and sympathise with the people's predicament. Sadly, our reason for sympathy is that because of all the links which bind Scotland and Ulster, the only one universally recognised today is the problem of sectarianism in our own society. That is a subject blown out of all proportion to its relevance in a Scottish context by the Glasgow-based media's obsession with the Rangers and Celtic football clubs. Sectarianism is a sexy subject there because of the glamour surrounding the big teams. It has little relevance to the rest of Scottish society and would probably have died a death here if it were not for the football dimension. Even with this element stoking it up, the difference in virulence within Scotland and Ulster was brought home to me by an Orange flute band player who had attended many marches in Scotland. 'It's just a day out for them [the Scots]. We live it all the time. They talk to their Catholics over there. We don't.'

Sectarianism here has weakened to such an extent that the bigots and the organisations which encourage bigotry are regarded as an annoying irrelevance by the vast majority of Scots. It was not always so and there were many violent incidents produced by the culture clash in the industrial west of Scotland, following yet another migration across the Irish Sea in the later nineteenth century. The comparatively successful integration of once explosive sections of our own society shows that a solution to Ulster's problems is not the absolute impossibility many perceive it to be.

What I have drawn from my work in Ulster is the awareness of a wider perspective through which to look behind the current debilitating and blinding myths. From that has emerged the realisation that for centuries the peoples on either side of the Irish Sea have interchanged and interacted and migrated back and forth, right through to the present day. Against that, the present sectarian Troubles are a drop in the ocean, albeit a bitter and tragic one. It is a relationship which deserves far greater attention than the narrow focus we have deigned to give it until now.

7

Empire, Religion and Nationality in Scotland and Ulster Before the First World War

GRAHAM WALKER

This chapter will be concerned, firstly, to discuss the respective relationships of Ulster and Scotland to the Empire, and to draw conclusions about national identity with reference to the period 1886 to 1914: the period encompassing the three Irish Home Rule Bills and much constitutional discussion about federation, the UK and the Empire. Secondly, it will consider, in some detail, the period 1911–1913 when events such as by-elections, Covenant signings and Church conventions produced a lot of evidence which helps us to interpret more searchingly the nature of the Ulster-Scottish relationship in all its political, religious and cultural dimensions.

I

In 1913 the Unionist (Conservative) Party in Scotland issued a confidential memorandum on the subject of Scottish Home Rule to its prospective candidates for a general election which they believed might be imminent.[1] The Unionists opposed Home Rule for Scotland, but recognised that the issue had to be handled carefully; that 'Scottish National sentiment is a strong force in all ranks of Scottish life' was admitted at the outset of the memo. However, the Unionists, as is clear from this document, felt that they could trump the Home Rulers by appealing to what they called 'the wider Imperial patriotism', and the need to harness Scottish national patriotism to the Empire ideal rather than the ideal of Scottish self-government. The memo stated that 'a parochial, parish-pump type' of Scottish nationalism, 'based more largely on jealousy of others than on pride in national achievements and capacities' had to be confronted by an appeal to imperial patriotism to which, 'when it is properly made, Scotsmen invariably show themselves ready to respond'.

In addition, it was urged on the candidates to stress that Scottish Home Rule would mean English Home Rule and that that would bring to an end something which had long been a source of Scottish pride, namely the success of individual Scots in reaching the top posts in London, in politics, business, religion, the press, the police and other walks of life. If the unitary state system of government was broken up, the memo argued, English posts would be kept for Englishmen, and the sense of satisfaction in Scotland regarding this brand of Scottish conquest would be extinguished.

The Unionists at this time and in stark contrast to the contemporary era, were in tune with the bulk of Scottish opinion on the matter. Indeed, the points made in the memorandum might be said to reflect very accurately the nature of the general Scottish national outlook on the eve of an imperial conflagration in Europe in which the Scots, in proportionate terms, sacrificed more lives than any other country in the British Empire.[2] The Nationalist fringe aside, Scots did not entertain any sense of themselves as a 'failed nation'; as J H Grainger has written: 'Edwardian Scots were a well-tempered people, quietly assured of certain moral superiorities, well instructed in fundamentals and quite unpersuaded that they were oppressed. Scotland had no linguistic grievances. The Empire provided ample opportunities for her soldiers, entrepreneurs and administrators.'[3]

The same could also be said of Victorian Scotland; there was no conflict of economic interests,[4] the Scots played a crucial political role largely through the Liberal Party of Gladstone, and, the British State and Empire provided opportunities for the full expression of *Scottish* qualities and talents.

Underpinning the desire to exploit the opportunities afforded to them by the wider context of the British State and Empire lay an undiluted pride in being Scottish and a belief that Scottish achievements in this context were a result of the superiority of the cultural and national distinctiveness of Scotland, a distinctiveness given form by the institutions of church, education and law. There was no need to struggle to assert a distinct national identity; it was assured, it was securely in place and it was a living, dynamic international influence.[5] As Adam Naylor, in an important unpublished thesis, has put it: '. . . no Scot need look to the nature of how he was governed to establish his national identity'.[6] Indeed, most Scots who did look favourably on the idea of Scottish Home Rule took the position of Lord Rosebery, one of three Scottish Prime Ministers in the period

1895–1905, that it would *strengthen* the UK state and Empire, leading to ulti-
mate Imperial Federation. Rosebery wrote in 1885:

> I cannot understand people preferring separation to Home Rule. I detest sep-
> aration and feel that nothing could make me agree to it. Home Rule, however,
> is a necessity for both us and the Irish. They will have it within two years at the
> latest. Scotland will follow, then England. When that is accomplished, Imperial
> Federation will cease to be a dream. To many of us, it is not a dream now but
> to no-one will it be a dream then.[7]

Rosebery was to be disappointed in not seeing his dream fulfilled, but
the federalist idea, both in terms of the British State and the wide Empire,
gained momentum among Liberals and even some Conservatives, like the
Scotsman Frederick Scott Oliver. It was an idea trumpeted in the pre-World
War One period by Glasgow Liberal MP Alexander McCallum Scott,
whose outlook typified the proud and idealistic 'Scot with a mission'.[8] The
expansive visions of the Liberal imperialists struck deep chords in
Scotland, although ironically, as we have seen, the Conservatives could see
ways of turning this to *their* advantage.

Perhaps the main reason why Scotland was fertile territory for imperi-
alistic appeals was the importance of religion in relation both to Scottish
national identity and to perceptions of Empire. Scottish Presbyterianism,
in its missionary character, stalked almost every colony, combining ethno-
centricity and paternalism with a drive in many cases for social justice and
improvement, and a radical egalitarian spirit. A Scottish view of Empire
which repudiated self-interest and celebrated the missionary heroics of
Livingstone and Mary Slessor, was deeply and widely felt, if self-indulgent
and self-congratulatory. The Scots believed that they took the task of
spreading Christianity more seriously than the English and that Scottish
Presbyterianism in general was more morally serious and less corruptible.

When John Buchan took up a post under Milner in South Africa, an elder
of his father's church, the John Knox Free Church in Glasgow, wrote to him
as follows:

> I feared for the future of South Africa where there has been so much corrup-
> tion, where Christian principles have been stifled by the craze for gold, and
> where there is the ever-present opportunity of the white oppressing the black.
> But if I knew that a man like you was helping to hold the helm, I should have
> confidence in its future. Rhodes and others are great men, possessed with large
> ideas, but they are hardly to be trusted in their treatment of the blacks and
> other questions. They see things only from a utilitarian point of view, and from
> the angle of their own advantage, consequently they do not like the mission-
> aries and their impractical notions. The ignorant sentimentality of Christian
> people (so they put it) is a thorn in their flesh, which they would fain be rid of,
> but which thank God is still of some power. If these empire-builders require to

use the black races as stepping-stones to further their plans, many people will say they are justified, but I cannot, and if I can do anything to hinder them I will do it willingly. It may do for the moment, but it is sure to end in disaster.

I believe, however, that Lord Milner will do what is right to the dark race, but he will need someone to help him, someone with the fear of God before his eyes.

The writer then ended by urging Buchan to remember Livingstone.[9] Buchan, moreover, made a clear distinction, as did Scottish Labour MPs in the 1920s, between the Scots' conception of themselves as, literally, the builders of Empire: the engineers, the road, bridge and railway builders, as opposed to that of the English which suggested 'public school men administering subject races.'[10]

Another Scot who epitomised a more enlightened attitude to Empire was William McGregor Ross, a civil engineer who rose to become Director of Public Works in Kenya by 1905. Ross, as his memoirs reveal, was a tireless social protester against the exploitation and degradation of the native people; he worked closely with the Church of Scotland mission to highlight social injustice and colonial government malpractice. At all times, however, Ross clung to the overall view that Empire could be 'a motive-power on the side of world progress'; racist attitudes and exploitation simply damaged the prospects of this.[11]

The Scots in general saw themselves as realising the constructive potential which the Empire offered,[12] and in this they might be said to have been expressing their sense of Scottish Nationalist identity while not repudiating the umbrella term of 'British'. However, their interpretation of English values and behaviour could often be critical and there was a pronounced sense of competitiveness about the Scots vis-à-vis the English in relation to their role in the Empire. In this connection, a distinctive religious identity was arguably the most important factor, especially since the dynamic of the Presbyterian democratic ethos was seen to lie behind the more egalitarian and anti-privilege orientations of the educational and legal systems.

Less idealistically, the British and Empire connection has also been viewed as attractive to Protestant Scotland on account of being added security against the encroachments of Roman Catholicism.[13] Fear of Irish Catholic immigration into Scotland had certainly exercised many Protestant minds, although it is not clear that outside the ranks of demagogues, often immigrant *Ulster* preachers, it produced any doubts about Protestantism's cultural dominance in Scotland; generally, until the First World War, Scottish national and religious sentiment flowed together and exuded confidence. Indeed, as Bernard Aspinall has argued, Scottish national identity was expressed significantly through a 'civic gospel' which the Scottish Protestant churches exported, not only to the Empire but also, very tellingly, to the USA. This 'civic gospel' was orientated to social problems and to the quest for Christian ethical values in modern urban life.[14]

There is no sense in this period of any lack of purpose or any doubt about identity and role in the world, on the part of Church and Nation. At the outbreak of the First World War, 90 per cent of all 'sons of the manse' volunteered for active service in His Majesty's forces, and John Buchan's propaganda contribution in the war was to be an exceptional one.[15] The Scots responded enthusiastically in 1914, echoing to a large extent previous episodes such as the Boer War which the Unionist memorandum of 1913 was doubtless referring to when it cited the Scottish propensity to respond to imperial appeals.[16] There was not at this time any real sense of Scottish destiny, whether economic, cultural or political, not being bound up firmly with Britain and the Empire.

II

The question of Ulster's national identity in this 'Home Rule era' has been the subject of much scholarly debate. Perhaps the most important contributions have come from the historians Peter Gibbon, David Miller, James Loughlin and Alvin Jackson.[17] Gibbon's analysis, the earliest of the four, has been rejected by the others in its assertion that an Ulster Nationalism emerged in the face of the Home Rule crisis and was shaped and led by the Belfast bourgeoisie who had displaced the landlord interest as the spokesmen of the Protestant Unionist community.

Miller, in a seminal work published three years later, argued that Ulster Nationalism did not develop but that the Ulster Protestants' sense of British loyalty was strictly conditional: that they were in a 'contractarian' type of relationship with the British State and that they would be entitled to withdraw their loyalty to the state if they perceived it to be breaking the 'contract' and acting against their interests. Miller holds that the Ulster Unionists preferred to make the focus of their loyalty the Crown and the Empire; the latter he sees as providing a convenient 'way out' for the Ulstermen in that it offered a focus for their loyalty which suggested that they were more than 'merely' British. Miller sees the Ulster Protestants as a 'special case' in the British context and argues that they themselves saw it that way, that they were deeply suspicious of British governments' intentions and so insecure as to always be ready to rely on their own resources and fight for their own community.

James Loughlin has taken issue with Miller's concept of an imperial identity as a substitute for a secure sense of British national identity on the part of Ulster. He has argued that their imperial identification followed naturally from what was a strong and committed sense of being British. He disputes that Ulster felt less 'completely' British than any other part of the UK and cites the example of Scotland as being the exception in this sense: in retaining separate institutions, Scotland subscribed in a far more limited degree to a 'complete' sense of UK nationality and sovereignty than the Ulster Loyalists did. In dismissing Ulster Nationalism, Loughlin says that it has often been confused with the existence of an 'Ulsterman' type or character which had developed without any Nationalist pretensions and with the purpose of sharpening ethnic divisions between the Loyalists and Nationalist (Catholic) Ireland.

Following Loughlin, Alvin Jackson has entered the debate to object to what he perceives as the former's relegation of Ulster to the status of a British regional identity; Jackson believes that an Ulster nation could be said to have existed in theory, although Ulster Nationalism did not develop in practice, and that it should be accorded similar conceptual status as other nations in the UK. Moreover, he is concerned to show that Ulster politicians in the Home Rule era were preoccupied with local Ulster issues rather than British or Empire ones, and he is critical of Loughlin's concept of British Nationalism, which he finds so 'flaccid' that even some Irish Nationalists might be able to accept it. Jackson concludes that, in relation to national identity, the impression received is too ambiguous to call: 'For, if there were two or even three nations in late nineteenth century Ireland, it would appear that each of these (and every combination) was represented within Loyalism.'[18] The Irish Unionist movement, North and South, in order to preserve unity, had to accept the ambiguities and instead gear itself to the negative end of defeating Home Rule. Class and religious denominational divisions within Unionism also demanded such a course.

Most recently, in a work of synthesis, another historian, George Boyce, has tried to classify the issue as follows:

> Ulster Protestants did not develop a 'nationalism' of their own, simply because they did not need to do so: the whole basis of their creed was a denial that nationalism was a genuine or tenable political belief. It was a sham and a fraud, since there had never been a united Irish nation in the first place. And from the 1880s until the 1912 Home Rule crisis it was possible for both northern and southern Unionists to maintain that loyalty was perfectly compatible with a wider British patriotism. Their claim was that Ireland was divided into 'loyal' and 'disloyal' Ireland.[19]

Elsewhere, Boyce has also written, *pace* Miller, that the Ulster Protestants' belief in a British nationality was tempered by the awareness that they might have to fight for the survival of their community and therefore had to assert themselves as a special breed, defenders of a British heritage in Ireland under threat from a Nationalist majority who were antagonistic to that heritage.[20]

In relation to the topic of this chapter some of these themes merit comment. Loughlin's criticism of Miller is persuasive; certainly, he is right to say that the 'contractarian' concept has at least as much relevance to Scotland. The popular understanding of the Union in Scotland in this era was very much like that of a contract: the Union was not seen, except by a few, as a bartering away of Scottish nationhood; rather it was a means by which Scotland could prosper.[21] If Scotland, by this period, had not done well out of the Union and Empire then it might be hypothesised that she would have sought to terminate the arrangement or at least adjust it. The Union at this time was widely viewed as a partnership, notwithstanding annoyance on the part of most Scots at some time or other over the English habit of seeing their country as synonymous with the concept of Britain. The Scots could accept the arrangement all the more for the retention of their national institutions and of a secure sense of Scottish nationhood. They, more than the Ulster Loyalists, were concerned not to be regarded as 'merely' British, and in this sense the latter's combination of a proclaimed British loyalty and a deep sense of Ulster independence cannot be viewed as aberrant or peculiar.

This sense of 'independence' was arguably related to the concept of an Ulster 'type' which Loughlin refers to: the cultivation of an image of the Ulsterman as resourceful, honest, determined and independently-minded in contrast to the feckless, untrustworthy, spineless and priest-ridden Nationalist Celt. It was undoubtedly true that the Ulster Protestant felt himself to be in a less secure position, in terms of the perceived Nationalist and Catholic threat, than anyone else in the UK, but while this situation called for the display of the personal qualities adduced above, it did not mean that the goal of British and imperial protection could not be pursued with the utmost vigour. This, it might be said, was the main reason for Ulster's commitment to Union and Empire: for the sense of security which would prevent them being at the mercy of an Irish Catholic regime intent on curtailing their civil and religious liberties, oppressing their culture and ruining their economic and social welfare.

Leave aside the argument that these were unreasonable fears: the point was, as will be illustrated below, that the Ulster Protestants believed their fate would be Catholic sectarian rule in a Home Rule Ireland, through the medium of the Ancient Order of Hibernians (AOH). Folk memories and cultural traditions revolved around episodes like the 1641 massacres, the 1688–89 siege of Derry and the Wexford massacre of 1798. The other side of this coin – the Orangeist triumphalism of the Boyne – was the defiant expression of this profoundly defensive mentality. Even if the Union and the imperial connection had not resulted in economic prosperity for Ulster, and much of course was made of this prosperity by Unionists, the hypothesis might be put that, contrary to the Scottish case, Ulster would not have repudiated the British link. In their case, religious and cultural factors counted for more. Their positive sense of national identity as opposed to their determination merely to resist Irish nationalism, was not clearly defined but multi-layered. There were, as Jackson argues, overlapping loyalties: Irish,[22] British, Ulster or Ulster-Scottish. Where Scots could regard the wider British and imperial contexts as opportunities to express their Scottishness and display the national qualities about which they were immodest, the Ulster view of Britain and the Empire was overwhelmingly conceived in terms of achieving solidarity and security.

In Ulster the view of an imperial role lacked the sense of keen rivalry with which the Scots invested it in relation to England. Thus while the following declaration by Arthur Balfour in 1914, equating Scottish and 'Ulster Scot' attitudes to Empire may ring superficially true, there was no way the Ulster Loyalists could divorce the Empire from the desperate plight in which they considered themselves to be, in order to hold the expansive vision depicted here of the Empire as a globally progressive phenomenon in its own right:

> Again, the Ulster Scot, like the Scot at home and throughout the Empire, has been true to his race and his tradition; but he has also opened his eyes to the larger vision of Empire, he has been loyal to the flag of the Union, and he has carried the British name with honour to every corner of the globe. Is it any wonder that the Ulster Scot refuses to barter away his share in the heritage of Empire?[23]

People like Milner and Bonar Law like to portray Ulster as 'holding the pass for the Empire' but again, this was in the negative sense of Ulster's cause being crucial to the prevention of imperial disintegration.[24] The Ulster view of Empire was more passive than that of Scotland; the Empire was something fixed as part of Ulster's inheritance.[25] The Scottish view was more active and crusading and suggested that Empire was something through which new achievements could be fashioned.

Neither did Ulster Unionists evince interest in, nor contribute significantly to the debates on imperial federation which were such a feature of British politics in this era.[26] The Ulster Unionists either viewed federal or 'Home Rule All Round' schemes as too vague and a diversion from the immediate reality of the Irish threat, or held that Dublin rule would still be unacceptable in a federal-type framework, or shared the constitutional conservatism of such anti-Home Rulers as A V Dicey who took the view that any devolution scheme would have the effect of weakening the integrity of the UK and the Empire.[27]

Ulster in the Home Rule era craved strong backing from both Scotland and England; the religious and political aspects of this will be discussed below. British solidarity was asked for, not more evidence of its diversity. The Empire thus tended to be viewed as a triumph of this kind of British

unity and solidarity, and indeed as a kind of 'Protestant front' encompassing all denominations. The Ulster Protestants covered up the divisions
within their own community which made a coherent Ulster Nationalism so
problematic and encouraged the other parts of the UK, excepting of course,
Nationalist Ireland, to forget theirs in lending them full-blooded support.
The Ulster Loyalists indeed, may have been the only ones to believe in a
truly British nation as well as a British state. Certainly, in the circumstances
of their conflict with Irish Nationalism, they found it easier to make do with
an Ulster 'Loyalism' which stressed British and imperial patriotism and
solidarity than to construct a distinctive Ulster Nationalism. Moreover,
Naylor's observation about the Scots, quoted earlier, might be inverted in
the case of Ulster: they *did* have to look to the nature of how they were governed to establish their national identity. Equally, it might be just as fair to
conclude that there were several Ulster Protestant identities,[28] most of
which managed to find a shared purpose in opposing Home Rule but not
all, for it should not be forgotten that there was also a minority who supported it.[29]

III

Of the different Ulster Protestant identities, that of the 'Ulster Scot', identified overwhelmingly with the Ulster Presbyterians, has probably carried
most historiographical and folkloric weight. While not losing sight of the
united Ulster Protestant campaign for British solidarity over the question
of Irish Home Rule, it is salutary to examine the Ulster-Scottish relationship at the heart of this campaign as illustrated by certain events in the dramatic period 1911 to 1913.

The Ulster Unionists had long felt that the kinship and religious ties with
Scotland, being so close and numerous, would bring them such committed
support from that country that the Irish question would swing decisively
in their favour. In 1886, in the midst of the first Home Rule Bill controversy,
James Henderson, proprietor of the Unionist *Belfast Newsletter* stated: 'It is
greatly to be desired that we should stir up the feeling of Scotland in favour
of this movement . . . I believe that if we can stir up religious feeling in
Scotland we have won the battle.'[30]

From the 1870s, with the coming of waves of Protestant immigrants
from Ulster, the Orange Order grew rapidly in Scotland[31] and along
with other smaller, friendly-society type organisations and particular
church congregations, formed an organised Ulster Protestant community in Scotland, largely in the industrialised west.[32] From the beginning of the Home Rule era, this lobby fought the anti-Home Rule cause
and undoubtedly received much sympathy from Scots who shared
their views about a Catholic Nationalist tyranny in Ireland. Indeed,

Orangeism spread significantly among the native Protestant working class in Lowland Scotland from this time, and soon came to have a political influence through the Conservative/Unionist Party, although this relationship was by no means always a harmonious one.[33] In certain constituencies the Orange Order could supply an important Protestant working-class vote for the Unionists, a factor perhaps most obviously evident in the Unionist triumph in the 1900 General Election. In December 1911, the Liberal government, committed to deliver Irish Home Rule, was defeated in a by-election in North Ayrshire and had its majority slashed in another contest in Govan, Glasgow. In both constituencies the Orange Order had a strong presence and both results were viewed by the Unionist press in Belfast as encouraging signs of Scottish support for the anti-Irish Home Rule cause.[34] In their papers they expressed the hope that by playing up 'the religious aspect of Home Rule' they would convince the Scots of the scheme's iniquity.[35]

However, it was not by any means a straightforward task to get the level of commitment and backing from Protestant, overwhelmingly Presbyterian Scotland for which the Ulster Unionists hoped. The Unionist press also betrayed very clearly their dismay regarding the strong support for Home Rule on the part of two traditional liberal and radical political constituencies: the Scottish Presbyterians and the English Nonconformists.[36] In Scotland, Ulster Protestant immigrants and their descendants expressed exasperation with the apparent indifference shown to their cause by some Scottish Protestants. The following outburst by the Rev. Victor Logan, an Ulster-born minister in Scotland, encapsulated their feelings and their view of what Irish Home Rule would mean:

> If the present generation of Scotchmen who wished to force Home Rule, that is to say, Rome Rule, on Ireland, could be lifted out of this glorious little country and set down for about three weeks in some central province in South America, they would come home again cured of their growing indifference for Protestantism and cured of a desire to force Ulster under the tyranny and the foot of the Church of Rome.[37]

Unionist frustrations of this kind were nonetheless tempered by the belief that their co-religionists would eventually come round to their way of thinking, that it only required increased propaganda efforts[38] and increased emphasis on historical and traditional bonds. In an editorial, the *Belfast Weekly News* painted the standard Unionist picture of Irish Home Rule as Catholic sectarian tyranny and stated: 'And this is the system of Government which the Nonconformists of England and the Presbyterians of Scotland are to be asked to set up in Ireland. We are confident that when they know the truth they will indignantly refuse to betray their Protestant fellow-subjects.'[39]

Referring to a proposed Presbyterian anti-Home Rule Convention in

Belfast, a columnist in the same newspaper, who styled himself 'Ulster Orangeman' testily declared: 'First the Presbyterian Church will make its protest against the betrayal which the Nonconformists across the water meditate. It should carry weight with the Nonconformists of England and the Presbyterians of Scotland who are up to the neck in the conspiracy to hand their brethren in Ulster over to the powers of Rome.'[40]

There was an element of simplistic naivety in these entreaties, whether they were expressed in terms of a comradely show of solidarity or a reproachful signal to these errant Protestants to remember their duty. They were appeals made without much regard for political, social and cultural realities in Scotland or England; rather they were based on timeless and, in a sense, romantic conceptions of a shared heritage and a common bond. Such appeals for support could also be made in terms of pure 'kitsch': for example, a postcard produced at the time of the third Home Rule Bill crisis entitled 'The Ulster Scot', bore a sketch of the stereotypical kilted Highland warrior, complete with claymore, and contained the rhyming verse:

> This land oor heritage by richt
> Priest ridden saints may grudge us
> Three hunner years we hae been here
> An Deil th' fit they'll budge us.[41]

The irony of an image popularly associated with Jacobite rebelliousness being used to promote the Unionist cause seemed to escape the propagandists, but it is doubtful if it would have escaped the Scottish target audience, overwhelmingly Lowlanders, who regarded such things as a music hall joke.

More seriously, these propaganda efforts, and much of the Orange Order-influenced press in Ulster, particularly the *Belfast Newsletter* and *Weekly News*, were either unaware of or disinclined to address the different characteristics of the political cultures of Scotland and England and especially the interaction between politics and religion which often produced liberal and radical effects. The dissenting Presbyterian churches in Scotland, such as the Free Church and the United Presbyterian Church and English Nonconformists, had a history of struggle against Establishment privilege and landlordism which resulted in a rigid antipathy to Conservatism in many areas. Among both groups and also some Established Church of Scotland Presbyterians, a body of radical opinion had reached the conclusion that Ulster Protestants had nothing to fear from Home Rule religiously and that if they were serious about Empire, Home Rule would not harm that connection either, given the expectation of federalist-type developments. The Unionist campaign with its heavy Orange colouring was handicapped in its appeals to many Scottish Presbyterians and English Nonconformists by its associations with Conservatism and landlordism. The paramount need, as the Unionists saw it, for unity against Home Rule concealed the extent to which a more liberal and radical Protestant, largely Presbyterian, presence previously hostile to Conservatism and with a history of struggle against landlordism and therefore much more likely to attract sympathy from these groups, was also exercised by the same fears of Home Rule and had sunk political and denominational differences in order to fight it.[42] Urged on by their fellow and generally more conservative Unionists, these Presbyterians sought to make this clear.

There thus occurred a remarkable Irish Presbyterian demonstration: the Convention, alluded to above, held in Belfast on 1 February 1912. It was a demonstration explicitly conceived to influence British 'progressive' and in particular Scottish Presbyterian opinion. There are many indications of this in the columns of the Irish Presbyterian journal *The Witness* in the weeks before the Convention. It was emphasised that it was not an Orange demonstration, that Presbyterians of all political persuasions would take part but that many would 'favour much of the policy of the Government apart from Home Rule'.[43] It was considered vital to counter the Home Rulers' propaganda among Scottish Presbyterians which was perceived to be systematic,[44] and which was making much capital out of the existence of Irish Presbyterian Home Rulers such as the Rev. J B Armour of Bally-money.[45] The paper also carried a 'Scottish Church News' column and urged the establishment of more links between ministers in Ulster and Scotland.[46] It was admitted that there were lay and clerical Presbyterians unhappy about associating with 'Tories, landlords and Orangemen', but stated: 'If there should be any error at all in such association, we think it would be for the sake of the country better to err with Sir Edward Carson than shine with Mr Redmond or Mr Devlin and those behind them; to err with the Unionist Council than shine with the United Irish League and the Ancient Order of Hibernians.'[47]

In its editorial written just before the Convention, *The Witness* high-lighted what it clearly believed was the heart of the matter: the imperish-able Ulster-Scottish bond. It stated:

> The Irish Presbyterians desire to appeal in the first instance to Scottish Presbyterians. The vast majority of them are descendants of the Scottish Presbyterians who were sent over three centuries ago to colonise and develop Ulster in the interests of civilisation and the kingdom . . . One of the resolutions makes a special reference to the Scottish Settlement, and a special appeal to Scottish Presbyterians, not to desert the descendants of those who were sent over to plant Ulster, and leave them to the uncovenanted mercies of Mr Redmond and the Irish Romanists, who threaten them with the strong arm because they are true to Scottish traditions, Scottish religion, and Scottish asso-ciations, and who have been systematically taunted and insulted as West Britons, and whom Mr Redmond has threatened to put down with the strong hand.[48]

The Convention attracted an estimated forty to fifty thousand male Presbyterians to Belfast, half of the adult male Presbyterian population in Ulster, according to the calculations of the *Glasgow Herald* which was very impressed by it.[49] The Convention issued an appeal to 'Loyal England and Scotland', but as is clear from at least one of the resolutions passed and the accompanying declaration, the main target audience was Scotland. The resolutions claimed that Irish Home Rule would:

1. imperil religious and civil liberties;
2. injure industrial and agricultural interests;
3. curtail the main philanthropic and missionary enterprises of the Irish Presbyterian Church at home and abroad;
4. endanger the congregations and livelihoods of ministers where Presbyterians (many of them consisting of settlers from Scotland) were in the minority in Ireland; and
5. increase the Roman Catholic hierarchy's power over education, which would result in the 'denominationalising' of education in Ireland leading to children of minorities suffering.[50]

The opening declaration of the Convention then went on to state:

In our opposition to Home Rule we are activated by no spirit of sectarian exclusiveness and we seek for no ascendancy religious or otherwise. Many of us were active sharers in the struggle which, over forty years ago, secured religious equality and initiated land reform in Ireland; and, if permitted, we are all of us ready to co-operate with Irishmen of every creed in the advancement of the social, moral, and material prosperity of our common country. Our demand is, as a matter of elementary right and justice, the undisturbed continuance of our present place in the constitution under which our Church and our country have so signally prospered.

Our Scottish forefathers, in their struggles for religious freedom and civil right, cast their burden on the Lord Omnipotent, who gave them signal victory. Facing as we do now, dangers similar to theirs, we shall follow in their footsteps and emulate their faith. In the profound belief that God reigns, we commit our cause in all confidence to Him.

Some comments might be made on these resolutions and the declaration. Apart from the explicit reference to Scotland in number four, it might also have been the case that resolution number three in its reference to missionary activities abroad was attempting to strike a chord with Scots who were so proud of their missionary work in the Empire, and that resolution number five was in part an attempt to play on the traditional Scottish Presbyterian emphasis on education and similarly fearful view of Papal power. The declaration, besides identifying with past Scottish struggles, makes pointed reference to the struggle for Church disestablishment in Ireland which was an assault on Anglican/Episcopalian privilege, and to the land reform struggle which was against landlordism. Clearly, Scottish Presbyterian sensitivities were uppermost in the organisation of the Convention.

Later speakers returned to these themes: much was made of Catholic educational separatism;[51] of the *Ne Temere* decree of 1908 which stipulated that mixed marriages were only valid if sanctified by the rites of the Roman Catholic Church and that the children should be brought up Catholic;[52] and of the Presbyterians' wish only for equality and justice and their traditional opposition to ascendancy which had led them to fight battles for Catholics in the past as well as for themselves.[53] Displays of prejudice and crude bigotry were, in fact, conspicuous by their absence, with several speakers taking pains to accord brotherly sentiments to their 'Roman Catholic fellow countrymen' while expressing their fears about Catholic Church aspirations.[54]

The chairman of the Convention, the Rt Hon. Thomas Sinclair, recalled Scottish assistance for Ulster Presbyterians during the persecutions of 1641 and expressed confidence that they would come to their aid again. Sinclair then went on to predict what a Home Rule parliament would be like and in so doing, identified the vehicle through which the Catholic Church would exercise domination: 'a body composed of men the great majority of whom would be the nominees of secret societies like the Ancient Order of Hibernians,[55] and utterly inexperienced in financial and industrial affairs'. The Ulster Presbyterians, as their historians have pointed out, took the view that they had escaped the Anglican ascendancy with its denial of the validity of their marriages and legitimacy of their children, and were thus not going to risk a situation where there would be a Roman Catholic ascendancy leaving Presbyterians again in a disadvantaged position.[56]

The Scottish flavour of the Convention was added to by the contribution of a minister from Edinburgh, Dr Salmond, who claimed he spoke for a great many Scots in expressing sympathy with the Protestants of Ireland in their quest to avert 'a great calamity to their beloved Emerald Isle, and a source of weakness to the Empire'. Salmond further declared that the Liberal government was dependent upon the support of people who did not have at heart 'the good of the British Empire', and ended by saying that 'as a Scottish Presbyterian conversant with Irish conditions, and mindful of many ancestral traditions – John Knox, Andrew Melville, Jenny Geddes, Thomas Chalmers – he said, "God shield and prosper you!".' Following Salmond, the Rt Hon. John Young identified the Irish Presbyterians with the Scottish Church, going so far as to say they were a 'Scottish colony' enjoying in the parliament of the United Kingdom 'civil and religious liberty such as was enjoyed in no other part of the world'. The imperial connection was stressed by a Dr R Henry and a William Colhoun, the latter declaring that they would not be driven out from their share of the heritage of the greatest empire ever known.

In Scotland itself there were signs that Scottish Presbyterians were responding to Ulster's appeals – messages were sent to the Convention from churches and individuals[57], although one well-wisher, William Whitelaw, the chairman of the Highland Railway, felt constrained to admit that political factors stood in the way of more solid support:

> In the coming fight the Irish Presbyterians will have the assistance and the sympathy of the majority of Presbyterians in Scotland, but I regret to say that I know that a large number of Scottish Presbyterians are so bound by hereditary devotion to the shibboleths of Radicalism that they will desert their Presbyterian brethren in Ireland rather than range themselves for once among the supporters of the Unionist party.[58]

The editorials of the *Glasgow Herald*, as befitted its Conservative disposition, came out in favour of Ulster and argued that if 'Glasgow and Clydesdale' were in the position of Unionist Ulster, 'we should talk and act much as do our kinsfolk across the Irish Channel.'[59] The Glasgow Presbytery of the Church of Scotland passed a motion of sympathy for Ulster later in February 1912,[60] while in October of that year a special meeting of the Presbytery of the more radically-inclined United Free Church (an amalgamation, effected in 1900, of the Free and United Presbyterian Churches) was called to 'correct' the impression given that they were not in sympathy with the Ulster Protestants.[61] This suggests that some movement may have been afoot among Presbyterians of a liberal and radical hue in favour of the Ulster cause, but much more work has to be done on the Scottish response to Ulster's propaganda efforts outside Conservative and Orange circles before this issue can be discussed with any assurance.

It was certainly the case, however, that developments such as the *Ne Temere* decree disturbed Scottish Protestants of all denominations and political views. Moreover, the impact in Scotland of the massive numbers who signed the Ulster Covenant pledging resistance to Home Rule in September 1912 may have been heightened by the event's conscious attempt to summon the historical inspiration of the Scottish Covenant. Certainly, the Covenanters were still a central part of Scotland's historical self-image, and tales of persecution and sacrifice continued to provide much fuel for Protestant militancy.[62] As a speaker, T G Houston had put it at the Presbyterian Convention:

> It was beginning to dawn on the people of England and Scotland that they had made a serious mistake about Ulster. They thought that they were listening only to an ebullition of jingoism. But to their astonishment and indignation they had found that it was not with the jingo spirit, but with the martyr spirit they had to deal . . .[63]

However, the magnitude of Ulster Unionist demonstrations could not entirely neutralize the Achilles heel of Protestant Home Rule support, whether in Ireland or in different parts of Britain. It was all the more galling, then, that a Scottish Presbyterian should stand on a Home Rule platform at a by-election in Derry City in January 1913. The candidate, Douglas Hogg, refused to take the pledge of the Irish Nationalist Party, but they nonetheless campaigned for him vigorously in the knowledge that such a candidate was grist to their propaganda mill, which proclaimed Home Rule as a non-sectarian cause. From the reactions of the Unionist press, it seems that they had some success in fomenting divisions between Presbyterians and Episcopalians in Derry, and that they astutely played up the Establishment Episcopalian credentials of the Unionist candidate, Colonel Pakenham. The *Belfast Weekly News* fulminated over 'the Scottish Lundy' whom they viewed as seeking to deliver them into the hands of 'the pikemen of the Hibernians',[64] and there were hints that Conservative/Orange disparagement of the Presbyterian Liberal tradition in Ulster might strain the unity of Unionism.[65] Hogg was duly elected by 2,699 votes to 2,642, a majority of 57. In the *Belfast Weekly News*, 'Scots Wha Hae' was rewritten and dedicated to Hogg as follows:

> What care you for kith and kin?
> Butter's thick and blood is thin
> Majorities are sure to win
> Minorities be hanged.[66]

Thus, it was as much characteristic of Ulster Unionism as a general movement to allege betrayal and accuse their 'kith and kin' of letting them down as it was to proclaim the imperishability of these kinship and religious bonds.

The Irish Presbyterian church, at their Assembly in June 1913, made it more than clear that their opposition to Home Rule was unimpeachable. The vote taken on it resulted in a 921–43 result against. Furthermore, the Moderator, in his address, struck an unambiguous note of British patriotism:

> Seldom, if ever, have any of us been ashamed to declare we are Britons . . . whatever quarrels with British policy members of the Assembly may have had from time to time, and whatever their views of the best solution of the Irish problem, the sentiment of loyalty towards and pride in the British inheritance and Commonwealth of peoples has been common to us all.[67]

The *Belfast Weekly News* could have had no complaint about that.

IV

Such was the internally protean nature of Ulster Unionism that it is difficult to sum up in a positive way its essence, as opposed, negatively, to its
vigilant defensiveness and defiance in the face of the perceived Home Rule
threat. Some have seen its essence as racism, a viewpoint most recently
expressed by Professor Joseph Lee.[68] Lee's contention seems to be based –
although it is not clear, since he does not provide empirical evidence –
on the cultivation of the 'Ulsterman' stereotype referred to earlier. Undoubtedly, there was implicit in this stereotype a suggestion of superiority
over the 'other Irish'. The Orange Order, which became increasingly
important both organisationally and culturally to the Unionist movement
in this era, certainly conveyed something of this in its imagery, its songs
and its catch-cries. However, it was arguably less concerned with boasting
about racial superiority than with decrying what it saw as the Catholic
Church's striving for ascendancy over Protestantism in Ireland and the
activities of the Orange society's mirror-image: the Catholic sectarian secret
society, the Ancient Order of Hibernians.

In many ways the Orange Order viewed the struggle as one between
tribal secret societies, a zero-sum game in which there could be no compromise; it was indeed a struggle which had its roots in the late eighteenth
century when the Orange Order was set up to fight the Catholic
Ribbonmen and Defender societies. It is a perspective caught well by
Houston, one of the most skilful of the Presbyterian Unionist propagandists, in a letter to the press in 1913:

> I have followed the controversy since the days of Isaac Butt, and I can find in
> it only one argument for Home Rule, an argument which was 'summarilly
> comprehended' in the concluding words of an Ancient Hibernian and an
> Orangeman after a heated discussion on the subject of Home Rule. 'We'll raise
> hell if you don't give us Home Rule.' 'You'll raise worse hell if we do.' That
> way of putting the case leaves, perhaps something to be desired in the matter
> of elegance of language, but nothing in the way of clearness and completeness
> in stating the point at issue.[69]

Besides Orangeism being essentially defensive rather than assertive of
racial superiority, it might be said that the component of the Unionist resistance exemplified in the Presbyterian Convention speeches quoted above
was a powerful influence against Unionism taking on the character of an
ascendancy caste protecting privileges. The Nationalist attempts to depict
it in this light, while admittedly successful in terms of propaganda
impac through the years, were disingenuous in their pretence that
Presbyterian liberalism or radicalism was wholly on the side of Home
Rule. Overwhelmingly it was not, although it must be said that many

Presbyterians of these political leanings in Scotland could not endorse their Ulster co-religionists' willingness to sink their differences with the Conservative and landlord wing of Unionism.

It should also be noted that the Orange Order, though still largely identified with the landed class and Established Church ethos of its origins, became a pan-denominational Protestant front organisation in the nineteenth century and was acceptable to many Presbyterians, especially after the disestablishment of the Church of Ireland in 1869. Its main function was to forge Protestant unity which was felt, in the circumstances of Home Rule, to be paramount by a majority in all Protestant denominations in Ireland. Finally, on the point of racism, it should be remembered that Irish Nationalists in this period were just as capable of it, and, indeed, some of the views of such figures as Arthur Griffith, founder of Sinn Féin, were far more explicit than anything recorded by Unionist leaders.[70] Unionism, in the manner of Lee, cannot be reduced to racism.

Similarly, it cannot easily be summed up in relation to questions of national identity. A plurality of identities has to be acknowledged, although it must again be emphasised that there was an unequivocal and positive identification with Britain and the Empire which was complemented, not contradicted, by the cultivation of a spirit of Ulster independence as befitting a people who saw themselves in 'the front line' or as 'under siege'; and by a specific appeal, on the part of arguably the most important sector of the Ulster Protestant community,[71] to an historic Ulster-Scottish bond forged through centuries of common religious – Presbyterian – struggle and social and cultural interaction.

Whatever the internal logic of Ulster Unionism, however, the image presented to the outside world could not avoid seeming insecure and muddled: threats of rebellion mingling with proclamations of loyalty; religious fears cutting across sacred political divisions. For all the appeal to history, the Ulster Protestant sense of what was historically significant could appear too diffuse and incoherent for even Scots Presbyterians to feel affinity with: if the Ulster Presbyterians were the backbone of Ulster Protestantism, they did not, ultimately, have a monopoly in defining its overall identity. No neat and tidy mythological narrative of their progress was constructed to match the kind fashioned by such as Patrick Pearse to serve the Irish Nationalist cause.[72] By comparison with the Ulster Protestants, the Catholic Irish story was all the more powerful for its capacity to be reduced to one of an oppressed people rising up and winning their place in the sun.

The Ulster Protestants made their appeal for support in this period with all too apparent anxiety and without the historicist confidence of the Irish Nationalists. Moreover, they made the strongest appeal to Scotland, a nation which at this juncture was perhaps at its peak in terms of a confident self-image as a great, ancient nation, possessed of internationally renowned traditions and institutions, and confident of its capacity to go on achieving greatness and influencing world developments. Scotland saw itself, at this time, as having the right blend of a working relationship with England and a cultural distinctiveness which included a Jacobite romanticism denoting potential rebelliousness and independence of spirit, and a thrawn, egalitarian Protestantism which facilitated engagement with the demands and challenges of the modern world at home and abroad.

The Scots' sense of their identity, enhanced through involvement in Empire to which their Protestantism was central, was of an expansive kind, in many ways too impatient with the insecurities, the complexities, the narrowness and the defensiveness of Ulster's outlook and preoccupations. This may have been an indication of how the Scots' conceit of themselves prevented consideration of the role that large numbers of Irish immigrants, both Catholic and Protestant, were playing in re-fashioning Scottish society and the overall sense of national and cultural identity. Beyond the self-proclaimed expansiveness of attitude, there perhaps lay an element of insularity which should have caused more critical self-examination than was evident.

8

An Ulster Labourist in Liberal Scotland: William Walker and the Leith Burghs Election of 1910

BOB PURDIE

William Walker, the Belfast trade unionist and socialist politician, was an opponent of Irish Home Rule who believed that the interests of the working class of Ireland were best served within the United Kingdom. He challenges the present day assumption that an Irish socialist must also be a nationalist and represented a political alternative which deserves serious examination. But perceptions of Walker have been overshadowed by the disgrace of the concessions he made to religious sectarianism in the North Belfast by-election of 1905, when he committed himself to supporting retention of the sovereign's accession declaration against transubstantiation, exclusion of Catholics from the offices of Lord Chancellor and Lord Lieutenant of Ireland, and said that Protestantism meant protesting against superstition and so was synonymous with Labour. The intellectual poverty he showed in his debate with James Connolly in the columns of *Forward* in 1911, also cast him in an unfavourable light, and, as a result, present day historical discussion has been almost as polarised as the one between Walker and Connolly. We are offered little more than an emotional choice between the hero-martyr of 1916 and the opportunist bigot of 1905.

Geoffrey Bell, for example, accuses Walker of 'leading socialism in Belfast along a religiously sectarian path',[1] while D R O'Connor Lysaght makes a similar point in a more sophisticated way: 'It is this irresponsible belief that religious bigotry can be accepted and then tamed, combined with a typical Social Democratic ignorance of the nature of imperial and colonial exploitation that constitutes "Walkerism".'[2] But apart from one incident in 1905, Walker consistently strove to keep Labour independent of both sectarian camps, and perceptions of his support for imperialism are based on a disputable construction put on one newspaper article. As this essay will show, he actually shared the socialist and radical position of opposition to colonial expansion. In any case these criticisms condemn Walker, but do not explain him.

C Desmond Greaves characterises him as a 'reformist' of the 'gas and water socialism' type, who saw no further than municipal ownership.[3] But James Connolly fought local elections on a platform of municipalisation, and we cannot assume that simply because Walker boasted of Belfast's progress in that field he thought it was sufficient: why would he have challenged the existing political establishment in the city if this were so? Bernard Ransome highlights the polarisation between Connolly, 'an unskilled worker and syndicalist theorist ... and Walker as a skilled tradesman and an official of the Amalgamated Society of Carpenters and Joiners.'[4] Actually, *both* were *socialist* theorists and Walker had a good record of supporting unskilled trade unionism. J W Boyle concentrates on Walker's personal qualities: 'As a political thinker Walker was unoriginal. Too much of what he wrote is concerned with long-dead problems. His powers of analysis were weak and when he generalised he became verbose.'[5] This is true, but it could also be said of a majority of the socialists of his or any time.

Henry Patterson relates Walker and his supporters to the alternative working class tradition of independent Orangeism, as embodied in the Belfast Protestant Association and the Independent Orange Order which, in the first decade of this century, challenged the domination of Protestant politics by the landlords and capitalists of Unionism. Walker, he suggests, picked up their theme that:

> ... traditional Unionism was now discredited by its reactionary voting record on social issues at Westminster. The best defence of the Union was the return of progressive Unionists who would ... demonstrate ... that support for the maintenance of the union was not the hallmark of landlords and other reactionary elements. The complementary notion was that Irish nationalism was the reactionary obverse of traditional Unionism.[6]

Patterson, however, does not prove that this was any more than an opportunist election tactic. He begs the question of why we should need such an elaborate explanation of Walker's actions. In reviewing his book shortly after publication, this writer pointed out:

> The problem is that this by-election and Walker's campaign become important for understanding Belfast Labourism in this period to no little extent because of the paucity of other sources. So much else of the day to day life of the labour movement and the evolution of the thinking of its rank and file has simply

gone unrecorded. Elections are a rather artificial time in the life of a political movement. Walker's propaganda about the need for 'progressive' Unionists to offset the record of the Unionist Party can be seen as a response to the campaign of his opponents, which, as Patterson shows, was focused mainly on the Home Rule record of Walker's election agent, Ramsay MacDonald, and that of the Labour Party at Westminster. The theme may have been borrowed form the I.O.O. [Independent Orange Order] but the circumstances tend to diminish the long term ideological significance of the appropriation.'[7]

It is worth noting that during this campaign Walker also made concessions to clerical opinion about atheism, accepting that they would be justified in opposing his candidature if he were not an orthodox Christian believer. This gives credence to electoral opportunism as an explanation, rather than ideology.

In most of these accounts, Walker is seen as part of an insular Belfast labour movement and Patterson, the revisionist, agrees with the pro-nationalists in portraying Walker as, essentially, a left-wing Ulster Unionist. Only Austen Morgan suggests that he has also to be seen in a British context, thus offering an explanation for the source of some of his political ideas. He also makes the point that:

> He warrants a place in Irish history for challenging conservatives in Belfast. Walker was the champion of independent working class politics, and he deserves the respect of socialists for his attempt to build a labour party . . . He of course belonged to the predominant community, and, despite his support for trade union organisation, was blind to the position of the Catholic working class. His anti-nationalism is not in doubt, but his labourism saw him leave working class politics rather than collapse into militant unionism.[8]

It ought to be acknowledged that Walker spent many years in unrewarded effort on behalf of the workers of Belfast: promoting trade unionism for unskilled and Catholic workers as much as for those from his own skilled, Protestant background; exposing exploitation and poverty and explaining the socialist alternative to capitalism. He suffered at the hands of Protestant extremists and he worked closely with James Larkin during the 1907 dockers' and carters' strike. This is not to endorse all of Walker's political views, simply to point out his complexity. The over-simplification to which he has been subjected robs us of vital insights into working class politics in Edwardian Ulster as well as a fuller understanding of Walker himself.

It is a virtue of Henry Patterson's work that he has a clear sense of conjuncture and puts Walker firmly into his historical context. He shows that Walker's political career began in 1893 when he joined the ILP and ended in 1912 when he took up a job with the National Insurance Commission. He was most prominent in the period between 1903 and 1911, a time when

Wyndham's Land Act appeared to have settled the old grievance of Nationalist Ireland. With a Conservative government in office, Home Rule was not in prospect, but there was great dissatisfaction with the Conservatives amongst Ulster Unionists when the government contemplated a scheme of devolution proposed by the Under-Secretary at Dublin Castle, Sir Antony McDonnell.

One consequence of this was shown by a letter written in December 1906 by Col. Fred Crawford, later to become famous for running guns into Larne Harbour for the Ulster Volunteer Force. He wrote to Lord Ranfurly, declining his offer to take up work in the Unionist cause, and telling him that 'Since the McDonnell incident we have lost a lot of staunch Unionist workmen in Belfast. They consider themselves betrayed . . . & have gone in for the labour and socialist programme. . . . The old unionist enthusiasm is dead among the masses here. These are facts and all in touch with the working man, like myself, knows [sic] it.'[9]

Six years later however, with the Second Home Rule Bill, the vast majority of Protestant workers had returned to the Unionist camp. It is necessary to keep this time frame in mind: Walker's politics were formed in a period when both nationalism and Unionism were relatively quiescent and when events had broken down old assumptions amongst Belfast workers. It should also be remembered that in dropping out of Labour politics, he also abstained from involvement in Unionist politics. We simply do not know his attitude towards the great traumas which racked Ireland between 1912 and his death in 1918.

Walker requires explanation. More precisely the link between his socialism and his Unionism needs to be interrogated and this is more complex and ambiguous than has yet been acknowledged. It is possible, for example, that at one time he supported Home Rule. According to an anonymous writer in *Forward* of 9 June 1917: 'It will be remembered that William Walker, a giant among socialist fighters, who as "Junius Junior" advocated Home Rule, considered it to be disastrous to his Parliamentary campaigns . . . to avow himself a Home Ruler.' There is no reference in any of the published literature to Walker having once supported Home Rule, and although the above seems to have been written by a contemporary, it cannot be confirmed. It is a fact however, that Walker joined the ILP in 1893, at the time of the Second Home Rule Bill and when the party, like the rest of the British labour movement, shared the Liberal policy of legislative independence for Ireland. At the very least, he must have cared less about the Union at that time than he did in 1905–7. His ideas need to be examined more closely and from other perspectives than those offered by the closed circles of Irish politics.

This essay will support Morgan's thesis that Walker is best understood as an orthodox British socialist, but will seek to prove this by considering him from a Scottish perspective. Such an approach offers new ways of comprehending his politics, firstly because it escapes from the polarisations of Irish political debate, in which Unionist and nationalist are opposites which do not interpenetrate. National feeling in Scotland has never exhibited this stark contrast and it has been quite possible to hold a strong allegiance to Scotland while supporting the legislative union with England; equally, it has been possible to move between support for the Union and support for self-government purely on the basis of perceived advantage. This pragmatism, this cultural ease with the idea of nationality, is quite absent from Ireland, but it offers a useful point of comparison. Moreover, Scottishness is a way of disaggregating the idea of Britishness. In Ireland it is out of the question for anyone with national consciousness to be influenced by Britain: you cannot be Irish and British. But no-one ever thinks of questioning Peader O'Donnell's nationalist credentials because he was converted to socialism in Scotland, still less those of James Connolly because he was born and grew to intellectual and political maturity there.

There is also the simple point that Walker was part of a labour movement which had close links with Clydeside and was strongly influenced by the Scottish socialist movement, some of whose leaders spoke regularly in Belfast; there was constant movement of labour and strong family ties between the two places. Walker became a trade unionist by joining the Scottish-based Associated Carpenters and Joiners Society; he was a member of the ILP which was founded in Belfast by a Scotsman and which was linked, for organisational purposes, with the Scottish region of the ILP; his debate with James Connolly was carried out in the pages of *Forward*, a Scottish socialist newspaper which circulated widely in Belfast; his last parliamentary contest was in a Scottish constituency, Leith Burghs. He was an Irishman who supported the link with Great Britain, but his perception of Britain must have been strongly influenced by his experience of Scotland. He cannot be understood fully, therefore, unless a Scottish perspective is brought to bear. Furthermore, he has a great deal of relevance to contemporary Scottish political debates.

This makes the debate about Walker relevant in a new way. In Ireland the discussion has been about the narrow issue of whether or not a socialist ought to be a nationalist. In effect, this has meant a debate about partition. This one-dimensional perception of the constitution obscures the full range of the problems which Walker and his contemporaries were trying to tackle. He can fairly be accused of helping to stultify socialist debate about constitutional issues in his own day: because he accepted the narrow terms of reference offered by Unionists and nationalists and because he believed that working people need only capture Parliament to abolish poverty and inequality, he thus left out of account the structural factors which had prevented the resolution of Irish grievances in the past. We have to explain, however, why he did so, and why his Scottish contemporaries shared his failure.

Walker's most substantial involvement with Scotland was his election campaign in Leith Burghs in 1910. Leith was a good seat for him to fight: like Liverpool's Kirkdale, the nomination for which he had unsuccessfully sought in 1907, it was a major port, with a vigorous shipbuilding and engineering industry and prospects of expansion with the building of large new docks. It was Clydeside on the Forth, cocking a proletarian snook at the great capital city of Edinburgh climbing the slopes of the Pentlands to its south. James Connolly contrasted the two places:

> The population of Edinburgh is largely composed of snobs, flunkeys, mashers, lawyers, students, middle-class pensioners and dividend hunters. Even the working class portion of the population seemed to have imbibed the would-be-respectable spirit of their 'betters' . . . Leith, on the other hand is pre-eminently an industrial centre. The overwhelming majority of its population belong to the disinherited class, and having its due proportion of sweaters, slave-drivers, rack-renting slum landlords, shipping federation agents and parasites of every description, might therefore have been reasonably expected to develop socialistic sentiments much more readily than the Modern Athens.[10]

The constituency also included the ancient fishing port of Newhaven and the burghs of Portobello and Musselburgh, strung out along Edinburgh's seaboard.

Walker was a good choice for the local Labour Party. He was an experienced and powerful speaker at a time when socialist campaigning relied heavily on public, often open-air oratory, and he was sponsored by his union, the Amalgamated Society of Carpenters and Joiners. His candidature got a fair wind from the local paper:

> Of Mr Walker it is only necessary to say that he brings his own credentials, which have not a blotch upon them . . . [he] gives evidence of earnestness of purpose and of having given much thought to political questions . . . he is entitled to a courteous welcome, a full hearing and the gratitude of his friends and critics alike for the light he will bring to bear on the point of view of the Labour Party.[11]

His Liberal opponent, R C Munro Ferguson, languidly noted: 'I see the Labour candidate is adopted for Leith. We'll have to look in there occasionally this autumn.'[12] Leith was a safe Liberal seat and was to remain so until 1945. Ferguson was a landowner with large holdings in Ross-shire and an estate in Kirkcaldy on the other side of the Firth of Forth. He had been MP since 1886, when he took the seat over from W E Gladstone; he was a former private secretary to Lord Rosebery, when the latter was Foreign Secretary, and he was Provost of Kirkcaldy. He was a Liberal imperialist who had supported the Boer War and, together with other right-wing Liberals like Asquith and Rosebery, he was opposed to the radical 'faddism' of the Liberal Party on matters such as Home Rule and land reform. The Liberal Unionist (Tory) candidate was Sir Robert Cranston, a former Lord Provost of Edinburgh.

Leith had a considerable Irish population, with two Catholic parishes and a Catholic secondary school. Almost all of the Irish worked in unskilled occupations and there was terrible poverty, but no tradition of anti-Catholicism or active anti-Irish bigotry. Walker was perceived in the constituency as an Irishman. *Forward* reported one of his speeches as being 'a splendid address enlivened by his Celtic wit and satire.'[13] The *Leith Observer* commented: '. . . his speech is his fortune. He is fluent, like many of his countrymen . . . '[14] During the by-election, Walker referred several times to his Irishness – at his adoption meeting he said he was 'a stranger amongst them'[15] and he was not above playing the stage Irishman, responding to one heckler: 'Leave him alone. I am a bit of an Irishman and I would like to throw down my coat for him to tramp on.'[16] He told another meeting that he had 'sufficient Irish blood . . . to give them trouble when he got there' (the House of Commons).[17]

At the adoption meeting on 12 August, Walker laid out the themes of his campaign. The Labour Party was a new force which had come into the political atmosphere and was uniting the workers. It was the only party pledged to social reform without regard to the interests of the monopolists. The main problem which 'ate at the vitals of the working classes' was unemployment. Labour was the temperance reform party and was 'a free trade party in the fullest sense of the term – that a man should not have a tariff put on him if he wanted land.' He asked, rhetorically, what would happen to Leith if a tariff was put on steel? The raising of prices would destroy shipbuilding in one year. Labour stood 'clear of all cavil' on the question of Tariff Reform and was the only party working for international peace. It was absurd to expect a man like Munro Ferguson or a Tory landlord (Cranston, who claimed to be a supporter of social reform), to remedy defects in legislation without 'a compelling power behind them'. He wanted that power to be 'inside the House, not outside.'[18]

This programme aimed at detaching radical Liberal voters and adding them to the potential Labour vote, a point borne out by a poster which has survived from the campaign. It shows Walker's head surrounded by thistles, with a scroll underneath hailing him as 'The People's Representative'. Below, two stereotyped, pigtailed figures in Chinese costume flank a quotation from Philip Snowden, linking landlordism with unemployment.[19]

At the August meeting, Walker referred to his record in Belfast:

> He might as well tell them at once, as he had heard diversities of opinion on that point. He had watched Belfast grow from a city of intolerance and bigotry until today Belfast was taking its place amongst the cities of the country, where neither religion nor class could debar men from having sympathy with one

another. He was proud to have been associated with those who had broken up the barriers of bigotry and who had helped to smooth the way of social progress in that city.[20]

This hints that he believed his record in Belfast might be controversial; at this point, however, he did not broach his views on Home Rule. He stayed in the constituency for about two weeks, addressing meetings and preparing for the election campaign. At a gathering in Newhaven Fishmarket he was asked about Irish Home Rule. He replied:

He did not believe in having a parliament in Dublin and another in England. There were too many parliaments already. If there was only one parliament for all Europe there would be no wars. To multiply parliaments would not improve the conditions of the people, and it would be more expensive. If Parliament was congested, the salvation was to confer extended powers on local authorities. As an Irishman he did not want to be divorced from his fellow-democrats in Scotland.[21]

At a meeting in Musselburgh in December 1909, during the election campaign proper, he said:

What was the Irish question? It was the demand of a body of men for better government . . . That was a cry that reached him and to which he responded in his own way by showing them that it was not by changing the place of the government, but by changing the men who governed them. (Applause) In Ireland they had the most wasteful and cumbrous system of government on God's earth. The Labour Party wished both Catholic and Protestant to realise distinctly that they were victims of a system that would not be changed by transplanting it.[22]

When asked elsewhere if he would vote against a Home Rule Bill in the House if he were elected, he avoided a commitment, saying: '. . . he was opposed to Home Rule for Ireland. The Irish landlord was the greatest curse the people had to endure, and every little peasant the moment he came into possession of the title deeds of a bit of land became a Tory with a vested interest.'[23]

This reply confused the issues of landlordism and petty proprietorship and had nothing to do with legislative independence for Ireland, but it seems to have satisfied his audience.

There is no evidence of any organised Irish opposition in the constituency, although at a December meeting in Portobello, he defended himself against claims that he was an Orangeman, pointing out that he had required nine months' police protection from the Orangemen during his time as an ILP orator at Belfast's Customs House. A United Irish League meeting in Musselburgh, called to discuss the forthcoming election, noted that he was 'an Ulsterman and opposed to Home Rule', but Ferguson was also attacked for not supporting Home Rule and it was resolved merely to await instructions from the Irish Parliamentary Party before advising the Irish on how to vote.[24]

James Connolly, during his debate with Walker in *Forward*, referred to a manifesto issued against the latter during the campaign by Irish socialists. There is no reference to this in the local newspaper, but at a demonstration against unemployment organised by Edinburgh and Leith Trades Councils in September 1909, and held in the King's Park at the foot of Arthur's Seat, there were cries of 'no' when a resolution supporting his candidacy was put, and a small disturbance when 'an apparently organised opposition' tried to get an amendment put to the meeting. His opponents were probably some of Connolly's old comrades from the Socialist Labour Party, and they may also have been responsible for the manifesto.[25]

The only difficult question Walker had to face about his Belfast career did not concern the 1905 concessions to sectarianism, but the dockers' and carters' strike two years later: he was accused of having been a member of a committee which had agreed terms with the masters to allow the carters to break the strike. Walker denied having been involved at all until the military were called out:

> After the first night's shooting he was on the scene. Next morning he wired Sir Antony McDonnell that if any military or police were found on a certain road (the Falls Road) there would be thousands of lives lost. . . . Sir Antony . . . withdrew the military and there was no trouble . . . Sir Antony . . . was appointed arbitrator in the dock dispute, and along with some others [he] arranged terms with him. The masters refused to see them.[26]

His account of the events was fairly garbled and he inflated his rôle in peacemaking and played down the extent of his support for the strike in its early days. But the questioner seemed not to have been aware that James Larkin himself had recommended the settlement to the carters. The evidence points to an SLP intervention, based on suspicion of him as a 'labour fakir' rather than on a detailed knowledge of the facts. In other words, it was not a manifestation of local Irish opposition.[27]

After December he made no further reference to Ireland and was not quizzed about it again. For the most part, his campaign concentrated on the themes of unemployment, the need for social reform and for a strong Labour Party in Parliament to represent the interests of the workers. He insisted that these were more important than the ostensible reason for the election – the rejection by the House of Lords of Lloyd George's 'People's Budget'. He told one meeting that he believed in the budget but thought it did not go far enough and would do nothing to solve unemployment. In this sense, he was fighting a fairly standard socialist campaign of the time:

counterposing social and economic problems to constitutional and international issues.

His stance on international affairs was a standard radical one. He opposed 'imperialism' in the sense of foreign entanglements and acquisition of colonies. He denounced his Liberal opponent for demanding the maintenance of British naval supremacy; but he referred to no specific foreign policy issue. On constitutional affairs he expressed support for proportional representation and for 'adult suffrage', in line with the 1905 Labour Party Conference decision. Adult suffrage was a way of enfranchising women but it was not a principled support for the right of women to vote, and he had to be pressed to endorse Keir Hardie's campaign against the brutal treatment of arrested suffragettes.

He identified himself as a socialist and defended socialism against an accusation by Munro Ferguson that it would destroy family life, but made it clear that he was standing on a Labour and not a socialist platform. His campaign culminated in a huge torchlight procession sponsored by Leith and Edinburgh Trades Councils, a campaigning method he had first developed in North Belfast. Two columns of demonstrators marching from different parts of the constituency met at the foot of Leith Walk, the main hub of Leith. The crowd of spectators was so thick that they had difficulty getting through, and at various points cheers were raised for Walker. 'Compliments were also exchanged between the processionists and a party of suffragists . . .' Walker arrived on horseback and, speaking to the crowd,

> urged the magnitude of the claim for social reform. He seeks to prevent the rash accumulation of wealth which is a disturbing factor in our industrial life, while at the same time securing a full measure of comfort, leisure and education for the large mass of our fellow citizens who are deprived not only of the luxuries of life but in an ever increasing degree of the necessities of life.[28]

During the campaign he had claimed that Labour was certain of 5,000 votes. This would have deprived Ferguson of his majority and Walker evidently hoped to squeeze the votes of both his opponents and get a majority on the basis of Labour converts and tactical voters. In fact, he got 2,724 votes, 18.9 per cent of the poll. Ferguson had lost 11.6 per cent compared with the 1905 result, so it seems likely that Walker did succeed in denting his vote.[29] In this sense it was a good result, given the circumstances of the election. His stance on Home Rule is unlikely to have had much effect on the Irish vote in Leith. He made no special appeal to it, nor did he do anything to alienate it but to state honestly his views on Home Rule. Except in special cases, like the support given to George Barnes in Gorbals by the radical Home Government Branch of the United Irish League, the Irish voted Liberal, on their leaders' orders. If James Connolly had been the Labour candidate in Leith in January 1910, the result would have been little different.

How does the Leith campaign compare with Walker's three contests in North Belfast? In his final speech during the 1906 General Election, Walker had said:

> When he used the phrase the Labour Party he did not mean the ordinary skilled or unskilled artisan. He meant the party that was seeking to elevate the working classes and the community in general out of the slough of despond in which they had remained for so long . . . He appealed to them on the platform of citizenship, did they not think that the system of party government which had been tried for the past 73 years ought to be displaced by some other system whereby the people would have the power and not the few. He appealed to them to try and alter the government of this country that the voice of the working classes would become effective in the Legislative Chamber of the Nation.[30]

This differed in no essential from his speech at the Leith adoption meeting. In Belfast his themes had been labour representation, opposition to tariff reform, temperance and vague sentiments of moral uplift. These were repeated in Leith and were similar to the themes of his presidential address to the Irish Trade Union Congress in 1904, when he was the first president to advocate labour representation from Ireland. In Belfast he had also opposed Irish Home Rule and he repeated this at Leith in precisely the terms he had used at home.

In May 1908, he delivered a lecture on the Irish question under the auspices of the North Belfast ILP in which he offered his own explanation for Irish grievances.

> It is a gross mistake to suppose that because we have a legislative union that we are thereby treated equally as England or Scotland. . . . We are subjected in our domestic affairs to the vagaries of the forty one central boards which control home affairs, and added to that we have that huge anachronism, Dublin Castle, with the Vice-Regal Office, standing as a perpetual bar to progress. Of the many recent beneficial acts which the British Parliament has adopted, Ireland fails to obtain advantage therefrom. Such acts as 'The Feeding of School Children', 'the Vaccination Amendment Acts', etc., all indicate that on questions which concern either the material salvation or the rights of conscience Ireland is treated different from England; in brief she is at the moment governed by the 'hangers on' of the political parties; for every new measure passed for Ireland establishes a new governing body, to which the favourites of the ruling party are appointed. . . . In fact every new departure or improvement on old policy must be subjected to the supervision of a specially nominated body, whose qualifications might be summed up in the phrase, 'they served their party well'.[31]

This was not a nationalist analysis, but it was nonetheless quite different from Unionism, which justified the Union in terms of sovereign right, not administrative and economic expediency. He went on to excoriate both parties:

> One camp strains every exertion to change the theatre of legislative action from London to Dublin, whilst the other camp, animated only by opposition to the first, refuses to admit that there is anything wrong, for fear that the 'Union may be endangered thereby.' ... Does it matter very much WHERE the legislation comes from so long as it is good? And can legislation by the British Parliament be made good and beneficial to Ireland? ... I am convinced that ... if the representatives of Ireland set themselves the task of dealing with the Irish problem as business men would in their private concerns, that we would get benefit from our legislative connection, not merely wasteful extravagance.[32]

Walker had demonstrated the logical absurdity of the belief that Ireland was necessarily badly governed because it was not governed from Ireland. He thus satisfied himself that he had disproved any connection between the Union and Irish grievances. But of course it does not follow that there is *no* connection between the geographical distance of a legislature and defects in government, and it was a fairly audacious piece of reductionism to present Irish grievances as simply a matter of government wastefulness. But, it should be repeated, this was quite different from Unionism. His campaign in Leith followed essentially the same themes as his three contests in North Belfast except for his response to the Belfast Protestant Association in 1905. Moreover, this was entirely acceptable to the local Labour Party and was not regarded as exceptional by the local press. Nor did his defence of the Irish Union provoke significant hostility from any section of the electorate, not even the Irish.

At his adoption meeting J R Clynes spoke in his favour and a letter of support from Arthur Henderson was read out. At the rally on unemployment in Edinburgh in September, he shared a platform with Keir Hardie. He had been sent a unanimous invitation by the local Labour Representation Committee (LRC) to put himself forward for selection and had sought Ramsay MacDonald's advice on the prospects,[33] MacDonald having been his 1905 election agent in Belfast. He had the support of prominent Labour leaders because he was considered a mainstream Labour candidate. He had, after all, been a delegate to Labour Party Conferences since 1905 and had been elected to the Standing Orders Committee in that year and the one following. In 1910 he became a member of the National Executive, rising to the position of Vice-Chairman; he was an assiduous attender, being present at all that year's meetings.

He spoke several times at Labour Party Conferences, but only twice on Irish matters. In 1906 there was a debate on the Party constitution which included a clause enjoining candidates 'to abstain strictly from identifying themselves with or promoting the interests of any section of the Liberal or Conservative parties ... ' Belfast Trades Council proposed an amendment to insert 'or Unionist or Nationalist' after 'Conservative'. James Sexton, of the National Union of Dock Labourers opposed, on the grounds that it did not recognise the Labour credentials of members of the Irish Party who had helped Labour on the Trades Disputes Bill. In supporting the amendment, Walker said:

> If the National Party travelled to London to vote on the Trades Disputes Bill, did not dozens of Liberals do the same? Did not Tories do the same? All parties would back Labour just in proportion to Labour's independence. . . . They must remember that the bulk of the men from whom they must draw their recruits in Ulster and in Lancashire were Tories, but how could they do that if it could be said that the Labour Movement was open to an alliance with the Nationalist Party. That Party had men in its ranks true on Labour questions, and they wanted those men to come out of that Party into their Party – the inter-nationalist Party.[34]

Walker was cheered and the amendment was carried with only a few voting against. Next day, Sexton struck back with an amendment to include the words 'and shall not include in their electoral addresses any expression of political faith other than that of the Labour Party.' In moving it, he said that he had intended to withdraw the amendment, but had changed his mind after the decision to 'accommodate the peculiar morals of Belfast'. He contrasted the refusal to endorse Will Thorne in South West Ham because he had proclaimed himself a socialist with the endorsement of Walker in North Belfast, despite the fact that he had described himself as a 'Unionist in politics'. He was given short shrift, the chairman described his proposal as a waste of time and 'absolutely ridiculous'; the amendment was lost.[35]

At the 1911 Conference Walker spoke in the debate on abolishing the 'pledge' obliging Labour candidates and MPs to abide by the constitution and accept the decisions of the Parliamentary Party. In the recent Osborne Judgement, overturning the right of trade unions to use their funds for political purposes, the Law Lords had declared this to be unconstitutional. The 'pledge' had always been repugnant to the Liberals and the NEC recommended that it should be abandoned as a diplomatic move to ensure government action to overturn the effects of Osborne. Walker was one of the minority who had opposed this, and he cited the 'pledge' extracted from the Irish Party, to which the Liberals had not objected. A miners' del-egate disputed his interpretation of that pledge, but no-one, not even Sexton, took issue with his attitude towards the Irish Party.

Walker's hostility was influenced by his opposition to Irish Home Rule, and this in turn was because of his Belfast Protestant origins. But his polit-ical stance was one of maintaining the independence of Labour and freeing it from entanglements with Lib-Labism. Benignity towards the Irish Party had kept Labour dependent on Liberal goodwill and he was with the mainstream on that issue. He was also at one with Larkin and Connolly, who had both objected to the relationship between the Labour Party and the Irish Party, which ignored the views of the labour movement in Ireland.

Other causes he took up at Labour Party Conferences included land nationalisation and state provision for injured workers. On both matters he was in a minority but his differences were tactical ones within a broad common approach. To reiterate, Walker was in the mainstream of the British Labour Party; it is only when Irish nationalism is made the test of political orthodoxy that he appears unusual. There is, however, another problem. It concerns the issue which, like the dog in the night, is significant for not barking – Scottish Home Rule.

The subject was entirely absent from the Leith campaign. Walker did not commit himself for or against, and he was not asked about it. At this time, the Labour Party's commitment to Scottish Home Rule was as definite as its commitment to Home Rule for Ireland: that is to say it was part of the old Radical agenda but it had never developed a distinctive stance on the matter. For most Scottish Labour leaders it was no more than a vague aspiration: in the words of John MacCormick, founder of the Scottish National Party, who began his own political life in the ILP:

> I think that most of them had a special sentimental compartment in their minds and it was there that they cherished as a somewhat distant dream the idea of Scotland governing herself. Many of them had begun their political lives as Liberals in the Gladstonian tradition and Home Rule was inherited along with other items of the Radical faith. As the years went on and as positions of power and influence opened up to them, they gradually forgot their Scottish sentiment and like so many other Scotsmen of their time concentrated their energies in a Party loyalty which transcended national considerations.[36]

MacCormick suggests that it was a simple matter of careerism. This was true in some cases, but the matter was more complex. By the end of the nineteenth century, the great amalgamated unions had appeared; Sidney and Beatrice Webb make an important point about the contrasting development of these unions in Ireland and Scotland:

> This tendency has been greatly assisted, especially in the engineering and shipbuilding trades by the remarkable industrial development of Belfast. Since 1860 a constant stream of skilled artisans from England and Scotland have settled in that town, with the result that it now possesses strong branches of all the national unions of both countries. With the shifting of the effective centre of Trade Unionism from Dublin to Belfast has come an almost irresistible tendency to accept an English or Scottish government [i.e government of the trade union] . . .

But there is a marked contrast between the unions of Scotland with England, and that effected by either of them with Ireland. The English or Scottish Trade Unions federate or combine with each other on equal terms. If complete amalgamation is decided upon it is frequently the Scotchman, bringing with him Scotch procedures and Scottish traditions, who is chosen to reign in England . . . Union with Ireland invariably means the simple absorption of the Irish branch, and the unconditional acceptance of the English or Scottish rules and organisation.[37]

Irish trade unionism suffered because of its subordinate status. J Dunsmore Clarkson reckoned that '. . . the Irish labour movement was, in 1907, almost a generation behind the British Labour movement.'[38] The lack of control over the central organisation meant that Irish members, involved in long drawn out disputes, were liable to be discarded in order to safeguard the union's assets. Thus in 1892 the Dublin and Belfast branches of the Gasworkers' Union were wound up, despite the fact that the leader, Will Thorne, had been exceptional in his level of interest in the Irish membership. A combination of the savagely hostile response of the employers during the Dublin Coalporters' strike of the previous year and difficulties for the union in England, meant that it withdrew to the London area.[39] Even James Sexton, who regarded himself as an Irish Nationalist, was unwilling to use the resources of the National Union of Dock Labourers in support of James Larkin's efforts to break the resistance of Irish employers to unskilled trade unionism.

The relationship of Irish and Scottish trade unionism to the British movement was an analogue of the United Kingdom: Scotland was a junior partner, Ireland was a tenant-at-will. Scottish trade unionists had a stake in the evolving British labour movement; they were allowed the benefits of relative autonomy and, at the same time, support from the much greater resources of a British movement. Irish trade unionists were unable to catch up fully with 'New Unionism' until they had created their own, Irish-based, unskilled unions. In doing so, they drew on Irish nationalist sentiment. Their Scottish counterparts did not need to appeal to nationalism, because any extra resources they required were forthcoming from trade unionists outwith Scotland. The 1913 Dublin strike and lockout was evidence that despite its large scale assistance to relieve hardship, the British movement was not going to provide the necessary resources to defeat the employers' offensive against the right of Irish workers to belong to a trade union. There was sympathy with the Dublin workers, but not effective solidarity.

The Scots had a strong political motive for abandoning an express nationalist commitment. There was greater resistance by Liberalism in Scotland to independent Labour politics, and the Scottish Liberals refused to follow English members of the Party in their electoral pact with Labour for the 1906 General Election. This meant that Scotland lagged far behind England in Labour representation in Parliament. It is significant that Keir Hardie and Ramsay MacDonald, both Scottish Home Rulers, had to rely on English constituencies to get into Parliament. The Scottish Labour Party had been founded in 1888 as part of a radical alliance, but by 1894 it had shed its Liberal and Irish Nationalist supporters and had combined with the all-British ILP. The separate Scottish Workers' Representation Committee was merged with the LRC in 1910, on the initiative of MacDonald. It is true that there was a reflorescence of Nationalist sentiment in the Scottish labour movement after 1918, influenced by the First World War, events in Ireland and the recognition of the rights of small nations in the Versailles Treaty, but the period from 1894 until 1918 was one of steady decline in Scottish nationalist commitment within the Labour movement; a decline which was resumed after 1922 with the Irish Treaty and the prospect of Labour attaining power at Westminster.

Keating and Bleiman show how commitment to Scottish Home Rule was closely linked to support for Irish Home Rule. When the movement ceased to give a priority to the Irish claim, the importance of the Scottish cause also dwindled in importance, although it was never dropped as a formal part of its programme.[40] They point to the role of trade unionists in redirecting the movement from a radical agenda to a concentration on parliamentary action to obtain social reform in the interests of workers. This was given a significant impetus by the failure of Gladstone's 1892–94 Liberal government to advance crucial social reforms because of its preoccupations with Irish Home Rule. The executive of the Scottish Labour Party reported to the fourth Annual Conference in 1893 that:

> The issues we represent are too momentous to be set aside for one moment to suit the convenience of any Party. It is evident that the Party now in power [the Liberals] means to burke all genuine Labour questions . . . Without deprecating the importance of Home Rule to the people of Ireland, it is of minor importance to the people of this country, and not to be compared with social legislation in the interests of the unemployed, and any attempt to make this latter question subserve the convenience of Home Rule or anything else will be bitterly resented.[41]

In an editorial in the *Labour Leader* of 17 November 1891, Keir Hardie had argued that Irish Home Rule was not in prospect due to the cynicism of the Liberals and the subservience of the Irish Party. The Liberal government was using its conflict with the Lords as an excuse to withhold social reform:

> We are certain that the Irish people have no intention of playing this little game of the privileged classes. Hence we have the ILP. If the people of Ireland had Home Rule tomorrow they would require to get rid of ninety per cent of their

present representatives before they got legislation in the interests of the poor. And as the interests of the worker in Ireland are the same as the worker in England or Scotland, it follows that their forces should be united . . . Before justice can be done to Ireland the present type of representatives, on both sides of the channel, will have to be changed, and then, and not before, will Home Rule be granted.

This line of argument eroded the significance of the difference between Walker and Hardie over Home Rule. If the overriding issue was Labour representation, it was not only tactically acceptable but a matter of principle to put other matters aside. As early as his first parliamentary contest, Mid-Lanark in 1888, Hardie had discovered the disadvantages of public identification with the Irish cause. He had been refused the support of the Irish National League, which had tipped the Irish vote to the Liberal, and he had suffered a backlash from Orange voters incensed at his pro-Home Rule propaganda. Ever the pragmatist, Hardie, while never disavowing support for Home Rule, kept it well in the background when it had no electoral utility. In his successful campaign in West Ham, for example, the claims of Ireland and Scotland to self-government were given very little emphasis.

And of course, both Hardie and Walker were socialists. Radicalism was a coalition of interests around a concrete political agenda and it was consciously reformist and pluralist. Socialism claimed to represent a single interest and it had a single solution. Whereas radicalism sought immediate and practical objectives, socialism sought an objective of the imagination, a new and better society based on fundamentally different principles than those of the existing capitalist system. In pursuing this aim, socialists sought immediate reforms and they actually represented a coalition of different working class interests with crucial support from middle class intellectuals; but they denied both realities and constantly counterposed the clean, clear world of the imagination to the day-to-day reality of muddy compromise. This made it all too easy to deny the validity or importance of any political issues other than those being addressed by the labour movement at any given time.

Just as socialism required an ability to think through to a new order of society, involvement in the labour or radical movements required parallel, but different, acts of the imagination. Radicalism was nation-bound because it depended on an alliance between rural and urban discontents. Radicals had to imagine links of common interest between disparate socio-economic groups, and that common link was often nationalism. Socialism required a similar act of the imagination – the concept of international proletarian solidarity. This, however, was too abstract to be of more than rhetorical value. It was practical, however, to imagine a community of urban, industrial interests which had less and less in common with the countryside.

A Scottish trade unionist and socialist could choose between two distinct political communities. On the one hand there was the nation: this implied an alliance with an ever-diminishing Highland and Island crofter community, with a Scottish Liberal Party which resisted independent labour representation in Parliament, and with Irish nationalism, whose interests had been served to the exclusion of the industrial working class. On the other hand there was the network of urban industrial communities of Scotland, England, Wales and Ireland which were linked together by the trade unions, by common experiences and problems and, increasingly, by socialist ideology. This network embraced Belfast, a fact signalled by the fact that the TUC met there in 1893, and it was possible to imagine it also embraced Dublin. By 1913 it was clear that it did not, but in 1893 that was two decades in the future.

William Walker is best understood as an urban socialist who made an imaginative journey into a new world of labour solidarity. His journey started in 1893 when he joined the ILP, and seemed to have reached its destination in 1904 when he received warm support from the ITUC Conference for his advocacy of Irish labour representation at Westminster. Thereafter he faced increasing frustration as the majority of the Irish labour movement refused to make the break with the Irish Party which the British movement had made with the Liberals. By 1912, his political world had collapsed and he retreated into private life.

He resembled his Scottish more than his Irish contemporaries; nor can he usefully be characterised as British, because although Walker was not an Irish Nationalist, he regarded himself as an Irishman, and his political programme was for the Irish working class as a whole, not simply for its Ulster Protestant fraction. Of course he was influenced by his background. In Belfast, 'Britishness' had layers of meaning which were absent elsewhere, and this gave him an incentive to counterpose participation in the British political system to the expression of a national identity, in mutually exclusive terms which Scottish ILP leaders did not find necessary. The similarities, however, were more important than the differences. Walker was an orthodox British socialist, not a left wing Ulster Unionist. But his socialism was created at a specific time, in specific circumstances, out of the dissimilar, though converging, experiences of working class leaders from the four nations of Britain.

9

A Fireman Writes . . . A Reporter's View of Scotland's Press and the Irish Question

ROBBIE DINWOODIE

A newspaper has no use for confidential communications it cannot transmit to its readers.

– from the memoirs of Henri de Blowitz

> Oliver's Army are on their way,
> Oliver's Army is here to stay
> And I would rather be anywhere else
> Than here today . . .
> – song by Elvis Costello

In the early hours of Tuesday, 5 May, 1981 I snatched a brief sleep in the Excelsior Hotel at Glasgow Airport before catching the dawn flight to Belfast to report on the climax of the H-Block hunger strike campaign. When the radio alarm went off five hours later, I discovered I'd missed the story. In the words of the Northern Ireland office: 'Mr Robert Sands, a prisoner in the Maze Prison, died today at 1.17am. He took his own life by refusing food and medical intervention for 66 days.' Ireland's tangled story is one I've struggled to catch up with ever since.

I make no claims to academic expertise in the history, sociology and politics of partitioned Ireland. But those of us who work as daily newspaper reporters sometimes think it helps to hint that such expertise exists, carrying through this bluff even at those thankfully rare moments when physical dangers overshadow the trade's perennial risks of alcohol and hubris. Of course, none of this effort is worth a damn, far less a monthly pay cheque, if the words, however sage and well-crafted, are not transmitted back to the office in time for a deadline which is never more than hours distant and at all the most trying times is invariably just minutes away.

This contribution does no more than outline one journalist's experience of trying to cover the Irish question, and attempts to offer some insights into the mechanics of filing for a daily newspaper when social tensions there are at their highest, but you should be wary of drawing too many inferences from the views of just one reporter. The term 'journalism' itself is unhelpfully broad, since sub-editing the local dog show results for a weekly paper, writing the caption under the bare breasts on page three of a mass circulation tabloid, covering an international arms control summit for Reuters or penning the Lex column in the *Financial Times* all qualify.

In my case, as a journalist on the *Herald* and previously on the *Scotsman*, I have usually been dispatched to Belfast as what is known in the trade as a 'fireman' – that is, a reporter sent in when a situation flares up, to provide a newspaper with staff coverage in preference to agency copy or contributions from freelances based in the area. Partly, this is a question of getting a known staff by-line on the story. Partly, it is to avoid using the same, necessarily somewhat bland agency copy as rival newspapers. But mainly, I would contend, it is about getting coverage which is specifically targeted at your own readership, which can both reflect and challenge shared assumptions.

As someone who has chosen to work for newsdesks in Glasgow and Edinburgh rather than in what used to be called Fleet Street, I would argue that to challenge the political and social power of London, and the ingrained British Establishment view of many broadcasters and newspaper journalists who see the world from there, it is vital that a different, distinctively Scottish perspective is put on issues such as Northern Ireland by Scots-based journalists, particularly given the strands of history and culture which bind us.

That doesn't mean going for the quick and easy cliché, interviewing yer man in the Glasgow Rangers scarf or the scrawny kid in the Celtic jersey, or photographing the first gable wall of the Shankill with a Scotland and Ulster mural. Rather, it should mean trying to empathise with both communities, to show that these are people remarkably similar to ourselves, human beings rather than the 'animals' or 'scum' or 'bastards' of the London tabloid headlines, driven at times to desperate and even hideous acts of inhumanity by many of the same forces of history which buffeted our own collective past. Cromwell's forces conquered Scotland too, even if it is a period of history rarely dwelt on in our schools, and had the military victory not been followed up by a rigorous campaign of bribery and economic coercion to bring about an assimilated 'North Britain', the later histories of Ireland and Scotland might have paralleled each other even more closely. Many will give thanks that this did not happen, and this is a view to which they are entitled, but 'Oliver's Army' still patrols the North of Ireland today, and in its ranks are many of Scotland's sons.

The degree to which the search for a humanising empathy between Scots and the peoples of Ulster is attempted, far less achieved, is a question I will return to later, along with the possibility that one reason for underplaying the parallels may be that they are too close for comfort, especially in the West of Scotland, where religious rivalries are so marked. But first it may be helpful if I outline some of my own experiences as a Scottish journalist covering events in the Six Counties, particularly in terms of the practicalities involved. If any of the difficulties make readers a little more forgiving of shortcomings in press coverage, fine, but this is not intended to excuse inaccuracies, flawed analysis or the lazy resort to cliché. Since first impressions are most vivid and tend to colour future interpretation, it is perhaps worth outlining my first few days there at some length.

When I arrived at Aldergrove Airport in May 1981, a few hours after the death of Bobby Sands, it was the first time I had set foot in Ireland, North or South. My personal politics were of the Left, but not aligned to any particular party, still less to any particular faction in Ulster. I believed then, as now, that the men and women of Ulster were Irish, and that the partition was a piece of post-colonial cowardice which had put off resolving the Irish question. At the same time, I understood Northern misgivings – mainly but not exclusively held by Protestants – about Dublin rule and the Republic's constitution.

Every journalist writing about the North knows it is impossible even to appear to be objective, for the moment you begin to handle terminology you offend somebody: Northern Ireland or the North of Ireland, Ulster or the Six Counties, Derry or Londonderry, even Derry/Londonderry and its derivative, 'Stroke City', the terms are loaded but you cannot avoid them. You may convince yourself of the factual case for a particular phrase, arguing that Northern Ireland is implicit in the name of the United Kingdom, or the North of Ireland is geographically correct, or Ulster should really mean all nine counties of the historical province, or that Derry City Council voted to drop the offending 'London' from its name. You still have to use a term which will be seen as biased, regardless of whether it was your own choice or your publication's house style imposed by sub editors.

In any event, the whole concept of objective journalism is bogus, dangerous and self-deluding. Leave aside for the moment broader issues such as a publication's overall editorial policy, the combined personal prejudices and opinions of everyone from the editor down through layout experts, headline writers, copytakers, text editors and those in charge of newsdesks and features departments, all of whom make subjective decisions which leave their mark.

Take the individual reporter once a task has been set. He or she defines and refines that task in the light of personal opinion and experience, decides on priorities, selects who to interview, what questions to ask, what background knowledge or materials to bring in, which contacts to find help from – the development of contacts being a highly subjective process in itself – and whose reaction to seek. Only after all this does the reporter decide what to include and what to exclude, what to emphasise, what to use in the introductory paragraphs, what to use as a clinching sign-off point and what to place down the story where it will be most vulnerable if there are cuts for reasons of space. Every part of this process is laden with subjective decisions. Of course you should include the views of people you may not agree with – especially if they damn themselves with their words! But while fairness is an excellent guiding principle, balance is a more dubious one, and objectivity is the fool's gold of journalism.

So how should a reporter approach as subjective an issue as the Irish question? As a Scottish socialist from a Protestant background, I hoped to be able to show a degree of sympathy to both sides and would try to file copy which would fit what I saw as the liberal traditions of the *Scotsman* (although not always so liberal on Ulster as we shall see). The newspaper's founders had promised 'impartiality, firmness and independence', to endeavour to be 'honest and useful' and to employ 'good sense, courage and industry'. Aside from doubts about impartiality, as at least a half-brother to objectivity, it seemed a decent target.

The problem was that I was unprepared for the assignment and was anything but street-wise. Journalists on the *Scotsman* had been on strike for a fortnight in the late spring of 1981 and had only just returned to work over that weekend. When told on Monday, 4 May to get myself from Edinburgh to Belfast, the first available flight was from Glasgow early the following morning. The IRA hunger striker Bobby Sands, his status enhanced by his election as MP for Fermanagh and South Tyrone, had been given last rites more than three weeks previously, and Belfast had sucked in the world's press and television crews during that period as they awaited his death. The Europa Hotel was full and had closed its waiting list, and the Wellington Park, the media's usual overflow, was also full. The *Scotsman* wanted to put me in a good hotel, but the only one available was well out of town, so I cancelled the reservation and instead booked into somewhere modest but central near Queen's University and within a few minutes' walk of the Europa which, because of its concentration of media people, acted as an informal press centre.

In the taxi on the way into Belfast from Aldergrove I experienced the *frisson* of the newcomer, reacting to the searches and questioning by armed soldiers and police officers with a mixture of apprehension and excitement, but equally aware of how intrusive living with this would be on a perma-nent basis. Coming into town, the outlying housing estates could have been peripheral council schemes on the outskirts of Edinburgh, the traditional red brick terraces were familiar from the North of England, the city centre's shops and impressive public buildings could have been Aberdeen, the backdrop of shipyard cranes could have been the Clyde.

But there were also security gates, armed police in reinforced Land Rovers, and troop carriers containing soldiers scanning pavements and buildings with loaded rifles. The impact of these repressive images fades very quickly, so I decided that for as long as they retained their capacity to disturb me and jar against everything that was familiar and commonplace, I would try to get this juxtaposition across. These people were very like us – how would we feel about living under arms? There was, in any event, little point in spending my newspaper's time and money on filing copy similar to that being provided by the Press Association.

Although I was able to make use of the *Belfast Telegraph* newsroom early each day because the evening publication was in the same newspaper group as the *Scotsman*, by late afternoon I found myself teaming up with other lone, morning paper journalists. I would send my stories by telephone to a copytaker in Edinburgh, sometimes in two or three sections with later evening additions. That first day's 1,200 or so words said – or more accurately, speculated – that the Provisionals were keeping the lid on their violent response until after Sands' funeral, recounted what rioting there had been and reported a little of the pretended historical expertise I mentioned earlier: 'Sands (27), was one hour and 16 minutes into his 66th day of hunger strike when he died in the Maze Prison, following Thomas Ashe, Terence McSwiney, Michael Gaughen and Frank Stagg into the history books.'

I completed the first day by sharing a taxi with Gordon Petrie, a *Glasgow Herald* reporter I had known from his days on the *Edinburgh Evening News*, and a reporter from the *Wolverhampton Express and Star*. For several days they had been making use of a driver, a former IRA man with a knack for skirting riot zones closely enough for them to get a look without becoming inveigled. Giving me advice and allowing me to share their taxi was typical of the camaraderie found among journalists, and my gratitude had nerve-wracking consequences the following night.

On Wednesday, because Sinn Féin's order to 'honour Bobby Sands' peaceful protest in a dignified fashion', was holding, we had very little to report. Our taxi spent the early evening taking us around some potential trouble spots before heading out through West Belfast to the Sands' family home at Twinbrook for the ceremony in which the coffin would be moved to the local church for the next day's funeral. On our way there we realised it was some time since we had made a check call to the RUC and we asked the driver to find us a payphone. We were passing a pub in the heart of Andersonstown and against his advice, we insisted on stopping.

Feeling I should repay the help I had received, I volunteered to make the call. I entered the bar and bought a drink, believing this was in some way the polite thing to do before moving over to the payphone. Above it was a formal, printed notice: 'Warning! In an emergency this phone may be needed. Anyone caught interfering with it will be dealt with by the

Provisional IRA.' I gulped and dialled the RUC press office number, looking round to make sure no-one was within earshot. Things were still quiet, the press officer said, but he understood the Army were issuing a statement from their HQ at Lisburn. Since I was being deliberately cold-shouldered in the bar, no-one seemed close enough to be listening, so I phoned Lisburn and got the statement, which said the standby 'spear-head' battalion was being flown into the province overnight from Aldershot. Hanging up, I left the bar at as moderate a pace as I could manage, jumped into the taxi and told the others the news.

Our collective nervousness was not helped at an IRA checkpoint near Twinbrook, when a masked man brandishing a revolver leaned into the taxi's rear window to check our press credentials. The ceremony itself, a highly-stylised paramilitary ritual foreshadowing the next day's funeral, was interesting and well worth reporting, but by the time it finished, dead-lines on the *Scotsman* and *Glasgow Herald* were looming. Our taxi driver helped out, taking us to his house to phone our copy. Thus stories which led on British Army reinforcements being sent into Ulster were filed from the home of a former member of the IRA.

The driver then took us out once more for a spin round the likely flash-points, and with unerring accuracy led us straight into a good-going riot in the New Lodge area, north of the city centre. Minutes before we arrived, at a security gate on the peace line between the Catholic estate and the nearby Protestant area of Tiger's Bay, a Scots-born RUC man had been gunned down by the Irish National Liberation Army. We found ourselves behind troops firing plastic bullets to drive back rioters whose bricks and stones were falling just short of our feet. One of the others pointed out that if a sniper opened up from Artillery Flats, my light-coloured trench coat would be an ideal target.

The deep boom of the baton-round launchers and the bright flare of the petrol bombs was colourful and a little unreal, the adrenaline buzz of the action undeniable. You had to keep trying to remember that people died in confrontations such as these, like a fourteen-year-old girl killed by a plastic bullet a few days later as she returned from buying a pint of milk. Eventually the rioters were pushed far enough back for the police forensic team to go in search of the bullet casings and other evidence in connection with their colleague's murder. We took the taxi back to the Wellington Park Hotel where my two friends were staying. I phoned over more copy, made a final check call to the police and had a drink before walking back to my own hotel. After less than forty-eight hours in the city, I felt like a veteran.

The next day I headed out early to Twinbrook because there were rumours that the area would be sealed off towards the time of the funeral mass at 1 p.m. Gordon Petrie was being relieved that day by Andrew McCallum, the *Glasgow Herald*'s chief reporter. They would team up to cover the Sands funeral before Petrie flew back to Glasgow, so one could cover the church service and the early part of the procession and then the other could take over. The mass lasted almost an hour, and I slipped in and out of St Luke's Church, listening for a few minutes and then taking notes outside on Father Liam Mullen's ambivalent sermon which called for 'peace, restraint, moderation and an end to violence' while at the same time praising Sands as a martyr. A uniformed IRA guard of honour appeared outside the church to drape the coffin with the tricolour, beret and gloves before the cortege set off for the three-hour procession to Milltown Cemetery in increasingly heavy rain and buzzed constantly by Army helicopters hovering over a crowd estimated at upwards of 70,000.

The scene at the Republican plot was macabre. A huge scaffolding was groaning and buckling under the weight of photographers and television cameramen, while others clambered onto gravestones to gain a vantage point – seized by 'collective necrophilia' as I later put it. The memory is not cause for pride in journalism. We could not hear the orations for the deafening beat of helicopters overhead, and I could no longer write anyway because pens had ceased functioning on sodden notebooks. It was almost 6 p.m. I had been on the go for more than eleven hours. I hadn't written a word of my story yet, and with no taxis to be found, I still had to get back to the city centre. I jogged down the Falls Road holding up my right thumb and my press card, and an American television crew stopped and gave me a lift back to the Europa. I grabbed some hotel stationery from the reception, bought a *Belfast Telegraph* to crib the facts of its report on a counter-demonstration organised by the Rev. Ian Paisley earlier in the day, and headed across the road to Robinson's Bar.

At a corner seat by the window, I sipped a pint and drafted a 1,200-word report. Unasked, the barman twice brought a fresh drink while I pressed on and completed the story before settling up and thanking him, then going out to the lobby of the bar to send copy from the public payphone. Twice, passing punters listened in as I sent over the story and tried to pick an argument. The second time, I snapped: 'Look I'll debate this with you all you like, but just let me finish this call first!' He wandered off, muttering, and I completed the time-consuming process of phoning over the copy, running perilously close to deadline for the third night in a row. Back over in the Europa, I called the police to check whether there was any sign of post-funeral rioting, but the heavy rain seemed to be acting as a dampener.

After my first full meal since Edinburgh I wandered along to the hotel bar which was doing a good trade for a Thursday night, and got into conversation with some of the other customers. One was a Catholic called Kelly who said he lived in Kashmir Road in Clonard, the area sandwiched between the Falls and the Shankill. 'Round my way they bomb shops and factories. I ask why and I'm told: "I've not got a job – why should anyone else have one?" Christ, the other night, when Sands died, I was handed a brick.' He paused and shrugged: 'I threw it.'

Kelly bought a round of drinks, and on his return he and his friends were obviously having a good-natured private joke at the expense of their naive Scots guest. 'You haven't twigged, have you?' he said, to laughter all round. I pondered on possible sectarian subtleties or allusions I was missing, then shook my head. 'You're surrounded by the only people in this community who don't give a fuck what religion you are.' We were in Belfast's main gay bar. It was a richly comic moment and I bought a round and listened to their tales of woe about life under the equally grim, would-be theocracies of both Catholicism and Paisleyism. It was, to use the local term for sparkling pub conversation, good crack, and Kelly ventured his answer to the Irish question: 'Basically, the Northern Irish are nice people. It's just that we're all fucking mad.'

Not too mad, evidently. On the way back to my hotel that night, I stopped off for a drink in another hotel bar and there was a leaving party going on for a woman who had made enough money in the building trade – presumably in spite of the widespread extortion – to sell up and buy a bar in Spain. By coincidence rather than invitation, one of her old schoolfriends came in and as they reminisced, it turned out that she was leaving Belfast too. In spite of being a linguist who possessed a law degree, she could not find work and was going to be an interpreter in France, following generations of Irish men and women into exile.

Not too mad either in West Belfast that night, with most people preferring to dry off indoors rather than take to the streets. But the rioting grew in intensity over the next twenty-four hours until no vehicles moved in or near the ghetto because of the level of hijacking and burning, which at one stage extended even to a fire engine and a gas board lorry. As reports of sniper fire increased, news emerged – with hindsight its genesis remarkably vague – that the RUC had uncovered a Republican hit list of leading politicians and figures in the security services. How serious was all this riotous activity? It seemed ferocious to me, but my problem was inexperience and the lack of any benchmark to compare it with. However, in his excellent diary of the period viewed from lodgings in the heart of the Lower Falls, *War as a Way of Life*, American journalist John Conroy makes clear it was not organised but was the result of emotionally wound-up teenagers for whom the hunger strikers had replaced pop stars and footballers as heroes.

For a daily newspaper journalist Saturday provides a respite from the tyranny of the deadline, but I wanted to cover the funeral of PC Philip Ellis, the former Scottish soldier from Banchory whose shooting in New Lodge on Wednesday night had made him the 2,076th victim of the modern Troubles. It wasn't just a question of the Scottish connection. He had moved to Belfast just a year before to become husband to a widow and father to her three children, and I wanted to gain some sense of cultural contrast to the images and rhythms of Sands' funeral. There were no foreign television crews and few journalists present in church to hear Dr Robin Eames, Bishop of Down and Dromore, say of an adopted son of Ulster that they had a right to ask the world's judgment: 'Is it to lie with the Philip Ellises of this world or those who use death as a form of blackmail, as intimidation of ordinary people of every creed?' The dead RUC man was then taken out into the Drumbo hills and quietly laid to rest in a picturesque, manicured graveyard. I had found the contrast I sought.

That afternoon I was determined to rest. My hotel room had no television, so I bought some beer and set up camp in the *Glasgow Herald*'s room at the Wellington Park to watch the English cup final while Andrew McCallum went shopping. He arrived back around five o'clock and suggested we use his hire car and 'take a look at Londonderry tonight.' We were heading up the M2 before I had a chance to think through just what we could safely 'look at' if we arrived with no plan of action. We stopped at the Everglades Hotel on the Protestant side of town and while elegant couples had dips in the pool before dinner, I began making phone calls back to Republican numbers in Belfast, eventually arranging through the National H-Block/Armagh Committee that we should go to a bar called the Rocking Chair and mention the name of Seán O'Hara, brother of INLA hunger striker Patsy.

The taxi from the Everglades would not go as far as the bar because the risk of hijack was too great, and we walked the remainder of the way, arriving about an hour before closing time. The interior was festooned with Republican posters of the 'Loose talk costs lives' variety and collecting tins were passed round. Andy had a way of delivering droll one-liners somewhat in the manner of the comedian Chic Murray, and the longer I watched him standing in his short white raincoat, sipping a half-pint, the more I thought he looked like a police detective. Our reception had been distinctly frosty and I was becoming nervous, but a representative from the local H-Block Committee arrived and we were escorted into the Bogside to a community hall, where we chatted to old ladies until a committee member arrived. He gave us a spiel to the effect that the hunger strike and associated rioting had thrust the Army back into the front line of law enforcement, wrecking the Government's 'Ulsterisation' policy of the previous five years which sought to put the RUC in control.

'No matter what the people who want peace say, the fact is that there is a situation in Northern Ireland which the politicians cannot resolve,' he said. 'You are from Scotland and you call yourself Scottish. People from England are English, the Welsh call themselves Welsh. But what do the Loyalists here call themselves? British . . . whatever that means.' He then called over a youth and said to us: 'We better give you an escort out of the Bogside. With that Scottish accent you'd never get out alive.' We got back across the Foyle and I slept as Andy drove us back to Belfast. If he had been nervous at any point, he hadn't shown it.

While riots, sniper attacks and mortar bombings continued over that weekend, another IRA man joined the hunger strikers to replace the dead MP. He was Joe McDonnell, who had been sentenced the same day as Sands for possession of the same handgun, and on Sunday, the National H-Block/Armagh Committee met in a Falls Road hotel and promised to step up the protest campaign. Between this story on the front page and three others inside – the police funeral, the Derry visit and a colour piece based on Thursday night's encounters – I filed about 2,500 words for Monday's newspaper, but at least I was now working from the relative comfort of a room which had become available at the Wellington Park.

On Monday, as a second hunger striker, Frankie Hughes, neared death, the IRA ambushed two soldiers in West Belfast, wounding one of them seriously. The Army's follow-up search of houses sparked off a riot. The following day, covering the funeral of a milkboy stoned during the riot the morning after Bobby Sands' death, it was odd to see a coffin not draped in a flag. Later, in anticipation of Hughes' death, I filed biographical details of the 25-year-old IRA man, once described as Ulster's most wanted terrorist. The Republican press centre was not contesting details of his 'active service' so there seemed to be no question of official disinformation over this.

Just before 6 p.m., I made a check call to the Northern Ireland Office and halfway through the conversation, word came in that Hughes had died at 5.45 p.m. After filing the story, I headed out to the Falls, but although the rioting was described as the worst for years, its impact on me was wearing off after just a week in the city. Even the bizarre events of the following day, when the RUC effectively hijacked Hughes' coffin to prevent it being paraded through West Belfast en route to his home village of Bellaghy in south Derry, did not seem as shocking and surreal at the time as they do now. The small matter of the Pope being shot now topped the front pages, but Northern Ireland was slipping down the news schedules anyway, a process which would become familiar. The sight of the funeral cortege winding through miles of country roads in south Derry, like a black ribbon across a patchwork quilt, was a memorable image overshadowed by the atmosphere of morbid hostility. A colleague arrived to take over the fireman's role.

What had I learned from this first foray into the Six Counties? Without overlaying the lessons with too much hindsight, I realised several things: the 'fireman' is tyrannised by the deadline, by definition sent only when the news situation is so hectic that there is little time to learn background or context; that, like it or not, you are caught in a propaganda war and that both your own capacity for shock and the interest of your readership – at least as perceived by newsdesks – wane all too swiftly. The response at the

Scotsman to my copy – colourful and thereby even more than usually value-laden – was generally favourable, but the brittleness of this was brought home less than two months later when the fireman's role involved covering the urban riots which swept England that summer.

Setting out to view Manchester and Liverpool through the same sympathetic/independent prism as Belfast seemed the right approach. Observing close up the riots on Moss Side – so closely that while phoning copy from a public booth around midnight, the front line shifted and I ended up between police and rioters – the parallels were obvious. The youths were obviously copying television images of Ulster, while Chief Constable James Anderton's Tactical Aid Group were using RUC tactics, albeit with Transit vans rather than armoured Land Rovers. Much later I discovered there had been rumblings within the *Scotsman* about this coverage being 'too political'. It was all right from across the water, but clearly this was too close to home. None of this came from the editor, Eric Mackay, always a robust sceptic when it came to the Establishment. 'Remember,' he said the following year, on dispatching me to Whitehall to cover the Falklands crisis, 'the Ministry of Defence will be the Ministry of Propaganda.' It was the sort of comment that doesn't tell you anything you don't already know, but is welcome in any case, as an encouragement towards independence and integrity.

It was six months after the first brief posting to Belfast that I was sent back to cover Ian Paisley's 'D-Day' of protest, denoting deliverance from the British-Irish Intergovernment Council and its implied 'totality of relations between these two countries'. Although my *Scotsman* card now said 'feature writer', it made no difference to an assignment of this kind.

Again, it was very much a fireman job, hopping across on the morning flight to Belfast Harbour Airport, writing a feature piece combining colour and analysis on the day's demonstrations and squabbles between Paisleyites and other Unionists, and then providing news coverage at night of 20,000 Loyalists drilling as the paramilitary 'Third Force' in the market square of Newtownards.

Next day I drove to Lisnaskea and Strabane to interview two clergymen: the Rev. Ivan Foster, a former cellmate of Ian Paisley who was now a minister in his church and a commandant in the 'Third Force', and Father Anthony Mulvey, a priest whose anti-IRA sermons had attracted both controversy and support. I got back to Harbour Airport in time to dump the hire car and phone over a news story about political reaction to D-Day while my flight was being called. The double interview was written up as a feature the following day.

While this sort of frenetic activity is exhilarating, it isn't always enlightening, so after settling into my new post at the *Scotsman* I applied for sabbatical leave to take a different kind of look at Northern Ireland, spending four weeks in Belfast without, for once, constantly running on the hamster wheel of daily deadlines. I had been greatly impressed by a book called *'Nam* by Mark Baker, which gave Vietnam veterans their say on events without editorial intrusion, and thought the groundwork for something similar on the Northern Irish Troubles might be laid. It soon became clear that such a book would take years rather than weeks or months and I abandoned the idea. Nevertheless, the trip was highly worthwhile, giving me the chance to get my bearings and meet people without the pressure of having to write.

Things which stick in the memory were the guided tour of the city in the car of SDLP Councillor Brian Feeney, whose driving was among the greatest dangers I ever encountered there, and the crack with Jackie Redpath and his community newspaper team who brought out the *Shankill Bulletin*. Jackie would talk endlessly about community politics and the struggle against poverty, poor health and bad housing in a genuinely non-sectarian way, but resented the way the British Left and the international community seemed to demand that he be ashamed of his Protestant heritage.

I also had a lot of fun with the local press corps and the Fleet Street reporters based in Belfast, including the excellent Press Association staff. The problem of blandness of agency copy I mentioned earlier is no criticism of them but results simply from the fact that the PA has to appeal to all its subscribers – morning and evening newspapers, broadsheet and tabloid, national and regional. My affection for the press regulars in the Blackthorn bar was genuine, but also practical. Visiting firemen need the goodwill and help of the experienced local hands. They also told anecdotes which showed the extent of the propaganda war we were all embroiled in, incidents involving the 'Lisburn Lie Machine', which were later resoundingly confirmed in the cases of Army information officer Colin Wallace, told by Paul Foot in *Who Framed Colin Wallace?* and Military Intelligence officer Fred Holroyd, in his own *War Without Honour*.

The off-the-record briefing is open to abuse at any time but to get too close to any sources, including the security services during an undeclared civil war, can actually make it harder for you to do your job. Who creates nicknames like 'Mad Dog' and slips them into the public domain? And for what reason if not to create a climate in which extermination is acceptable? I haven't patrolled in the back of an Army Saracen or RUC Land Rover, not because I lack sympathy for the difficult job the security forces do, but because I have my own job to do, and if I am going to receive statements, I would rather they were attributable and provable. Official or Government access, however flattering and seductive, should be treated with scepticism. An example of the *Scotsman*'s coverage of the modern resurgence of the Troubles from 12 October 1968 shows precisely what ought to be avoided. The front page article by the newspaper's Close-Up Staff, supposedly an investigative team, started, without qualification or attribution:

> Factions of the Civil Rights Movement in Northern Ireland are being infiltrated by known sympathisers of the banned Irish Republican Army, Trotskyites and agitators with criminal records. They are using social and economic problems to create unrest and the Government have 'reliable information' of acts of planned sabotage.

The quotation marks around the term 'reliable information' were not intended to indicate scepticism, nor were they later when the article, still unsourced at that stage, stated: '. . . the Government think "there may be something" in information that the IRA are receiving guns from behind the Iron Curtain.' Well down the story it transpired that these unsubstantiated hints – claims would be too strong – were being made by the Northern Ireland Home Affairs Minister William Craig. The article continued: 'We had coffee while he talked of the agitators at work in the Civil Rights Movement.'

Note the claim masquerading as fact amid the obsequious chink of china in the article, whose first two cross-heads, words in bold type between paragraphs to break up the text, could have been dropped into place by the Lisburn Lie Machine: AGITATORS and 'TROTSKYITE', the latter inside the ubiquitous quote marks. At no point over the coffee did they question the Minister about his tactics in banning the demonstration in Londonderry the previous weekend, or the behaviour of the police in breaking the heads of peaceful demonstrators for the benefit of the world's television cameras. In other words, this was not an interview, it was an audience, and I believed that, 15 years on, we should at least be asking questions.

So throughout the 1980s, the *Scotsman* continued to use me to fight the Ulster fire. Sometimes there was enough notice to put in a few calls in the preceding days to set up interview possibilities. Sometimes it would be a question of taking a taxi from the office to Edinburgh Airport via home to pack a bag: then on to witness the Orange marches and Republican funeral parades, the urban squalor and the misleading mask of rural idyll, the Loyalist strikes, the Provo bomb outrages and the tit-for-tat, that playground phrase concealing random horror. Always, you find yourself wondering whether you can retain your capacity for both horror and humanity in order to find something worth saying after Enniskillen, the Milltown attack or the lynching of two off-duty soldiers.

The sudden attack on the funeral of the IRA's 'Gibraltar Three' in March 1988 was an example of the impossibility of planning coverage in advance. It also involved a classic breach of the principle laid down by the Victorian journalist Henri de Blowitz and cited in his memoirs: 'A newspaper has no use for confidential communications it cannot transmit to its readers'. One Scottish journalist was ideally placed to report the attack on mourners by a Loyalist gunman but did not file a word. The reporter, whose name and newspaper I won't identify, was on a trip to Belfast as a guest of the security services and watched the gun and grenade attack unfold on closed circuit television screens inside Andersonstown joint RUC/Army base. While most journalists were ducking behind gravestones to avoid bullets and shrapnel and were for a time bewildered about what was going on, this reporter had the only overview. While his counterpart on the *Belfast Telegraph* was grabbed while running for a phone and mistakenly roughed up by mourners, the reporter in the police operations room had it all on a plate, but felt unable to write a sentence then or since, because he was there as a guest of the security forces. If they gave access that good to everybody, who knows, perhaps they could eliminate coverage of the Troubles entirely.

Since moving to the *Herald*, my brief forays to Ulster have followed the familiar admix. One involved forward planning, a feature examining Co. Monaghan's position as part of historic Ulster in the Republic. The other was vintage firefighting, when I was sent at short notice to Co. Tyrone to write a background piece on tit-for-tat killing in the area. It was late lunchtime when I arrived in Castlederg and none of my phone calls from airports and car hire offices had succeeded in setting up interviews. Mild panic was setting in, so I bought the local newspapers and went for a pint. As I circled names in the papers as likely interview subjects, I was aware of a big, dark, bearded man dressed all in black eyeing me suspiciously, so I identified myself and explained that I was trying to compile a newspaper article, not a sectarian hit-list. He took my business card, phoned my office in Edinburgh to check me out, then took me to meet his brother, local Sinn Féin Councillor Charlie McHugh, whose election agent had been the most recent murder victim.

McHugh in turn had a copy of a study by the University of Ulster's Centre for the Study of Conflict, which had examined the effect of sectarian tensions upon the town and surrounding area. Ideally, the next step would have been to get hold of someone from the Protestant community, but I was pulled over by RUC officers who didn't like the company I had been keeping, and valuable time was lost. Fortunately, I had a copy of Colm Toibín's book, *Walking Along the Border*, in which a Protestant farmer poured out his feelings about Republican genocide against his community. By borrowing from this, properly attributed of course, and combining it with the academic study, the McHugh interview and some details gleaned from the local newspapers, I was able to rush back to Belfast and file the article just inside deadline. 'Veneer of calm that hides the hatred in a town's blood feud', the sub editors headlined the article, which managed to make it sound much more profound and better informed than it actually was.

Should the readerships of Scottish newspapers be getting more or better coverage of Irish issues? The *Daily Record* relies primarily upon the coverage of the staff reporters of its sister paper, the *Daily Mirror*, while the editors of both the *Herald* and the *Scotsman* concede that in an ideal world they would like to have their own staff in Ireland. 'Any newspaper would benefit from having its own staff correspondent there. Unfortunately, we have to live in the real world,' says Arnold Kemp at the *Herald* where the cover comes from two 'stringers', freelance journalists based in Belfast and Dublin.

He acknowledges the historical and cultural links between Scotland and Ireland, but believes notions of empathy between the two nations is somewhat romantic. 'In the West of Scotland you have a substantial body of readers with first-hand knowledge of Ireland, you can find cab drivers with their radios tuned into RTE, so you are dealing with a better informed audience than many other newspapers. It is very important for the *Herald* to show it understands Irish politics and our coverage of Ireland has to be at a higher level than some others.'

Magnus Linklater also uses Irish-based freelancers to provide coverage for the *Scotsman*, but he concedes that it is difficult to find correspondents whose work will be precisely what the newspaper seeks. He also has reservations about the use of staff reporters as firemen, given the difficulties and potential dangers involved. He is convinced, however, that Scottish newspapers have a part to play in reflecting a distinctive view of the Irish question which is different from that of London publications. 'If you are in London with a Fleet Street paper, you have very much a British-dominated view of Ulster,' he said. 'The Scottish view is less dominated by the British Establishment view and there is a sense of shared perceptions with Ireland. It is undoubtedly the case that you get in Scottish newspapers a less predictable response to Irish issues.'

The editors of both newspapers, while recognising the importance of the Irish question as a major issue deserving extensive coverage, also volunteered the view that readers were often reluctant to hear about the story. As Linklater put it, the problem was one of 'the intractability of the story, of the sense of déjà vu. It is a harsh view, but I don't quite know how you get round that.' Kemp also spoke of the Troubles as a turn-off factor for many readers. 'It doesn't sell papers,' he said. 'There is a comparable phenomenon in the Republic of Ireland, where often people just don't want to know.'

The impression must be faced that the Irish question is just too close to home for comfort. In the wake of the 1992 General Election and the Scottish constitutional debate, influential Conservatives have talked about appealing to working class Protestantism – 'playing the Ibrox card' – and becoming more overtly Unionist. The SNP has a morbid fear of being linked with its kindred Nationalism across the water. The *Orange Torch*, official journal of the Orange Lodge in Scotland, takes a keen interest in the media and has taken to task writers on the *Herald* for their perceived sympathies in relation to coverage of Northern Ireland. My own view is that these parallels, alarming though they may be, are better confronted openly and debated in an informed historical context.

Good coverage of affairs in the North can only benefit that process, but is this likely to improve? In truth, there is scant cause for optimism. In spite of the wishes of Scottish editors, this is a time of shrinking journalistic resources, smaller staffs, increasing casualisation and ever-tighter control on budgets. It would be good to think that these constraints will ease once the recession ends , but this remains to be seen. If Scottish readers want good coverage of the undeclared civil war on their own doorstep, they should let their newspapers know.

10

Thin Red Line? – Scottish Soldiers in the Troubles

IAN S WOOD

Early on the morning of Wednesday, 10 March 1971, three bodies were found beside a lonely stretch of road leading to Ligoniel in North Belfast. Two of them were identified as Joseph McCaig, aged 18, and his 17-year-old brother John, both of the First Battalion of the Royal Highland Fusiliers. They were lying one on top of the other and they had both been shot in the back of the head. So, too, had Fusilier Douglas McCaughey, 23, who was propped up against the grass verge with a pint glass still clutched in his hand.

The three had been on leave and had gone drinking in the centre of Belfast the previous night, which off-duty soldiers could still do, even though the army's relationship with the city's Nationalist community was already under strain. In Mooney's bar, they had fallen into conversation with three men who were members of the Provisional IRA's Ardoyne unit. One of these was almost certainly Paddy McAdorey, who was killed in a gun battle with the army following the introduction of internment five months later. After a time, the Scots agreed to move on to another pub where they were invited to a party. They accepted lifts in two cars, which stopped for them to relieve themselves at the side of the road. While doing so, they were shot dead.

Nobody was ever charged with the killings, which produced a wave of revulsion in the press on both sides of the Irish Sea. The Belfast Brigade of the Provisional IRA never claimed responsibility for the murders since its 'rules of engagement' at this time precluded the shooting of off-duty soldiers. In reaction to what had happened, Harland and Wolff workers marched in protest into central Belfast to call for internment without trial of republican suspects, and a thousand additional British troops were sent to Northern Ireland. Just ten days later, the Unionist Prime Minister, Major James Chichester Clark, resigned as the killings and bombings increased.[1]

Gunner Robert Curtis of the Royal Artillery had already been killed by an IRA sniper on Belfast's New Lodge Road on 6 February 1971. He was the first soldier to die in the present Troubles , but his death and that of the three Royal Highland Fusiliers were inevitable, given the rapidity of the deterioration in the army's relationship with a Nationalist population which had originally welcomed it to the streets of West Belfast and Londonderry. It is still difficult to be precise about the chronology of this breakdown, but it almost certainly dates to Easter 1970, when army units in West Belfast allowed a series of Orange Walks to come dangerously close to Nationalist areas such as Ballymurphy and New Barnsley. The period remains controversial, though the case against the army's role has been set out in some detail.[2]

One unit heavily involved in the Ballymurphy disturbances was the Royal Scots, the oldest foot regiment in the army. Three months later, they were deployed in the curfew and sealing off of the Lower Falls area of West Belfast. This began on 3 July, with one company of Royal Scots searching for and seizing, in Balkan Street, some arms belonging to the official IRA. Some people in the street resisted, claiming that the army should be searching for Loyalist weapons in the Shankill Road area, barely a mile away. In fact, Balkon Street had come under Loyalist fire during the riots of August 1969 which had brought troops onto the streets of Belfast.

A total of six battalions was brought in to reinforce the original company, 13 soldiers were wounded, houses were wrecked and three people were killed. The episode was a public relations disaster and prompted a huge demonstration from all over West Belfast, both to protest at the army's action and to bring food and milk into the area. One Royal Scots lieutenant recalls how his men were accused of deliberately smashing statuettes and religious objects during the Balkan Street search. In reply, he was able to produce figures showing that in fact almost 40 per cent of the battalion were Catholics, many from West Lothian where the regiment had been recruiting actively over the previous year.[3]

In the Royal Scots' regimental magazine, a general view of the battalion's role in these events, probably written by a senior officer, takes a benign view of the Lower Falls curfew:

> The effect of this battle – it was nothing less – was traumatic. The locals were stunned, the IRA was rocked and the heat was taken out of the situation. Although dissident elements tried to whip up hate against the soldiers, it petered out quickly. The 'Twelfth' passed without incident and the Battalion's tour in Belfast ended in peace, as it had begun.[4]

The same issue of this magazine contained another report of operations in the Lower Falls, written by an officer of C Company who had clearly been very directly involved in the Balkan Street searches and the reaction they had provoked. It makes rather different and ominous reading:

> We arrived in March when hopes of peace were in the ascendant, we left in July after some of the bitterest rioting seen in Belfast for many years. We left a city with a deep wound of hatred and suspicion which has been there for many centuries, but it was thought it had at least closed, if not healed. Now again it is wide open and will take many years to close and heal again. For a soldier, it was an experience of great sadness which none of us will ever forget.[5]

One observer of the immediate aftermath of the Lower Falls curfew was Conor Cruise O'Brien, who wrote vividly about it. 'There was always something unnatural or brittle in Catholic approval of the British Army,' he argued. He could claim to have seen at close quarters the collapse of this guarded approval, although he did not deny the role of the republican movement in helping to bring it about. He also recalled watching army vehicles driving up the Lower Falls after the curfew with soldiers who must surely have been Scots, singing 'The Sash' at the tops of their voices. 'They were making an essential point for the IRA more effectively than the IRA could do themselves.'[6]

More Scottish battalions, including the Royal Highland Fusiliers, followed the Royal Scots into the province as the situation worsened. In July 1970, it fell to the King's Own Scottish Borderers to shoot dead Danny O'Hagan on Belfast's New Lodge Road. He was the first rioter to be killed by the army and a former senior officer of the KOSB recalled how his men were greeted in Nationalist areas with placards reminding them not just of O'Hagan's death, but of those killed on Dublin's Bachelor's Walk in July, 1914, when the regiment had opened fire on a hostile crowd.[7]

Training for tours of duty in Northern Ireland has become an intensive and in some ways sophisticated business now, but in the early days of the Troubles, battalions could be pitched in with little warning. One former sergeant recalls parading on the barrack square at Redford, Edinburgh, to hear his Company Commander announce that they were about to 'go Paddy bashing'.[8] That was November 1971, and those who have served more recently recall the rigours of preparation at camps in England where street patrols are practised in mock-up tin cities where surveillance and ambush techniques are taught. A former private in the Royal Scots felt that some basic political education about the conflict would have opened his mind on his first tour of duty at the end of 1975, but he recognises that this might cause a problem for the army. 'They could end up simply explaining all the IRA's reasons for trying to kill us. So they settle for teaching you how to get the IRA before they get you.'[9]

A trooper in the predominantly Scottish Fourth Battalion of the Royal Tank Regiment told a newspaper: 'When we were trained to come out to

Belfast, we were told that the only way to win was not to antagonize the people, always to be polite. In the training, they practised provoking us, swearing at us, but it was nothing like as bad as the real thing. If you're on duty and say a nice "good morning" to someone and they turn round and shout "Shut your fucking face", young girls and kids too, it gets to you.'[10]

Initial impressions of Northern Ireland's Troubles remain clear in the minds of many Scots who have served there:

> My first patrol in 1975 was in Crossmaglen. We operated out of the old RUC station there right in the middle of the town. The place was already a byword for IRA activity and attacks on the security forces, and we were almost disappointed to see no burning cars or wrecked houses. It seemed just like an ordinary wee town but it was a normality in which we knew from our training we could never relax.[11]

A paratrooper from Edinburgh recalls his own uncertainty on his first morning out onto the streets of West Belfast in 1978:

> On your first tour, you don't know what to expect: because of the intensive pre-tour training you half-expect a contact every time you leave the base. Although apprehensive, I was also as proud as Punch going out on my first patrol with my red beret on, much the same as I felt as a young lad going to an away match with the Jambos [a nickname for the Heart of Midlothian football club]. After a couple of times on the streets, however, you begin to settle down and a routine develops.[12]

Recollecting his arrival with the platoon he commanded in the Lower Falls in 1973, another Scot wrote:

> One can feel the hostility in the air. It bursts out when one stops a boy in the street and within five minutes, ten or more people are standing around hurling insults or worse. Yet these same people are as equally capable of laughter, fun and dancing as they are of harbouring gunmen, creating aggro and generally supporting terrorism . . . My first impression is of a dying community. The population of the Lower Falls has halved since 1969. Close to 200 houses are derelict or demolished. The squalor reflects a total inability or unwillingness to get on terms with an appalling situation. How can they believe that fighting is the only way to end their troubles?[13]

For some new arrivals, the first glimpse of their operational area would be from the air. 'The helicopter banked and hovered,' recalled a lieutenant in the Argyll and Sutherland Highlanders,

> while below us unfolded a relief map of dozens of mean, smoky little streets fenced in, as it were, between the two main east and west arteries, the Crumlin and Shankill Roads. This was our patch, bordered by steep green hills in the

west and an area of razed houses close to the city centre in the east. Even from 200 feet, one saw the decay and sensed despair, although perhaps some of the despair was in one's own heart at the prospect of four months plodding amongst these mean and dirty streets.[14]

Scottish regiments have never been recruited on a denominational basis, although over the years, several have maintained kirk sessions and masonic lodges. These badges of Protestant allegiance have not prevented Catholics serving on an equal footing, quite apart from being promoted and commissioned. One Catholic from the west of Scotland, serving in Northern Ireland with the Argyll and Sutherland Highlanders, had no problems over his loyalties, despite having played as a teenager in a republican accordion band in his home town near Glasgow. 'I still can't understand how any Catholics would do what the IRA does or give them support. To me it's just terror. I'll tell you one thing, though, when I was out on street patrols in Belfast, I was never worrying about whether the boy covering me with his rifle was a Catholic or a Protestant.'[15]

What could sometimes affect Scottish Catholics was the ostracism with which they were liable to be treated in republican areas.

> I know that some of the friendliest people in the world live in Belfast, but they all just seem to avoid me when I'm there. I have met with lots of friendly people in the province, but because of who I am they were all Prods. I used to see a priest in the Turf Lodge area and I always said 'Good morning, Father' but he ignored me. He may have thought I was winding him up but I expected more than that from a priest because I am, after all, a Catholic.[16]

At the start of the Troubles, Scots, like British troops generally, viewed the demands of the minority community with a good deal of sympathy. The rapid erosion of this sympathy, however, did not create much affinity with the Unionist majority, although there have been individual cases of Scots who have been disciplined for unauthorised contacts with Loyalist paramilitary organisations. Until recently, a senior member of the Ulster Defence Association whose role was to co-ordinate its fundraising in Scotland, was himself a former member of the Argyll and Sutherland Highlanders who had served in the early period of the Troubles.[17]

Other Scots have been sceptical of the approbation sometimes heaped upon them, and the army more generally, by the Loyalist population.

> On the Wednesday after internment, we came down from Ballymurphy along the Shankill Road and the pavements were lined with Protestants cheering us, throwing us packets of cigarettes, wearing Union Jacks. Our driver, a Jock, stopped the wagon and shouted at them: 'Don't you start, you bastards. Because it's your turn next. It'll happen to you as well because you're just as bad.'[18]

Scottish troops, without regard to the denominational composition of their units, could of course find themselves under orders to head off Orange Walks and territorial Loyalist parades from routes which could cause provocation and serious disorder at 'interfaces', i.e. meeting points between Protestant and Nationalist working class areas. One such interface was the Boyne Bridge at the western end of Sandy Row opening onto the Grosvenor Road and the Lower Falls. Over many years it had been the scene of vicious sectarian clashes, and in the summer of 1972, the Queen's Own Highlanders found themselves sealing the bridge against a column of flute bands and Orange lodges.

Ulster Loyalist flute bands, of course, have strong Scottish links and regularly cross the water to play at Orange Walks in Scotland. Many of the bandsmen on this occasion, a former sergeant remembers, were in fact wearing regimental cap badges which his own company had given out to them earlier in its tour of duty. He is equally clear in his own mind that his company would have stopped the parade with whatever force deemed necessary, but his relief was still palpable when the parade marshals decided to co-operate with the army and march the bands and lodges back along Sandy Row and into the safely Loyalist village area.[19]

The same sergeant was in the province two years later when much of it had been taken over by the Loyalist paramilitaries, co-ordinated by the Ulster Workers Council, in the May strike against the Wilson government's attempt to make a success of the power-sharing executive provided for by the 1973 Sunningdale agreement. 'I couldn't believe it,' he says,

> when UDA men with hoods and pick handles started to operate their traffic checkpoints right outside our battalion base on Broadway. You began to ask yourself who was the law now. UDA pickets even stood talking to army patrols, sounding off about trouble in local discos and how they should be allowed to handle it. In fact they were defying an elected government, and we should have moved against those road blocks. I still see it as a black day for the army that we didn't.[20]

Another Scot with commissioned rank who did three tours between 1972 and 1975 still has uncompromising views abut the Unionist community.

> In my time in the army, I've served with Americans from the deep South and Arabs and Jews in the Middle East, but I believe that there is not a more bigoted, unreasoning population anywhere than the Ulster Protestants. I say this knowing the many reasons and historical justifications for it, based on fear and now desperation or something close to it, and I know too that there are many individual and honourable exceptions. Outside Ulster, I have many Catholic friends from the province, but no Protestant ones as far as I know – terrible, isn't it?[21]

Scottish regiments in Northern Ireland have often had a reputation for tough and drastic methods in dealing with the population in republican areas. The army's regimental system, of course, allows different units to cultivate their own style and self-image. An ex-sergeant in the 2nd Battalion of the Scots Guards claims that on his tours of duty in Belfast and Londonderry between 1971 and 1974:

> On no occasion did I see a guardsman being even unkind to ordinary Irish people in the street. I know of a guardsman in my battalion up in Ballymurphy who was fined £15 for swearing at a dog. His section commander reported him because local people heard him and that's what happened. We were gentlemen, gentlemen of the Guards and I always tried to line up to that ideal, even when we had lads killed. Hearts and minds was the operational principle we started from at that time.[22]

This former sergeant has given some thought to the different approaches of army units but admits that he still thinks in terms of the standards applied by the Scots Guards when he was with them:

> Every unit in the British army likes to think it's the best, so all attitudes among them are comparative and competitive. I watched the Royal Marines and the Parachute Regiment in action and there's no doubt that they were manifestly and outwardly aggressive. The Paras, especially, did intimidate and encourage fear, though I felt their bark was often worse than their bite. Under attack of course and off the leash, they were professionals who would kill without compassion.[23]

Regarding his regiment's attitude towards the Irish Republican Army, he recalls:

> We were not trained to hate the IRA, only to know them as an enemy. I remember, back in 1971, a young fellow was brought into Springfield Road RUC station while I was there. There had just been an ambush in which one of our lads was killed and this fellow was later charged for his part in it. They spread him up against the wall, arms and legs apart, quite professional and nothing out of the ordinary – standard procedure. One guardsman asked him if he had any fags and he indicated he did in one of his pockets. The guardsman took out a packet, took a fag from it and returned it, just like that. That told me something about the relationship with the IRA we were trying to work from.[24]
>
> I know there were numerous occasions when interrogation was carried out by what I'd call SAS methods, lights, intimidation, bullying, methods after all used since time immemorial, you could say, by the British army around the world. But that was no part of our business as ordinary guardsmen. It was outside our remit. We were soldiers on the ground, there to make arrests as and when we could, but the experts were there to take over from us for actual interrogation.[25]

The act of killing could, it seems, co-exist in the minds of some Scots, especially in the early phase of the Troubles, with the need to look for ways out of an increasingly deadly impasse. When a platoon of the KOSB First Battalion shot dead petrol bomber O'Hagan in the New Lodge area of Belfast on 31 July 1970, rioting which had already started lasted for another full week and the regimental magazine described the whole sequence of events. Yet the same issue devoted several pages to the need for equal rights for both communities in the province, integrated schooling, the teaching of toleration and real investment in the social infrastructure. Much stress was laid upon the battalion's attempts to improve community relations in North Belfast. These had included the building of a swing park in Ardoyne, football fixtures with local teams and pipe band performances at schools in the area.[26]

This preoccupation of many army units with a hearts and minds approach lingered on even as attitudes hardened within the Nationalist community after internment and Bloody Sunday. The Second Battalion of the Scots Guards produced a newspaper during their 1972 tour in Londonderry. Called *The Rose and Thistle*, it combined detailed regimental news for families in Scotland and in West Germany with a good deal of coverage of community relations work in what had been the city's 'no go' areas. In one issue, a major with the battalion set out the case for the effort involved in this work and looked back over his tour recalling how, amongst other things:

> We have given matrimonial advice to a local who by no stretch of the imagi-nation could be described as being on our side and, at short notice, we organ-ised a missing dogs service. The battalion has seen an improvement in relations with some of the people of the area, particularly the old and the very young. In short, we set out to establish some form of communications with influential people, and although they may not like us or our role here in Londonderry, the more moderate among them respect us for at least trying. We shall of course never know how much aggro and other trouble we may have been saved by the efforts of those civilians who were deployed to defuse a situation before we had to intervene.[27]

Some who have served in the Troubles have indeed realised, especially when most regiments in the 1970s were doing four month tours, how much the varying demeanour of different units could affect the situation locally. A Black Watch officer made this point forcefully in the regiment's maga-zine in 1974:

> Although this is our fifth visit to Northern Ireland since the outbreak of the Troubles, we could never fully imagine what it must be like to live the life of an Irishman. We come and we go. The people whom we now control have lived this life for five troubled years. Every four months, 'their' soldiers

change. The training that we do prior to a tour in Northern Ireland may be standardised, but the temperament of each and every regiment will change according to its territorial background and character. This results in a basic communication between the army and the people having to be re-established every four months.[28]

Much of course can depend, as it always has done, upon particular situations, and the way soldiers, often young ones, react or over-react. At the time of writing, two young Scots Guardsmen are awaiting trial for the murder of a teenager in Belfast's New Lodge area.[29] On 27 December 1973, Private Hesketh, an 18-year-old serving with the Queen's Own Highlanders, was shot dead in an IRA ambush during a period of high tension in West Belfast. Some of the battalion reacted strongly when the news was released:

Paddy bashing took off for the next few days. Our patrols would lie in wait at night outside the church youth clubs and discos for when the boys came out and they got the shite beaten out of them. You can get in a fair head butt with your helmet on and its visor down. One night, some of them with a girl fought back outside a disco on Broadway. One of our lads hit the deck, so one of my platoon used the muzzle of his rifle across the girl's face. He split it open right down the side. She'd not get a boyfriend for a while after that one.[30]

Another informant on his first tour of duty in late 1971 was assigned to guarding Musgrave Park Hospital:

We used to patrol the actual wards and there was one IRA boy with 13 bullets from a Royal Marines patrol who was still alive and able to taunt us. Somehow or other, his blood drip was disconnected one night and he died. When the hospital came under fire, as it did then quite often, we would make a point of putting IRA 'patients' right in front of the windows.[31]

The following year, his battalion were on guard duty on HMS Maidstone in Belfast harbour while it was a prison for internees. 'I wouldn't like to have been wakened up the way we wakened some of the boys there during our night searches of the sleeping areas. We made sure, too, that a fair lot of their food got specially treated. What went into it was nobody's business.'[32]

A former Royal Scots private recalls:

We didn't like being called Brits, and on my tours we tried to go easy on the rough stuff with local people. Partly, that was to be different from the English, of course, or so we thought. As Scots, we half-understood what the IRA was fighting for, so we didn't put the population in our areas under as much pressure as the Paras and Royal Marines did.

On 8 May 1981 however, three days after the death of Bobby Sands, he was on riot duty in West Belfast as part of a battalion snatch squad:

> We arrested a young woman and she struggled quite a lot. We duffed her up a good bit, but when we got her back to our base it was decided we had wrongly arrested her. It made me feel extremely small and extremely rotten. We had really duffed her up and she was only a bystander. We had hit her arms with our truncheons to immobilize her. Her upper arms were very badly bruised, also the upper part of her legs. We later drove her to the Royal Victoria Hospital, where she had to go on crutches. We're not perfect. We make mistakes.[33]

Scots, of course, have served in units other than Scottish regiments, including those which, over the years, have built up the most aggressive reputations in the Troubles for their willingness to 'terrorise the terrorists' and impose their will upon the communities within which the IRA operate. One former Royal Marine from Edinburgh was with 45 Commando in Northern Ireland in 1971 and 1972. His tour included Operation Motorman on 31 July 1972, when the army moved against the IRA-controlled 'no go' areas in Belfast and Londonderry. He was with his unit in Andersontown and remembers most of all the sound that accompanied the operation:

> As soon as it began, the women appeared on their doorsteps, banging metal dustbin lids together. There was a marked absence of men about, just these yelling witches banging dustbin lids together. It was an infernal racket but after a few minutes, as with most things, I got used to it. In retrospect, I feel this din was created to bolster the morale of the population who, after all, were witnessing the clinical destruction of what they believed was a safe republican area.[34]

This informant is not critical of the way the Royal Marines operated, though of course since then they have been at the centre of much controversy:

> We were highly disciplined in a way that the army was not. We were subject to the same provocations and taunts as everyone else. Yet we did not indulge in fits of murderous temper as did the Parachute Regiment on Bloody Sunday. We were briefed exactly on the circumstances in which we could open fire and the consequences of what would happen to us as individuals if we killed anyone without entirely justifiable reason in law. At one point, my company was stationed in Newry which, as you will know, is a largely republican area, but we had very little trouble. It was made clear that we would kill anyone who tried to kill us, and on these terms we got on very well with the local population.[35]

The Marines' reputation may have hardened as the Troubles dragged on, to the point where Mary Holland could write, in the aftermath of the IRA's 1989 bomb attack on the corps' music school at Deal, Kent:

Since June, the marines have been in west Belfast, where their behaviour has been, to put it mildly, a cause for some unofficial concern. Brian Feeney, a local SDLP councillor strongly opposed to the IRA, told me that every week he receives a sheaf of complaints from local priests and social workers about the regi-ment. He was under no illusion as to how the news of the Deal bombing would be received in west Belfast and it would not be discouraging for Sinn Féin.[36]

A former marine from Edinburgh who served three times in the province with 45 Commando, tells of how, in 1981, they made free with baton rounds and plastic bullets:

We got issued with a white card but I don't think anyone ever read it. I certainly didn't. There was little or no control over rounds fired. If you caused a fatality, you got together and agreed on a story, and in a riot who can say who fires the plastic bullet that kills, when three or four guys are firing them. There were very few ways in which we could be held accountable. I remember a guy being shot in the kidneys with a plastic round and being very badly hurt. There was an investigation that got nowhere. It was a slow business getting any evidence heard and the guys involved had ample time to agree on their story.[37]

The men of 45 Commando went in hard in their TARs (Tactical Areas of Responsibility):

Beating people up for the hell of it was almost a nightly occurrence. *An Phoblacht*'s claims at the time were nearly all true. In Turf Lodge, people wouldn't come out on the streets after dark because they knew we'd fill them in. I watched some fierce beatings that put people into hospital. At the time, I've got to say that I wasn't too unhappy about it. On Land Rover patrols it was better still because you could nip into another TAR, beat one or two locals up, then let the responsible unit take the shit, if there was any.[38]

The Parachute Regiment, because of the style it cultivates on the streets and its quick reaction tactics, has never been far from controversy since it was first deployed. Twenty years on from the event, its actions on Londonderry's 'Bloody Sunday' continue to be examined and former members of the regiment have written brutally frank accounts of their time in Northern Ireland. 'During house searches, they vented their anger on their victims, smashing down doors, breaking up furniture, kicking and rifle-butting anyone who resisted,' one declared, adding to this the obscene talk of his platoon to women in the houses and their regular threats to children . . .

The circumstances of our training, coupled with the peculiar nature of our existence in Northern Ireland, turned us into savages. We begged and prayed for a chance to fight, to smash, to kill, to destroy: we were fire-eating berserkers, a hurricane of human brutality ready to burst forth on anyone or anything that stood in our way.[39]

He was writing of the 1970s when the army operated with little reference to the RUC or civilian concepts of policing. Scots who have served with the regiment more recently think that its ethos has not changed fundamentally. Recalling his first experience of Northern Ireland in 1978, one Scot still serving says:

> The attitude of the regiment then and to a certain extent now, was to go in hard and let them know who was boss. This meant that a few of the local hoods and players got filled in. Harsh, yes, but they didn't trouble us thereafter. Consequently, we had a really quiet tour. The locals were definitely scared of us but still gave us a hard time verbally, especially the girls. If you tried to be civil they still gave you shit, so in the end you gave as good as you got and it's actually quite a good laugh.[40]
>
> I missed what I term the good old days, 1970 to 1976, when the army had total control of the province and the police were conspicuous by their absence. Listening to the stories of the old sweats about those days, some of them no doubt apocryphal, could make you jealous. In 1978, we were coming to the end of that era and the police were beginning to take a more active role.

Yet this, in his view, did not cramp the regiment's style too much. 'We do have a reputation within the local community and the press, for being tough and occasionally out of control. The former is quite justified and nothing to be ashamed of. We are, after all, soldiers and our job is to go in hard and aggressively.'[41]

Another Scottish paratrooper contributed his recollections and thoughts in the aftermath of some well-publicised incidents involving his battalion in the tour of Coalisland, Co. Tyrone, in May 1992. These led to an officer of the battalion being suspended, a brigadier being transferred to other duties and the battalion being taken off the streets. Ken Maginnis, an Ulster Unionist MP who has served with the former Ulster Defence Regiment, joined the SDLP in criticism of the paratroopers' actions which, he warned, could only harm and alienate the local community.[42]

Claims of a rampage by his battalion through Coalisland are disputed by this Scot:

> There were a couple of incidents which gave 3 Para a really bad press and almost got us sent packing from the province: in one incident, a young officer was sent home and in the second, some shots were fired at a rioting crowd. Both incidents were, in the opinion of the lads on the ground, set up by Sinn Féin. In the first, a patrol was bricked by some youths who then ran into a pub. The patrol gave chase to make an arrest. There was a bit of a barney and a few blows were exchanged. That was it. According to the press the next day, the Paras had sealed off both ends of the town and had then run amok. This was supposedly in retaliation for one of our lads who had his legs blown off earlier in the day. The fact that both incidents happened almost simultaneously and that the patrols in the town could not have known about him were not allowed to get in the way of a good story.[43]

The Parachute Regiment was withdrawn from Coalisland and replaced by the King's Own Scottish Borderers, but tension remained high, as indeed it had been since the killing of four local IRA men in an SAS ambush in the town earlier in the year. On Sunday, 17 May, a KOSB foot patrol accepted a challenge to a fist fight with some local men outside a bar and in doing so, allowed bystanders to seize a rifle and a general purpose machine gun they had been carrying.[44] This, and other incidents, brought the Paratroopers back in support of the KOSB and another Scottish paratrooper takes over the story:

> What I did not see mentioned in the press was the fact that the man who had the rifle taken off him was almost killed by it. Luckily, the unreliability of the SA 80 saved his life in this instance. As a member of the crowd attempted to cock it, the rifle jammed. Patrols from 3 Para were sent in later to find the weapons and they were set upon. Warnings were given to no avail, and only when a soldier was being dragged down an alleyway were shots fired, some by the commander, over the crowd's heads. A burst was fired by the lad the crowd were trying to drag away. That was the burst that caused some injuries. I think the action of the soldiers involved was justified, but none of this came out. Sinn Féin used the incident for PR purposes and we got a mauling in the press.[45]

In the one instance where Scots were tried and convicted of murder while serving in Northern Ireland, there were sharply divided reactions. This was in January 1981, when one former and three still-serving soldiers were brought to trial in Belfast for murders they were charged with having committed nine years earlier. The victims, Mick Naan, a civil rights supporter with no known IRA connections and a simple-minded young labourer, Andrew Murray, were found dead with multiple stab wounds on a farm near Newtonbutler in Co. Tyrone, on 24 October 1972.

RUC men who found the bodies worked from the premise that the killings were a Loyalist reprisal for IRA attacks in an area near the Irish border where they were increasingly active. News reports began to refer to the case as the 'pitchfork murders', because of the deep wounds from which the two men had died, but nobody was charged with the killings. The pitchfork theory was, however, called into question the following year in a book by two Belfast-based journalists on political and sectarian murder in the province.[46]

The recently re-formed First Battalion of the Argyll and Sutherland Highlanders had in fact been patrolling the Newtonbutler area at the time of the farm murders and between early September and the end of November, 1972, eight of its men had been killed there.[47] Six years later, the battalion was at Catterick, Yorkshire, during the succession of macabre murders later proved to be the work of Peter Sutcliffe. A telephone call to the police by a former Argyll alerted them to a possible link between the regiment and one of the current murders. Many serving and former members were questioned by both military and civilian police, but no light was cast upon any victim of the man later to become known as the 'Yorkshire Ripper'.

The trail started by a single phone call from a much-troubled Argyll led back to the lonely farm near Newtonbutler and to a renewal of the RUC's interest in the case. Sergeants Stanley Hathaway and John Byrne were found guilty of murder and sentenced to life imprisonment. Former Lance Corporal Iain Chestnut pleaded guilty to the lesser charge of manslaughter and was given four years' imprisonment. Captain Andrew Snowball received a one year suspended sentence for withholding information about a crime. Later in 1981, the army let it be known that he had resigned his commission.

The case necessarily involved gruesome evidence about the ferocity with which the two victims had been bayoneted to death by the Argylls. It also prompted much comment in the Scottish press about the power of regimental loyalties and the effective veil these had thrown over a brutal episode for more than six years. Of the informant whose telephone call to the police had set the eventual trial in motion, a detective in the RUC was quoted as saying:

> We feel he is in a rather delicate position. He belonged to a regiment with a great family tradition, probably the strongest in the British army, and loyalty amongst the men is something of which they are extremely proud. I am sure some of them know who he is, and as far as they are concerned, he broke a strict barrack room rule and squealed.[48]

Other former Argylls feel the same, and one who served with the convicted men is confident that the police informer will, in due course, get his deserts from 'the regiment'. He recalls Chestnut as a man easily led, with a grudge against the battalion which had court-martialled him for random shooting at civilians in Newry. Sergeants Hathaway and Byrne were, in his view, much affected and unsettled by the death of a fellow sergeant shortly before the Newtonbutler murders. He knew nothing of the murders at the time, though he mentions a great deal of talk by those who had served there about the brutalities they had got away with against the population in Aden during that emergency.[49]

Chestnut's father-in-law, Mr John Bews, was quoted after the trial as saying: 'How did you expect them to behave? It was cold fury at seeing their pals getting blown up.'[50] This view was echoed by some Scottish contributors to an angry newspaper correspondence. One Church of Scotland minister wrote to the *Scotsman* to declare 'deep distress at the savage sentences handed down to the young men of the Argyll and Sutherland

Highlanders.' He went on to stress the pressures under which they served in the province and how they were

> walking targets for totally unscrupulous and inhuman foes . . . as for the young officer who held his counsel in this matter, he has my fullest sympathy. He must have weighed how this was not a killing for gain or revenge, not one of the sordid butcheries we see reported almost daily where sex or drugs are the motive. He must have known the men involved and believed it to be a tragic error, one which would do no good at all to expose to the kind of process we have seen acted out in our courts. He must have known that the morale and honour of the regiment and the Army was involved and was not as ready to sap both as some have been in the name of 'justice'. His family and brother officers have no reason to feel other than profound sympathy and comradeship towards him.[51]

The minister, the Rev. Dr the Hon. Malcolm Mackay, a former naval officer and Minister of State for the Navy in Australia, contributed a second letter, claiming that a sheaf of correspondence in support of his views was arriving with every post, much of it from the families of soldiers serving in Northern Ireland. He was bitterly attacked however, by those who thought they detected a double standard in his response to the sentences. 'How', one of them wrote,

> can one compare the deaths of two Irish farmers to the honour of the Argylls? These two men who wickedly and wantonly got themselves murdered in order to besmirch the honour of a fine body of the Queen's soldiers were, after all Irish, Catholic and Republican (a bad mixture) and obviously not made in God's image as are the gallant Argylls, the Queen and, of course, the Rev. Dr the Hon. Malcolm Mackay.[52]

The year 1981 was a bad one for the Argylls. In October, eight soldiers of its First Battalion received sentences of imprisonment from Belfast Crown Court for theft, burglary and handling stolen goods. In one break-in, in March 1976, at a Shankill Road restaurant used as an office by the Ulster Volunteer Force, they removed a safe containing £1,600 as well as a list of names. They shared out the money and left the list, which could have been immensely useful to the security forces, in a derelict house nearby. 'You actually suppressed documents which you believed to be valuable information about the UVF, in order not to betray your theft,' the judge told them, adding that they had 'disgraced themselves and an historic regiment.'[53]

The pressures and temptations of army service in Northern Ireland are no different for Scots than they are for any others, but Scottish regiments, at least on occasions, have been frank in recognising them. Writing for the regimental magazine in 1974, about duty in Andersonstown, a Black Watch officer showed understanding of just how much was expected of the men serving under him:

> It is extremely difficult for the young soldier suddenly to realise that the occupants of our area are normal people. Where they differ is not in themselves but in the conditions created by the present political impasse. He is ordered into the streets of Belfast with a weapon in his hands, live rounds in his pouches, enormous powers at his disposal, and then told that he is dealing with normal British subjects. He has been trained as a soldier, how to observe, how to seek out a target, how to shoot. Suddenly he is thrown into a situation where he has to make the terrible decision to kill in self- defence. He is put through tremendous demands on his personal endurance resulting from the long hours and the peculiar strains and pressures of his position. At the same time, he must show almost superhuman patience and self-restraint when controlling and attempting to help a community that to him appears only to be antagonised by his presence.[54]

The degree of empathy with the community shown here by this officer is not, of course, echoed in every response to service in Northern Ireland which one encounters among Scots who have served there. Attitudes can harden and become embittered by the protracted routines of patrols, house searches and the ever-present danger that goes with them.

> I know that West Belfast has some of the best council housing in Europe, but also that most of the people there seem to be involved in some kind of criminal activity and that they hate my guts, whether I'm sympathetic towards them or not. So now I detest both sides equally and think Britain should wash its hands of the scrounging, murderous bastards.[55]

A generalised contempt for everything Irish often surfaced among Scottish regiments in the early years of the conflict and is on record in regimental magazines. *Thin Red Line*, the Argyll and Sutherland Highlanders' journal, announced a photographic competition in 1973 for the First Battalion serving in the province, with special prizes for anybody 'who can contribute a picture of an intelligent Irishman.'[56] The same issue also ran a somewhat laboured feature about the supposed educational subnormality of people in one of the areas where the battalion was operating:

> Once upon a time in a far-off land inhabited by idiots, there was a town called Newry. Newry was a very peaceful town where the locals amused themselves by demolishing their buildings and burning cars. This was regarded as sensible practice by the not-too-bright inhabitants. One day, some strangers arrived in Newry and tried to stop the locals from changing their own landscape. This, they said, was naughty. These strangers were very different, they could tie their own laces, use long words when they spoke and could even write other people's names. The Paddies decided all this fantastic brainpower came from

the hats the strangers wore . . . One day the strangers left, much against their wishes (ho ho), and the Paddies lived happily ever after, happily blowing up buildings, themselves and cars.[57]

The Scots Guards ran a magazine, already quoted from, that covered their 1972 tour of duty in Londonderry in which some articles by senior officers strove to be serious about the town's problems and the 2nd Battalion's peace-keeping role. This, however, was combined with much knockabout humour featuring the local population. It included spoof letters to the editor, written in semi-literate style, one singling out a family who thought the bath in their new council flat was a pig trough. In another issue, a mock-up travel advertisement celebrated the delights of the Costa Del Bog with its 'Ristorante Leprechaun' and local traditions such as the Festival of the Brick, observed nightly by 'fun-loving natives at Free Derry Corner.'[58]

Others, looking back over their time served in the Troubles, feel they can detect a change in their attitudes. A Royal Marine commando remembers his response to the 1981 Republican hunger strikes:

> The fact that people were starving themselves to death in prison for a cause just didn't bother me. It never got through to me, except that the next death could mean my platoon being called out on the streets at 3 o'clock in the morning. I never thought of it in human terms at all. Yet that same year, I know I began to feel something for the West Belfast people, even for the IRA units they as a community were harbouring. There was the thought that they were mostly young guys like us. Most wars, after all, are fought by people with a lot in common and Northern Ireland was, after all, no different. But the trouble was that nothing in our training taught us to think of it as a political or moral problem. [59]

One informant, already quoted in this chapter, admits that once out of the army, he began to think a great deal about his experiences, especially after August 1989, when Channel 4 re-ran the Granada series *The Troubles*, to mark the 20th anniversary of British troops' deployment.

> That made me wish that I had known more about the history of it all and the sources of the conflict. Maybe I'd not have been quite so hard on the people in the republican areas where we operated. I don't know. I can see, though, that a united Ireland will have to come and that it should come, but I'll never accept the IRA's methods. Don't forget I've seen the results of their methods.[60]

The ability of soldiers to distance themselves from crude anti-Irish stereotypes could, of course, be linked to a growing respect for the IRA's tenacity and military skill. This was how the KOSB magazine described a gun battle in the Turf Lodge area of Belfast early in 1972:

A well-planned and frankly unlucky attempt to ambush two of our patrols failed. The contact involved initially two separate groups of enemy gunmen and developed into a Wild West shoot-out lasting some hours with hundreds of shots exchanged. At least two gunmen were involved and their persistence under heavy fire distinguished them as hard core (not the boyish enthusiasts normally encountered).[61]

A survivor of some heavy action between the IRA and the Scots Guards in 1971 and 1972 still feels it was right to recognise the quality of an enemy who rapidly increased his operational skills:

I always gave them the respect one soldier should give another. You need to know your enemy. The chap with a gun is by definition part of some kind of fighting machine. I'd always treat him as a soldier, regardless of his beliefs or values, and it's always best to overestimate your enemy rather than to under-estimate him. There's a few soldiers and RUC men dead just because they underestimated the IRA. There's a lot of IRA men, after all, who have been in the British army. The IRA train their men as soldiers, they teach them to know their weapons, which ones to use and when. It would have been silly not to appreciate them as soldiers.[62]

Generous praise for the enemy came from a paratroop sergeant refer-ring to the operation carried out by an IRA unit against a KOSB-manned border checkpoint at Derryard, Co. Tyrone, in December, 1989. 'Brilliant – a superb professional job. The army couldn't have done it better'[63] he said of the attack which killed two Scots and critically wounded another. The initiative had achieved maximum surprise and used a multiplicity of weapons, including a rocket-launcher, to confuse the defenders. Only their ability to return fire despite suffering casualties prevented the complete destruction of the base, but the IRA were able to withdraw intact.[64]

Officers with long experience of the Troubles, whether in riot control in the early days, street patrols or undercover surveillance operations, will sometimes allow a distinction between Belfast-based IRA units and those that operate in rural and border areas. One senior officer in the KOSB obviously had great respect for the latter:

I can actually identify with them as a soldier because, within the limits of their training, they operate with military skill. They know the ground and they use good fieldcraft. Francis Hughes, whom we shot in 1976, was a case in point, a real soldier and a skilled guerrilla. There's no question about that, capable of living rough for days and weeks at a time. He was a hard bastard of course, and many of his victims were Protestant farmers or farmworkers around his home at Bellaghy or across the Tyrone border, off-duty UDR men or RUC reservists there for the taking.[65]

The same source recognised weaknesses, too, in the IRA's operational methods:

> They have the funds to get reliable mortars any time off the shelf, instead of which they persist with dangerous home-made ones of their own because making them is a cottage industry they feel they should support. They'll stay in business though, because there is still injustice in Northern Ireland but not, in my view, enough to justify the continued price of armed struggle. It's going to be a long war, but one which the army can keep a degree of control over for so long as the IRA don't choose to become a suicidal guerrilla outfit on the Middle Eastern model. God knows what answer we would have to truckloads of high explosive driven by people ready to blow down a whole base on top of themselves.[66]

A number of books have now drawn upon the reminiscences of soldiers of all ranks who have served in Northern Ireland.[67] Scots often like to think their cultural affinity with that community gives them a better understanding of its sectarian tensions which, in a modified form, are a reality of life in the west-central belt of Scotland. Listening to the accounts of their service in the Troubles by men selected because they are Scots creates doubts as to whether their perceptions are in fact much different from or more searching than anyone else's.

Two decades of communal violence and insurgent warfare directed against them have now claimed several hundred soldiers' lives as well as wounds and long-term disability to more than five thousand others. Scottish regiments and Scots in other units have suffered their share of this toll and the survivors inevitably reflect upon the fact of their survival. 'It makes me think a lot now,' a former Royal Marine says, 'of the randomness of death. Things I did and thought then worry me much more now than at the time.'[68]

> When you are 18, a lot of what you do is role-playing and you act tough without realising it. Not until late in 1981 did I realise fully that Northern Ireland was the real world with real people getting killed. Near death was something we laughed about. On a patrol in Belfast, a friend of mine once had a bullet miss him by a couple of inches. We put around the joke that if it had gone through his head, he was so thick he would never have felt it. It worries me now that I didn't, or couldn't, take in the reality of it at the time. The Royal Marines training had worked on me whether I knew it or not and I became a lot more aggressive while I was over there, something I'm certainly not now.[69]

Death passed close to a Royal Scots private who, during his 1981–1983 tour wanted to go home for a weekend's leave to attend his sister's wedding in Edinburgh. He had used up his official leave allocation but paid a friend £20 to cover for him on weekend patrol duty. The friend's coffin returned to Scotland within days. He had been caught in an IRA ambush. 'Did I pay that guy £20 to get killed in my place? Should it have been me? Was it fate, or was I just lucky?'[70]

All army service, whether in conventional or guerrilla warfare such as that prevalent in Northern Ireland has a life of its own in the memories of those who experience it. The Royal Scots private whose friend accepted £20 to get killed in his place, finds it hard to escape from his mental images of Northern Ireland.

> When I've had a few drinks, it all starts crawling back into my brain and I think: 'God almighty, was that what really happened? Did I actually do things like that? Was there a different way without hurting people too much?' It's too late for me to do anything about now that I'm out of the army, but at least I took no lives. That would have troubled me for a very long time. I might have killed in self-defence but never just for the hell of it. Conscience would have held me back before I pulled the trigger on someone put on this earth for a reason.[71]

Other survivors of service through the Troubles have found themselves mentally re-examining the nature of patriotism, both their own and that of the Irish republicans they encountered.

> I happened to be with a patrol in the vicinity of Bernadette McAliskey's house near Coalisland in 1980, when she and her husband were shot by Loyalists. We were first on the scene and called up cover while we went into the house. She was close to death and the action of an army medic without doubt saved her life. What sticks in my mind though was her attitude. Close to death and with the medic frantically trying to save her life, she was still ranting and raving at us in the foulest language. We all wished then that we had let the bitch die, a sentiment that has come back to me after more recent incidents in Coalisland involving contact with committed republicans. I think as Brits we find it difficult to understand such deep feelings. Unlike the Irish, or even Americans, we have no tradition of dying for the flag. Sure, we die in our country's wars, but we fight for our own pride and for our 'muckers' which, in my opinion, makes the British soldier the world's most effective.[72]

A deepening aversion to violence as a means of furthering political goals has been one recognisable effect of service in Northern Ireland.

> I developed a lasting hatred for the IRA which is reinforced with each outrage and I don't expect it to lessen. I am a black-hearted cynic with few abiding principles, but one of these is a belief in pluralist democracy which allows for orderly social and political change. Fanaticism, like that of the IRA, knows only violence as a source of change.

This is the unchanging view of a former Royal Marine commando who says he led a sheltered middle class life in a Scottish city before joining up in 1970. Northern Ireland was, for him, part of a maturing process. 'I witnessed violence, hatred and death for the first time but it did not trouble me then and does not now. I now have a greater experience of all these features of human existence as a police officer than ever I got in Northern Ireland.'[73]

Wholesale death and young lives abruptly cut off leave images in the mind that for some can never be erased. A survivor of the 1979 Warrenpoint ambush which killed 18 soldiers in the IRA's biggest single 'victory' over the security forces, had to struggle to describe a sergeant major sitting down helpless with grief over the dismembered remains of his platoon who had walked straight into a second bomb explosion prepared for them as they arrived by helicopter to help paratroopers already ambushed:

> Some of the boys who hadn't been ripped apart by the blast were twisted so much out of shape that we had to break limbs to get them into the body bags. Our C.O. (Lieutenant Colonel David Blair) got a great funeral in the Canongate Church in Edinburgh, but I can tell you there wasn't a lot of him in that coffin because he took the full force of the bomb when it went off.[74]

Since then, and over the more than 20 years of the army's deployment in Northern Ireland, much has changed. Infantry battalions can complete a tour of duty there without engaging the IRA at all, while surveillance and covert operations now account for many more 'contacts' with the IRA than the uniformed army. This twilight war can be a squalid business, relying as it so often does upon relationships between informers and their handlers, but much of Northern Ireland's conflict has indeed been a dirty war, contaminating many of those drawn into it.

Some live uneasily with their memories, unlike Rifleman Harris, who wrote long ago of his service in Spain, in bloody battles against Napoleon's armies:

> I look back upon that portion of my time spent in the fields of the Peninsula as the only part worthy of remembrance. It is at such times that scenes long past come back upon my mind as if they had taken place but yesterday. I remember even the very appearance of some of the regiments engaged and comrades, long mouldered to dust, I see again performing the acts of heroes.[75]

No battle honours have been added to regimental colours from an intractable and probably unwinnable war in Northern Ireland which has prompted Scots, like soldiers from elsewhere in these islands, to act with much bravery and often, too, with brutality. Patience and endurance have perhaps been more important than either, and remain so amongst young men walking streets where their fathers' generation patrolled and manned interfaces in 1970 and 1971. These qualities have been needed in equal measure by the wives and families of those who have served in the Troubles, and consequently had their lives cut short.

One of the many Scots to whom this happened was James Novosad, 'Nifty' to his friends, a young trooper in 'Scotland's own' Fourth Battalion of the Royal Tank Regiment. In March 1978 he met his death while on duty in central Belfast during the Queen's University Charities Day procession, shot dead by assailants bizarrely disguised as Arabs, who had mingled with student collectors in fancy dress. On a wild and rainy day, his body was brought back for burial to Leven, Fife. 'The ground was wet and muddy and the undertakers had surrounded the grave with bright green artificial grass. The piper led the procession with a wailing lament and the mourners followed the coffin. Novosad's wife looked so young that it was hard to believe she was a widow and not a schoolgirl.'[76]

Six of Novosad's company who had been closest to him had volunteered to act as pallbearers, but had to return to Belfast the same night for patrol duty the following day. 'While we're away,' they told a newspaper, 'other lads have to work even harder than usual. Still, they'll be glad to hear that we gave Nifty a right good send-off. That's important to everyone.'[77]

11

Scotland, Ulster and You

OWEN DUDLEY EDWARDS

Is this book history? Is it history in the telling, or in the making? Some of its essays are historical in content, some of its authors are professional historians, and all believe that the present is meaningless without knowledge of the past (or else have been wasting time at your expense), but this book is not intended to give the comfort of academic study.

It may be, indeed, that students of history who read this book will gain some of their most profound insights into their craft from the formally non-historical work: you will know more about the assessment of journalistic witness as evidence from coming to your conclusions about what Robbie Dinwoodie has told you of the way he recalls his Scottish-oriented data on Ulster being accumulated; gain a very different basis for study of Scottish observation of Ulster from Sarah Nelson; and suddenly discover ordinary soldiers' perceptions marching at you under the command of Ian Wood.

These things will tell historians of the future – which is to say you, whether you fulfil that destiny or not – things they need to know but which previous histories will not tell them. And you will find that the writers actually concerned with history as their theme communicate with you on another level by their way of telling you what they have to tell, sometimes because of the lives they have had: Dr Bob Purdie apparently takes the most specialist of all historical problems in his choice of topic, William Walker and the Leith Burghs election of 1910, but he draws lessons – or silently lets you draw them – which throw startling light on the permanent relationship of Scotland and Ulster, above all in such a masterstroke of analysis as: 'Scotland was a junior partner in the United Kingdom, Ireland was a tenant-at-will'. If it's been put better by anyone else, I haven't seen their work. But Dr Purdie can do this from his own experience of Ulster and Scotland over the last quarter-century as political activist and subsequent self-critic. Admittedly, his brand of self-criticism is exceptional in its constructive capacity.

There is also a question of what you are to make of the fact that people are saying certain things. When Dr Ian Adamson, for instance, writes: 'In 1655 Cromwell despatched his son, Henry, to be ruler of Ireland and under his firm but mild government an increase of liberty was granted to Catholic, Presbyterian and Episcopalian alike', he raises the interesting problem as to whether Henry Cromwell and his father would be more incensed at this claim than would be the mass of the Irish observant Catholics whom they ruled in permanent denial of the liberty to be observant Catholics. But the fact that Dr Adamson conscientiously believes in the truth of what he is saying throws most important light on Ulster at the present day, both on the many Protestants who would agree with him and on the many Catholics who would not. Or again, when he says, 'for the twelve years following 1670, there was nothing that could be remotely described as persecution in Ulster' you may be left wondering whether the Roman Catholic Archbishop of Armagh, St Oliver Plunket, imprisoned himself in Dublin Castle during the Popish Plot in 1678, indicted himself for treason before a chorus of obliging London trial lawyers and judiciary, made his way to Tyburn and hanged, drew and quartered himself. But Dr Adamson was not thinking about Catholics, and it is very useful for us that he was not. He was thinking about Presbyterians, and Catholics simply became invisible to his historical view.

Scotland and Ulster in recent centuries have been dominated for much of the time by self-perceptions from Presbyterians and other Protestants, in which Catholics became invisible. The Northern Ireland Premier Terence O'Neill was given the credit or debit of pioneer liberalisation in Catholic-Protestant relations in the 1960s – and it is a pleasing reflection for the Rev. Dr Ian Paisley and sundry other of his critics that he owes his gossamer-thin liberal status almost entirely to them – but it was much more characteristic of him and his inheritance that he preached an identity for his substate entirely congruent with Protestant, indeed 'Scots-Irish', historical contours. On the other side of the North Channel, the then prevalent version of Scottish history devalued medieval history outright and promulgated a version of Reformation history which correctly noted a Reformation far more popular in character than the pallid English obeisance to Tudor sexuality (Henry's, Mary's, Elizabeth's), so often dignified with the term 'Reformation' but which denied the very considerable popular support for episcopalianism, both Protestant and Roman Catholic.

Modern Scottish historiography has rediscovered a multi-faceted and multi-dimensional past, largely through the work of Ranald Nicolson, Leslie Macfarlane, Geoffrey Barrow, Gordon Donaldson, Michael Lynch and others, in which the work of the *Innes Review*, founded by the late Fr Anthony Ross, played the vital part of asserting Scottish Catholicism's right to its historical identity by placing its investigation on an impeccably scientific footing, and moving the work of the historical rediscovery of

Scottish Catholicism from an apologetic, filio-pietistic and yet triumphalist ethos to a pursuit of truth to be welcomed whatever its findings. Ulster benefited from the professionalisation of historiography associated with the foundation of the journal *Irish Historical Studies* in 1938; and yet if we look at the second and third (medieval) chapter of Jonathan Bardon's welcome and massive *A History of Ulster* (1992), we find in contrast to its excellent first (archaeological and pre-Viking) chapter how long a distance popular accounts of the Ulster past still have to go. In those pages, Bardon is still largely writing in the old imperial vein, where pre-Reformation history is impatient dismissal of aboriginal antics with alien artefacts. In fact, it is the imperial approach which was painfully parochial: celebrants of the reality of medieval perspectives can point to a European sense on the part of Scots, and perhaps some Ulster persons, which is in urgent need of recall. Whatever the merits of the United Kingdom, it appears more deficient in a European sense than any other power in the European community.

There is a Chinese-box situation here. England proposed a history for the archipelago in which Wales, Scotland and Ireland figured as gravel on the wheels of progress: dirty, delaying and very occasionally, usually accidentally, dangerous; but if put to proper function, such as in the more suicidal military regiments (see Shakespeare, *Henry V*), capable of helping to get a grip on the road to facilitate the triumphant onward march. Naturally history should waste little space on gravel and therefore English history has much to make invisible. The Thatcherite satrap of education, Sir Keith Joseph, was previously distinguished for such *aperçus* on Scottish history as that Scottish devolution was wrong since together the Scots and English had defeated the Spanish Armada. Mrs Thatcher could hardly have made a more brilliant symbolic statement of her priorities than his appointment. The Glorious Revolution of 1688 was celebrated in its tercentenary by a tacit assumption of its bloodlessness, and if it were retorted that it was bloody in Scotland, Ulster and the rest of Ireland, the answer was presumably that these were bloody places anyway: the periphery is permitted occasional visibility to receive its *congé*.

Whether it be immigrants looking at the host culture or peripherals at the metropolis, the sight fixed most firmly is all too often the dismissive, repressive or contemptuous face. Hence to gain status, if only as enemies, the search for peripheralist identity involved an attempt to gain status with the metropolis by assuming a countenance like its own. Peripheralist Nationalism thus shapes itself in colonial or post-colonial form. This can apply with obvious variants, to Welsh linguistic preoccupation, Scots institutional separateness, Ulster settler tradition, Irish Catholic varieties of self-expression.

In terms of history, it means that as with the English pattern, a national ethos is determined, usually to the exclusion of its own margins. A former religious regime, in this context, becomes particularly peripheral: it is repugnant to national ethos as having survived its sell-by date in all senses. So Ulster historical identity is asserted without Catholics and, where necessary, without Monaghan, Cavan and Donegal, and so forth. Irish historical identity is asserted to assume a national unity in which Protestants were looters, defectors, a garrison or – preferably – Nationalists in apparent sympathy with Irish Catholic identity. In both Scotland and Wales, the undoubted Nationalist contributions of episcopalians were obliterated respectively after Presbyterian capture of the state church in Scotland in 1689 and Welsh disestablishmentarian annexation of the Nationalist agenda in the later nineteenth century. The Spartans show their illustrious title to nationality above all in their conquests and their courage in defeat, but also in silent denial of participation to the Helots.

Once we bring the episcopalian dimension into play, we perceive a new complexity. Episcopalianism intermittently persecuted, or at least degraded, Presbyterianism in both Scotland and Ulster in the seventeenth century, but thereafter the roads diverged. In Scotland, Presbyterianism won, and so vaunted over its rival driven from power and edifice that the Scots Protestant episcopalians seem to have supplied the main thrust of the Jacobite rising of 1715. In Ireland, Presbyterianism thought it had won a fight in alliance with the episcopalians against the Jacobites, only to find itself betrayed by its greedy and faithless former partners. Irish Catholics might have nothing other than penal laws to expect from the Hanoverian overlords – what do you expect from a pig but grunts? – where Irish Presbyterians had every right to expect far more. The existence of Presbyterian triumph in Scotland so close at hand gave both an emotive cutting edge and an intellectual depth to their Irish counterparts. Professor A T Q Stewart has brilliantly charted the intellectual complexity of Scots-Ulster Presbyterian links in the eighteenth century in his invaluable *A Deeper Silence* (1993), showing how the Scottish Enlightenment can claim both to have derived in part from Ulster antecedents and to have informed and transformed Ulster Presbyterian growth in self-awareness and self-perception.

The fascinating point made in our own book by Dr Linde Lunney as to the want of folk-awareness of their Scottish origins in Ulster Protestantism may have much to do with the uniqueness of Presbyterian Irish identity. In general, the migrant takes the place of origin to be a culturally rich but economically poor and usually politically deprived antecedent and hence requiring that its pieties and sanctities be passed on in a more fortunate land where Mammon might displace God; but in Scotland and Ulster, a condition possibly unique in migration history had occurred. The lost homeland had made good, the emigrants had suffered degradation. Moreover, the very same settlement which had conferred power and status on Scottish Presbyterianism had treacherously hurled their Ulster co-religionists into subjection for another century. They did not want to talk about Scotland in folk-culture. They did, as Dr Lunney points out, want to read about it, or at least their intellectuals did. In the process, the Scots Presbyerian migration to Ulster and thence to North America, became one of the most cohesive and intra-communicative known to historical scholarship. Its very formality and self-consciousness in writing may have eroded the spontaneity at the heart of non-literary and pre-literate cultural communication.

There is another matter which made Ulster Protestant folk culture rather watchful. The growth of national identity alongside deepening racial concepts and religious administrative rigour has taken many pains to elim-inate the sectarian frontiersmen in sexual, as opposed to military or fac-tional, expression. Everyone assumes the sects in Scotland and Ireland kept themselves to themselves and a Victorian respectability is also erected as a yardstick for ancestral conformity. Nobody, not even Joe Stalin, was a more ruthless manipulator of the past than an ethno-religious group anxious to silence the derision of contemporary opponents, usually by standards dic-tated by those opponents. There, the Irish girl was pure, implacably and eternally, irrespective of whether she had been or not, and the Irish man bedded and married his own. If the historian will only listen, it may be pos-sible to hear through the stifling Victorian atmospherics the long, lecher-ous giggles of the eighteenth century.

What is the real truth behind the local Tyrone tradition that the great Catholic-born novelist William Carleton had an illegitimate, Protestant father? Why, when his maternal forbears, the Woodrows, stretch so strong and inspirational into the Scottish Protestant past, do we hear nothing at all of the paternal ancestors of President Woodrow Wilson before that Wilson grandfather who came so suspiciously from a countryside thronged with the sept of Mac Liaim? What does the violently anti-Catholic H G Wells mean in his *Experiment in Autobiography* when he speaks of his drunken innkeeper grandfather George Neal (né O'Neill?) as 'probably of remote Irish origin' whereas his wife 'sounds good English'? What is signified by Kipling's, Stanley Baldwin's and Edward Burne-Jones's maternal Macdonald ancestry, romantically spoken of as refugees from the '45, fleeing to heavily Catholic Fermanagh whence they emerge in the late eighteenth century with a Wesleyanism by its own definition new to them? Modern Ulster Catholics and Protestants alike have an interest in blotting out the ancestors who crossed the sectarian lines on which posterity built its taboos. Modern Scottish Presbyterians have an interest in diminishing the longevity of episcopalian ancestry, especially if the episcopate in ques-tion climaxes in Rome. If your grandmother married a monster from Outer Space, you may find it best to stress your supreme terrestrialism.

Dr Adamson very justly stresses the incredible antiquity of the inter-connections between Scotland and Ireland, whether the inhabitants make their initial landfalls as visitors, sojourners, migrants or immigrants, and very often, the permanent entrants had no intention of remaining. We may do well to remember, before we become too besotted on the beauty of our golden links, that slavery, piracy, brigandage, rapine and God knows what built up the connection. The case of St Patrick – he, or one of him, may be conveniently allowed to be Scots for purposes of argument – is unanswerable. Modern Irish pint-patriots, who object to the geographical expression 'British Isles', should be reminded that the words 'Irish Sea' may have symbolised a far more terrible and longer lasting history of oppression. The Irish invasion swelled into a nineteenth century torrent, whose terrifying potential Thomas Carlyle so vividly agitated in his *Chartism*.

The 1800 Irish Act of Union made for one country in law whose effects meant that Catholic aboriginals, often primarily non-Anglophone, were let loose on Scotland whose own aboriginals, non-Protestant and non-Anglophone, had been so conveniently deported to the colonies and the army. They made their mark, witness the various careers of the murderers Burke and Hare; the socialist national revolutionary James Connolly and the migrant labour historian Patrick MacGill in his novels *Children of the Dead End* and *The Rat-Pit*. But, as Dr Lunney says, 'perhaps our ancestors had no concept of boundaries between countries, even of the "otherness" of a new place, as we perceive them today'. Scotland seems to have been much more perceived as different in non-Ulster Ireland than in Ulster, Protestant or Catholic: Burke, Hare, Connolly and McGill were all Catholic. Certainly the Irish county you came from was more a badge of identity before the great famine than your Irishness; certainly it was more important to a Scot that s/he was Highland or Lowland than that s/he was Scots. The metropolis, the host country, called you Irish or Scots – usually 'Scotch'. You worked out what that meant; frequently you did so in terms of, and with variations upon what they meant. An Ulster Catholic migrant might become more like the Ulster Protestant migrant with whom an insensitive host classified him/her. To move into Mr Finn's patch, Celtic *is* Rangers.

Similarly, migration creates its conflicts within the one coven. The history of Irish Catholic migration to Scotland is the history of bitter resentment between the indigenous Scots Catholics, courageously surviving through the havens of Banff and the Western Isles, and the Irish invaders. The Gaelic languages are mutually comprehensible between Donegal, so fertile a breeding ground for seasonal migration, and the Western Isles, much more so than between the Donegal and Kerry dialects. But to comprehend each other, and to share one another's Catholicism, did nothing to improve the affections in which the Hebridean and Hibernian navvies held one another in the late eighteenth and early nineteenth centuries. The battles were as bad as any with the nominal sanction of confessional difference or linguistical ignorance. The 'invisible man' situation we noted in the case of prevailing national historic myth, came to apply intensely as

Ireland extended what the Catholic bishops, in imitation of their metropolis, liked to call her 'spiritual Empire'; the Irish clerics favoured Irish laity and fostered other Irish priests. 'What' said one Irish-born priest venomously to the Scots Catholic Archivist, the Rev. William James Anderson, 'would the Scottish Catholic community be without the Irish?' 'Small, but select', replied the Scotsman. The Irish domination of western anglophone Catholicism militated against any Scots preference for restoration of their Catholic hierarchy while the all-powerful Cardinal Paul Cullen was still alive: his relatives and friends would promptly pick up the jobs, and the new Scottish Catholicism would be an Irish colony. As it was, Irish Catholic priests and journalists kept Irish questions at the top of the Scottish Catholic agenda.

Elaine McFarland's fascinating discussion of Orangeism in Scotland brings out that for it, as for Catholicism in Scotland, the wars of 1919–21 and the treaty which followed proved the decisive point in transformation. Suddenly a country of origin, hitherto the womb, became the afterbirth. Politically, the Irish Catholics left Liberalism for Labour, while ultimately the Orangery turned sour on Toryism. Culturally, the fissure widened rapidly. An Irish identity in Scotland, proclaimed through the well-lubricated larynxes of the Glasgow Celtic supporters, was proof of attendance at a 'foreign game' in the eyes of the Irish Gaelic Athletic Association and with it, Irish nationalism at its holy of holies. Donegal, birthplace of so much Irish Catholic Scotland still, was now in a foreign country and its emigrant priests and people awoke to discover themselves with no land save the one they were in. The very things which had maintained the links now vanished, notably the relevance of Irish agrarian agitation to Scottish crofter needs. The Irish Catholic identity in Northern Ireland, ecclesiastically part of an autonomous Irish Free State and later of an independent Irish Republic, showed some signs of distancing itself from the constitutionalism it had retained while the rest of Ireland was going Sinn Féin. As it swithered between defiance and conciliation of the new Ulster substate, rejection or collaboration with republicanism, its problems took it far from Scotland's necessities. Meanwhile, Orangeism, frequently seen in Scotland as an immigrant eccentricity, was in turn cut off from its parent and hence became often critical of the Northern Ireland respectable establishment whose Lodges sang of 'Lady Clark, Blithe as a Lark' in place of their early egalitarianism.

In the late 1950s Scottish Orange lodges protested on the 12th of July when the Ulster Orange establishment excluded from its Finaghy Field platforms a promising young preacher whose mouth was in the right place: in any case, what sounded more appealingly Scottish than the Rev. Ian Richard Kyle Paisley? But while it was the beginning for Big Ian, it seemed an early death-throe to his Scottish supporters. Nor has twentieth century Scottish anti-Catholicism been easy in Orange company. The Church of

Scotland might rant at the country's alien Irish Catholic population in 1923, ironically just at the moment when that population had discovered it had no choice but to be Scots, but neither its demand for repatriation nor the violence of Edinburgh Councillor John Cormack in the 1930s, nor the Protestant crusade of Pastor Jack Glass in recent years, was ever happy at an Orangeism certain to reassert the non-Scottish antecedents of Scottish Protestantism. Scottish anti-Catholicism wanted to capitalise on the national non-Catholic historical myth: it asserted the alien as the enemy and hence could hardly embrace it as a friend. Even Big Ian won little following in Paisley – or Kyle.

Certainly there were figures who could find an Ulster Protestant and a Scottish Protestant identity with no sign of conflict, notably Andrew Bonar Law. Dr Graham Walker's informative account touches on this point. Bonar Law united Scotland and Ulster in a Unionist Protestantism, to which his Canada added its own financial and managerial strengths. Law was unusual in that he really was a capitalist perceiving profit from the Ulster *status quo*: Belfast businessmen without Scottish connections were the most lukewarm Unionists of the lot. They would not quarrel with their workers nor their best customers on such an issue, but privately few of them had doubts as to their capacity to run a Home Rule Ireland in which Dublin incompetence might surely be trusted to ensure their seizure of real power. It was an embattled workforce, the most militant in these islands, which closed the door on Home Rule then, and closed it again in the mid-1970s; and it was that force's manipulators, the apparently doomed agrarian capitalists, who prolonged their own order by making Northern Ireland their survival capsule, defying Pope and time alike. Unlike his office-hungry British Tory colleagues in their flirtation with treason, and Carson, with his priority for the terminally-ill Irish Unionism rather than Ulster Unionism, Bonar Law was very serious about Ulster. As such, he represents a surviving Ulster-Scotland élite which seems to have survived in some sort of acknowledged existence up to the 1970s.

One of the greatest strengths of the Union had been the simple fact that the ruling class had its estates in both the major islands of the archipelago, and where individual members were so unfortunate as to lack a British estate, they had kinsfolk who did. The Hamilton Dukes of Abercorn who progressed from solipsism to plurality during the course of the nineteenth century, had as their Scots relatives the Douglas-Hamilton Dukes of Hamilton, and so on. Such a class readily traded its name for business status in a manner so memorably recorded by Anthony Trollope in *The Way We Live Now*. As a result, quite a few political figures flickered through Unionist machine politics on both sides of the North Channel: Dr Purdie shows how this could happen in Labour politics before 1914, and there were one or two echoes of Walker's Leith candidacy, but it was never the way of life that Scots-Ulster Unionism could be. Neither form of élitist

Unionism looked too closely at the darker side of its neighbours: Scots Catholic Unionist aristocrats or business leaders worried themselves little about the sufferings of their Ulster co-religionists. Indeed, on the outbreak of civil rights agitation in Northern Ireland in 1968, Antonella, Marchioness of Lothian, demanded an oath of allegiance for her fellow Catholics there, failing which they should promptly be deported to the Republic.

Robbie Dinwoodie's document from the *Scotsman* reportage of the 1969 Ulster crisis, via the courtesies – such as they were – of Minister for Home Affairs William Craig, is a reminder of the meaning of that Scots-Ulster establishment. At that time, the *Scotsman* was still very conscious, first and foremost, of serving the best and the nicest, if not necessarily the best and the brightest. It did not like to review books adversely, as this distressed nice advertisers. It did not like to question the actions of the English who ran Edinburgh University, since this encouraged the hooligan elements. It assumed its priorities were those of its Ulster equivalent even if, as Mr Dinwoodie points out, its Thomson stablemate was the *Belfast Telegraph* which, though Unionist, was much more uneasy about the Ulster Unionist establishment than was the *Scotsman*. The sudden division between those old friends emerged before Scots eyes when the great Scottish judge Lord Cameron, presiding over his Commission on Disturbance in Northern Ireland, found his summons to attend refused by the same Right Hon. William Craig, PC, MP, a rejection only matched by four other Unionist dissidents, one of them, naturally, being his Reverence Dr Paisley.

Nobody was more vociferous than Lord Cameron in condemnation of the *Scotsman* in the same period, when it actually began to feature reports of rebel student discoveries and accusations. But the identical process which led him to condemn the Ulster Unionist establishment was leading the newspaper to question the Scottish establishment. In a sense, the wretched Bill Craig, by his outspoken abuse of the power he and his colleagues had engrossed, was telling the *Scotsman*, did he but know it, that it had to choose its own destiny. It could either be an establishment mouthpiece, or a newspaper: it could no longer be both. Mr Dinwoodie is correct in saying that reportage of Northern Ireland in Scotland is today handled with caution, and rightly so: in the present state of the situation, loud mouths take lives. But the impact of the 1969 crisis may have been a turning-point for the identity of Scottish journalism, with consequent effects in enabling the Labour party to become a Scottish élite in its turn and Scottish nationalism to progress from a sideshow to a proof of human existence.

Is the distinguished folk historian Billy Kay correct in hazarding that the erosion of Scottish sectarianism may be comparably related to the fate of Northern Ireland? It is a daring speculation and it has the danger – an almost lethal danger as more hardened commentators such as Sarah

Nelson would recognise – of optimism. Nobody has done more valuable work than Billy Kay in celebrating such ignored but vital aspects of Scottish life as the Donegal migrants, but he has the instinct, born of love of the infinite variations of song and speech, to believe a formula must exist. He tells us: 'The father of modern Irish nationalism, Daniel O'Connell, gave the stamp of approval to this limiting vision of Irish nationhood when he described Protestants as "foreign to us since they are of a different religion."' Paternity is not a matter of giving stamps: if the birth registrar is another name for the father, it might be so, but he gives no such examples.

Excisemen are another matter, as the poet Burns indicates. The repetition of stories about him in the works of Kay and Lunney are valuable reminders of his significance – even if they seem to give a new credibility to his title as the wonder of all the gay world – moving as his songs and poems did, into the vacuum created by the death of Irish as a folk language. If Dan O'Connell had been a stamp-giver, the stamp would have borne Queen Victoria's face, Protestant as she was. Arguably, his delight in her fecundity as a national symbol gave hints of incipient senility, but she certainly would have been a symbol with which to unite his own Catholic followers and the descendants of settlers from the English and Scottish monarchical traditions. What O'Connell meant was that his own making of an articulate political force of the mass of the Irish Catholic people, the first such mass movement in history, arose partly from their retention of integrity in clinging to a proscribed religion whose abandonment would have brought immediate material benefits to the apostate. The profiteers who flourished as a result of the Catholics' disability were literally regarded by their victims as alien dispossessors. O'Connell was not stamping approval but asserting a fact. You might as reasonably accuse Galileo of stamping the solar system with his approval: maybe the Inquisition did. But Billy Kay, naturally, would like to sanitise Irish history in retrospect and hence shares an inquisitor's desire to save the souls of his subjects. Is his wishful thinking, touchingly representative of how a lover of folk-culture instinctively yearns, liable to impair his judgement on the future? Possibly – probably, even – but possibly not. At all events, it is an area of comparative analysis which greatly merits exploration.

As C Vann Woodward said in the study that convinced his students' generation of the impermanence of segregation, *The Strange Career of Jim Crow*, the American South should look at South Africa with more understanding than censure because it had itself escaped from the apparently inescapable condition of the man on the cliff who cannot go up or down and would die where he was. Woodward may have been premature in seeing the South as off the cliff by the time of writing in 1955, but he proved a true prophet. Scotland could no more hope than the American South that Northern Ireland would directly follow its example: the stories are too dissimilar. The final nail in the coffin of Scottish sectarianism was driven in by the Papal visit of 1982, less by His Holiness himself – I speak as a Roman Catholic – than by the Protestants and agnostics, Jews and atheists and others who welcomed him. The Pope's visit to Ireland seemed more a reaffirmation of monoculturalism, while in Scotland he symbolised polyculturalism. This may be a starting point for some constructive reflection.

We must remember not only that we are part of a larger archipelago, but of a still larger continent, and of an even larger world. Canada, so remarkable a proof of the Ulster and Scottish imprints, takes much of its identity still from not being British, not being of the USA and – let's all be honest, shall we? – not being French. Ulster – Northern Ireland variety – takes much of its identity from not being Irish and not being English. So, rather more silently, does Scotland. But of course, in certain ways Ulster and Scotland are both Irish and English and we do some violence to history in making exceptions. As our editor Ian S Wood makes clear in his fine Studs Terkel-like evocation of the voices of Scottish soldiers in Northern Ireland, it is not always easy to distinguish such reactions from those of English soldiers, or Welsh, or Irish-from-the-Republic-via-Blighty-take-the-Saxon -shilling. Again, at the heart of Sarah Nelson's searing, shattering perceptions is her memory of Miriam Daly, victim of her own INLA intransigence and a Protestant murder squad, to whom it seemed the 'loyalist people . . . were incidental', and by the incidental Miriam died a dreadful death. But some 40 years ago I knew the then Miriam MacDonnell as a Dublin student. Hers had been something of an ideological Odyssey: at one time in moderately conservative Dublin politics, subsequently widowed at a young age before entering on what seemed a triumphant scholarly fulfilment, only to end so far from how I remember her – as a laughing red-haired girl, battling on the tennis court with zest and exchanging rapid-fire repartee with her fellows under a shady tree while I listened, in 12-year-old admiration. Those were no shadows cast before of her future battles and rapid fire – and that is the reminder of how the unreality of her death had its roots in its evolution from an abstract, Dublin, problem, even as Ian Wood's soldiers derive from London deployment and in some respects, London culture. Neither Ulster nor Scotland is the thing it seems to be, and we have to make long journeys to understand home. Thank God I never knew Miriam when she followed her dreams into the madness of republican warfare. Thank God I can find her in so moving an epitaph from a writer of such compassion and understanding as Sarah Nelson. In its way, that compassion, that understanding, however tragic and hateful the circumstances, is the finest of all connections between Scotland and Ulster.

Notes

Preface

1   J Buchan, *Mr Standfast* (London, 1919), p. 86
2   J McGee, *Northern Ireland: Crisis and Conflict* (London, 1974), p. 51
3   *The Young Unionist*, May 1987, no. 5
4   T Clyde (ed.), *Ancestral Voices: the Selected Prose of John Hewitt* (Belfast, 1987), p. 125

1 The Ulster-Scottish Connection

1   W C Mackenzie, *The Races of Ireland and Scotland* (Paisley, 1916)
2   G M Trevelyan, *A Shortened History of England* (Harmondsworth, 1974)
3   Peter C Woodman, 'The Mesolithic in Ireland', *British Archaeological Report* 58, 1978
4   Seán P O Ríordáin, *Antiquities of the Irish Countryside* (London, 1973)
5   T F O'Rahilly, *Early Irish History and Mythology* (Dublin, 1984)
6   Lloyd and Jennifer Laing, *Celtic Britain and Ireland* (Dublin, 1990)
7   Liam de Paor, 'Roots', *Irish Times*, 15 July 1975
8   J P Mallory, 'The Origins of the Irish', *The Journal of Irish Archaeology* II, 1984
9   Peter Woodman, 'Prehistoric Settlers', in Patrick Loughrey (ed.), *The People of Ireland* (Belfast, 1988)
10   O'Rahilly, *Early Irish History*
11   *Ibid.*
12   T Fowler, *Introduction to Vita S Columbae by Adamnani* edited from Dr Reeves' text, (Oxford, 1894)
13   Tomás Cardinal O Fiaich, 'The Beginnings of Christianity', in T W Moody & F X Martin (eds.), *The Course of Irish History* (Cork, 1984)
14   Ian Adamson, *Bangor – Light of the World* (Belfast, 1979)
15   Proinsias MacCana, 'Mongán Mac Fiachna and Immram Brain', in *Eriu*, vol. XXIII (Dublin, 1972)
16   Charles Thomas, *Britain and Ireland in Early Christian Times* (London, 1984)
17   G Chalmers, *Caledonia* (London, 1807)
18   John MacQueen, in 'Welsh and Gaelic in Galloway', *Transactions of the Dumfriesshire and Galloway Natural History and Antiquarian Society*, Third Series, vol. XXXII, 1955
19   Fowler, *Vita*
20   Liam de Paor, 'The People of Ireland', in Loughrey, *People*
21   Edmund Curtis, *A History of Ireland* (London, 1970)
22   Denis Kennedy, foreword to T M Healy, *The Great Fraud of Ulster* (Tralee, 1971)
23   Rev. George Hill, *An Historical Account of the Plantation in Ulster at the Commencement of the Seventeenth Century, 1608–1620* (Belfast, 1877)

24   P L Henry, *Ulster Dialects* (Belfast, 1964)
25   F J Bigger, 'From Uladh to Galloway and from Galloway to Uladh', *The Red Hand Magazine*, vol. 1, no. 3, November 1920
26   Trevelyan, *History of England*
27   Lord Macaulay, *The History of England from the Accession of James the Second* (London, 1913)
28   E Wright, in *The Ulster–American Connection* (Belfast, 1981)
29   W H A Williams, 'Irish Traditional Music in the United States', in *America and Ireland: 1776–1976* (Westport, Conn., 1980)
30   Robert McCrum, William Cran and Robert MacNeil, *The Story of English* (London, 1986)
31   Estyn Evans, *The Personality of Ireland* (Belfast, 1981)
32   Bob Quinn, *Atlantean* (London, 1986)

3 Sporting Symbols, Sporting Identities

1   J Sugden and A Bairner, 'Observe the Sons of Ulster: Football and Politics in Northern Ireland', in A Tomlinson and G Whannel (eds.) *Off the Ball* (London, 1986); J Sugden and A Bairner, 'Northern Ireland: Sport in a Divided Society', in L Allison (ed.), *The Politics of Sport*, (Manchester, 1986.) More recent analyses can be found in J Sugden and A Bairner, *Sport, Sectarianism and Society in a Divided Ireland* (Leicester, 1993); J Sugden and A Bairner, 'National Identity, Community Relations and the Sporting Life in Northern Ireland', in L Allison (ed.), *The Changing Politics of Sport* (Manchester, 1993)
2   The use of sectarian is too misleading: see G P T Finn, 'Racism, Religion and Social Prejudice: Irish Catholic Clubs, Soccer and Scottish Society – I, The Historical roots of Prejudice', *International Journal of the History of Sport*, 8, pp. 70–93, 1991a. Ethnic or ethno-political has been used to categorise the different communities in Northern Ireland. See for example E Cairns, 'Intergroup Conflict in Northern Ireland', in H Tajfel (ed.), *Social Identity and Intergroup Relations* (Cambridge, 1982). In this essay communities or groups will be more commonly used, but the divisions in Northern Ireland and Scotland can correctly be conceptualised in terms of ethnicity
3   See, for example, B Murray, *The Old Firm. Sectarianism, Sport and Society* (Edinburgh, 1984)
4   See M de Búrca, *The Gaelic Athletic Association. The Official Guide* (Dublin, 1980); M de Búrca, *Michael Cusack and the GAA* (Dublin, 1989); W F Mandle, *The Gaelic Athletic Association & Irish Nationalist Politics 1884–1924* (London, 1987). The Scottish connection is made clear in de Búrca, 1989. See also G Jarvie, *Highland Games. The Making of a Myth* (Edinburgh, 1991)
5   This point is well made by Mandle, *The GAA*
6   For the complex history of the GAA bans and the regional variations in their application, see Mandle, *The GAA*
7   *Ibid.*
8   *Scottish Football Association Handbook, 1882–3*; M Brodie, *100 Years of Irish Football* (Belfast, 1980); J Rafferty, *One Hundred Years of Scottish Football* (London, 1973)
9   Brodie, *Irish Football*
10   Brodie, *Irish Football*; E Corry, *Viva! Ireland Goes to Italy* (Dublin, 1990); Finn, *IJHS*

11   Brodie, *Irish Football*; Corry, *Viva!*, p. 11
12   M Tuohy, *Belfast Celtic* (Belfast, 1978); J Kennedy, *Belfast Celtic* (Belfast, 1989)
13   Corry, *Viva!*, p. 11; Tuohy, *Belfast Celtic*; Brodie, *Irish Football*; Kennedy, *Belfast Celtic*
14   *Ibid.*, and see Sugden and Bairner 'Observe the Sons', footnote 4
15   M Brodie, *Linfield, 100 Years* (Belfast, 1985)
16   *Ibid.*, p. 64; Kennedy, *Belfast Celtic*, p. 59
17   Brodie, *Linfield*; Kennedy, *Belfast Celtic*; Tuohy, *Belfast Celtic*
18   I Adamson, *The Identity of Ulster. The Land, the Language and the People* (Belfast, 1987); M Crozier (ed.), *Cultural Traditions in Northern Ireland* (Belfast, 1989)
19   Brodie, *Linfield*; G Walker, '"There's Not a Team Like the Glasgow Rangers": Football and Religious Identity in Scotland', in G Walker and T Gallagher (eds.), *Sermons and Battle-Hymns. Protestant Culture in Modern Scotland* (Edinburgh, 1990)
20   See Sugden and Bairner, 'Observe the Sons', on Glentoran fans affecting Catholic/Nationalist identities. This suggestion has been disputed by a number of Northern Irish fans. What is certainly correct is that some Linfield supporters can take support for any other team as a sign of less than whole-hearted commitment to Northern Ireland
21   See Sugden and Bairner; M Tichener, 'Taking Sides on the Bogside', *When Saturday Comes*, no. 10, Sept/Oct 1987
22   D Armstrong and H Saunders, *A Road Too Wide. The Price of Reconciliation in Northern Ireland* (Basingstoke, 1985)
23   Sugden and Bairner, 'National Identity', have noted that Cliftonville's record is much better than many other clubs and that more violence has taken place at matches between Linfield and Glentoran. Newspapers have also commented on this imbalance: see *Sunday Press*, 26 February, 1989
24   In 1989 Protestant schoolchildren did display Derry City scarves and I observed some supporters returning to predominantly Protestant residential areas after Derry's home matches. Sugden and Bairner also refer to City supporters' buses being the targets for missiles. My incomplete survey of newspaper reports in 1989 only came up with incidents outside Derry
25   Sugden and Bairner, 1993, provide a good summary. See also both *Irish News* and *Newsletter*, 19 February, 1990. Criticism of the policy of switching matches from Nationalist to Unionist areas was made by both newspapers
26   Sugden and Bairner, 'National Identity'; *Sunday Life*, 5 January, 1992; also *Blues Brothers* fanzine no. 8 for the response of some Linfield fans
27   Corry, *Viva!*; Brodie, *100 Years*; Sugden and Bairner, especially *National Identity*, provide a very good summary
28   Healey made this statement on a BBC 2 programme on Derry City and Rangers
29   See G P T Finn, *IJHS*; G P T Finn, 'Racism, Religion and Social Prejudice: Irish Catholic Clubs, Soccer and Scottish Society – II, Social Identities and Conspiracy Theories', *International Journal of the History of Sport*, 8, 370–397, 1991b and 'Racism, Religion and Social Prejudice etc. . . . . III, Rangers and the Conspiracy Tradition', *IJHS*, 1994a, in press

30   Adamson, *Identity of Ulster*; Crozier, *Cultural Traditions*; R Fitzpatrick, *God's Frontiersmen: the Scots–Irish Epic* (London, 1989). Ulster–Scot was also used as an ethnic label

31   *Irish Times*, 14 October, 1989. McGivern's survey of opinions and preferences is cited in Sugden & Bairner 'National Identity'

32   For various accounts of Scottish identity and Scottish football, see H F Moorhouse, '"We're Off to Wembley": the History of a Scottish Event and the Sociology of Football Hooliganism' in D McCrone & S Kendrick (eds.), *The Making of Scotland: Nation, Culture, Change* (Edinburgh, 1989); R Forsyth, *The Only Game. The Scots and World Football* (Edinburgh, 1990); A Macpherson, *Action Replays* (London, 1991); S Cosgrove, *Hampden Babylon. Sex and Scandal in Scottish Football* (Edinburgh, 1991); R Giulianotti, 'Scotland's Tartan Army in Italy: the Case for the Carnivalesque', *Sociological Review*, 39, 503–27 (1991); R Giulianotti, 'A Model of the Carnivalesque? Scottish Football Fans at the 1992 European Championship Finals in Sweden', *Working Papers in Popular Cultural Studies* no. 6 (Manchester, 1993); R Giulianotti, 'Scoring Away from Home: a Statistical Study of Scotland Football Fans at International Matches in Romania and Sweden', *International Review for the Sociology of Sport*, 4 (1994, in press)

33   A Tomlinson, 'Going Global: the FIFA Story', in A Tomlinson and G Whannel (eds.), *Off the Ball*, Pluto Press (London, 1986)

34   The English role was one that emphasised the dominance of that country. Even its defeats could be celebrated as acts of giant-killing by other, smaller, but still British nations. Mandle (1987) notes that when England lost to Australia at cricket, this was seen to demonstrate the power and value of the Empire. Defeat by another part of the *British* nation was even less threatening to an English/British sense of identity. For many years England lagged behind Scotland in soccer victories between the two countries. Defeats by truly 'foreign' nations, such as Hungary, caused concern: yet Scotland then still had a superior record over England

35   J Mitchell, *Conservatives and the Union. A Study of Conservative Party Attitudes to Scotland* (Edinburgh, 1990). Mitchell stresses the centrality of the Irish question to the development of Scottish Conservatism in the twentieth century, leading to Unionism and Protestantism becoming its dominant force until the last quarter of the century. Unionism also celebrated Scotland's union with England, which was seen to allow for a discrete Scottish identity within a beneficial union with its larger neighbour

36   Many more details of the following analysis can be found in the three parts of G P T Finn, 'Racism, Religion and Social Prejudice', *IJHS*; G P T Finn, 'Faith, Hope and Bigotry: Case-Studies in Anti-Catholic Prejudice in Scottish Soccer and Society', in G Jarvie and G Walker (eds.), *Ninety Minute Patriots? Scottish Sport in the Making of a Nation* (Leicester, 1993)

37   S Bruce, *No Pope of Rome. Militant Protestantism in Modern Scotland* (Edinburgh, 1985), p. 36. For further details on Hope and the 3rd Edinburgh Rifle Volunteers, see Finn 'Faith, Hope and Bigotry'

38   When the Tailteann Games did eventually occur in 1924, the first event featured a shinty match between Ireland and Scotland, won by the Scots

39   *Hibs Monthly*, 1992, no. 48; also see a letter in the *Edinburgh Evening News*, 22 February, 1992

40   BBC TV Scotland, 'One Afternoon in Lisbon', 25 May 1992. Match commentator Kenneth Wolstenholme also refers to 'a kilted gentleman' celebrating on the pitch after Celtic's second goal

41   R Boyle, '"We Are Celtic Supporters . . ." Celtic F C, Celtic Supporters and Questions of Identity in Modern Scotland'. Paper presented to the International Conference, Soccer, Culture and Identity, Aberdeen, 1992

42   D Bell, *Acts of Union. Youth Culture and Sectarianism in Northern Ireland* (London, 1990)

43   See G P T Finn, review of A Tomlinson and G Whannel, *Off the Ball*, in *The International Journal of Sports History*, 4, 253–258 (1987). Also see Finn, 1991a. Walker, *Glasgow Rangers*, argues convincingly that not all Rangers supporters are Unionists or Conservatives. However, this chapter does not dispute his account of the part played by Rangers officials

44   For a fuller analysis of Rangers, see Finn, 1991a; 1991b; 1994a, 1994b, both in press; also G P T Finn, 'In the Grip? A Psychological and Historical Exploration of the Social Significance of Freemasonry in Scotland' in G Walker and T Gallagher (eds.), *Sermons*

45   See C F Graumann and S Moscovici (eds.), *Changing Conceptions of Conspiracy* (New York, 1987) for analyses of conspiracy ideologies

46   Walker, *Glasgow Rangers*

47   See Bruce, *No Pope*; T Gallagher, *Glasgow: the Uneasy Peace. Religious Tension in Modern Scotland, 1819–1914* (Manchester, 1987); C Holmes, 'Alexander Ratcliffe: Militant Protestant and Antisemite', in T Kushner and K Lunn (eds.), *Traditions of Intolerance. Historical Perspectives on Fascism and Race Discourse in Britain* (Manchester, 1989)

48   See both Vanguard and Govan Press in late 1933 and especially in early 1934. On the dispute in Northern Ireland, see G Walker, '"Protestantism before Party!" The Ulster Protestant League in the 1930s', *Historical Journal*, 28, 961–967 (1985)

49   The dispute about the flag is well summarised in B Wilson, *Celtic, a Century with Honour* (London, 1988)

50   *Vanguard*, 1 October, 1933

51   See Finn, 'Faith, Hope and Bigotry'

52   G Souness with K Gallacher, *Graeme Souness. A Manager's Diary* (Edinburgh, 1989)

53   See A McCoist with C Brankin, *Ally McCoist. My Story* (Edinburgh, 1992), chapter 13; A Macpherson, *Action Replay*; Souness, *Manager's Diary*, gives a very different account, which is totally contradicted by McCoist. Souness claims, unsurprisingly, that Rangers made no move until early July, after Celtic finally withdrew from the deal. It is also worth noting that in a recent club video, Butcher, then the Rangers captain, admits that Johnston's arrival was not well received by some of the club's Scottish players or by some others employed by the club

54   See *Newsletter* (Belfast) in July and August 1989 for local reactions and interview with McMurdo

55   S Cosgrove, *Hampden Babylon*

56   Walker, *Glasgow Rangers*

57   See H F Moorhouse, 'On the Periphery: Scotland, Scottish Football and the New Europe', in J Williams and S Wagg (eds.), *British Football and Social Change. Getting into Europe* (Leicester, 1991). Moorhouse presents some useful background as to why Rangers had to change the club's anti-Catholic image abroad, though he neglects the dialectical opposition between tradition and modernisation. However, so far, despite rumours of the religious persuasions among the playing staff at Ibrox and Moorhouse's assertion, no other known Catholic has been signed by Rangers

58   *The Herald*, 27 March 1992 and 2 April 1992. Murray explained that his involvement was because of his business interests; the best known is Rangers

59   Moorhouse, 'On the Periphery'

60   *Scotland on Sunday*, 27 September 1992 and 4 October 1992

61   *Ibid.*

62   G Souness, *No Half Measures* (London, 1987) and Macpherson, *Action Replays*

63   P Davies, *All Played Out, the Full Story of Italia '90* (London, 1991)

4 Ulster Attitudes to Scottishness

1   Angélique Day and Patrick McWilliams (eds.), *Ordnance Survey Memoirs of Ireland*, vol. 2, Parishes of Co. Antrim (1) (Belfast, 1990), p. 63

2   John A Oliver, 'Some Ulster Scots and their origins in Scotland', in *Familia*, 2:3 (1987), p. 104

3   Samuel Ferguson, 'Attractions of Ireland. No. 3. Society', *Dublin University Magazine*, 8: xlviii (December, 1836), p. 663

4   John Gamble, *Sketches of History, Politics and Manners in Dublin and the North of Ireland in 1810* (London, 1826), p. 168

5   Whitehead Extramural Study Group (eds.), *Ordnance Survey Memoir for the parish of Templecorran*, p. 47

6   Samuel Davidson, *Autobiography*, 1899, no page ref, quoted in Eull Dunlop, 'Back to "Bonnie Kellswater" (2)', *Familia* 2:6 (1990), p. 91

7   L E Cochran, *Scottish Trade with Ireland in the Eighteenth Century* (Edinburgh, 1985), p. 146

8   Cochran, *Scottish Trade*, p. 16

9   R N Smart, 'The provinces of the Scottish universities', in G W S Barrow (ed.) *The Scottish Tradition* (Edinburgh and London, 1974), pp. 102–103

10   L M Cullen, 'Scotland and Ireland 1600–1800: their role in the evolution of British Society' in Robert A Houston and Ian D Whyte (eds.), *Scottish Society 1500–1800* (Cambridge, 1989), p. 230

11   Henry Joy McCracken, 'The social thistle and shamrock' in R R Madden, *Literary Remains of the United Irishmen of 1798 and Selections from other popular lyrics of their Times* (Dublin, 1887), p. 167

12   Anon, 'Friendship, or Wallace's last wish', in Madden, *Literary Remains*

13   Sir John Forbes, *Memorandums of a Tour in Ireland* (London, 1853)

14   Ferguson, 'Dublin University Magazine', 8: xlviii (December, 1836), 663

15   *Ibid.*

16   J Gamble, *Sketches of History*, p. 168

17   Gamble, *A View of Society and Manners in the North of Ireland in the Summer and Autumn of 1812* (London, 1813), p. 80

18   John Fullarton, 'Life of Thomas Beggs', *Ulster Magazine*, June 1861, p. 243

19   Edward L Sloan, *The Bard's Offering: A Collection of Miscellaneous Poems* (Belfast, 1854), p. i

20   George Hill, 'Notes and Queries', *Ulster Journal of Archaeology*, 2nd series, 1:2 January 1895, p. 149

21   T House [?], letter of 3 March 1791, in Trinity College Dublin MS 7257, p. 72

22   *Northern Star*, 21 April 1792

23   Samuel Thomson, 1794?, TCD MS 7257, p. 150

24   Thomson, TCD MS 7257, p. 151
25   John Rabb, letter of 14 March 1794, TCD MS 7257, p. 174
26   Luke Mullan, letter of 15 May 1797, TCD MS 7257, p. 11
27   Mullan, letter of 4 February 1797, TCD MS 7257, p. 5
28   Mullan, letter of 15 April 1797, TCD MS 7257, p. 14
29   John Salmon, 'Notes and Queries', *Ulster Journal of Archaeology*, 2nd series, 1:1, September 1894, p. 77
30   Mullan, letter of 29 September 1796, TCD MS 7257, p. 3
31   Fullarton, *O'More: A Tale of War and Other Poems* (Belfast, 1867), p. iv
32   J Getty, letter of 27 May 1811, TCD MS 7257, p. 101
33   Abraham Hume, 'The Irish dialect of the English Language', *Ulster Journal of Archaeology*, 1st series, 6, 1858, p. 50
34   Benedict Kiely, 'Dialect and literature' in Diarmaid O Muirithe (ed.), *The English Language in Ireland*, (Dublin and Cork, 1977), p. 90
35   David Herbison, *The Snow Wreath* (Belfast, 1869), preface
36   'Civilis', *Belfast News Letter*, 8 June 1792
37   John Graham in W S Mason (ed), *A Statistical Account or Parochial Survey of Ireland Drawn up by W S Mason from the Communications of the Clergy*, I (1814), p. 592
38   Hume, *UJA*, 1st series, 6, 1858, p. 51
39   *Belfast News Letter*, 20 March 1787 and 15 July 1796
40   *Belfast Mercury*, 19 March 1784
41   *Manson's Pronouncing Dictionary and English Expositor . . . corrected by a teacher*, 9th edition (Belfast, 1816), advertisement to the present edition
42   David Patterson, *The Provincialisms of Belfast and the Surrounding Districts Pointed out and Corrected* (Belfast, 1860), p. 5
43   *Belfast News Letter*, 8 September 1797
44   Henry R Montgomery, *An Essay Towards Investigating the Causes which have Retarded the Progress of Literature in Ireland and the most Efficient Means of Promoting its Advancement. Read before Belfast Rhetorical Society by a Member*, 25 November 1840
45   Thomas Beggs, *The Second Part of the Minstrel's Offering* (Belfast, 1836), preface
46   Robert Huddleston, *A Collection of Poems and Songs on Rural Subjects* (Belfast, 1844), p. ix
47   Hugh Porter, *Poetical Attempts by Hugh Porter, A County of Down Weaver* (Belfast, 1813), p. xi

The author wishes to thank the board of Trinity College, Dublin, for permission to quote from MS 7257.

I also want to thank colleagues and friends, especially Dr James Lunney, Professor Gordon Herries Davies, Dr C J Woods, Brendan Dixon and Dr Brian Walker for help with ideas, proofreading, computers and sources. Thanks are also due to very many librarians, in Trinity College, Dublin, Queen's University, Belfast, and the Royal Irish Academy, Dublin.

5 'A Mere Irish Faction'

1   I M Bishop, 'The Education of Ulster Students at Glasgow University during the Nineteenth Century', MA thesis, The Queen's University of Belfast, 1987

2   Address from the Four Belfast Societies of United Irishmen to the Scottish Friends of the People, in *Belfast Politics* (Belfast, 1794), pp. 100–104

3   See T B and T J Howell, *A Complete Collection of State Trials*, vol. xxiii, col. 224

4   *Drennan Letters*, nos 652 and 668, March–July 1797, T.765, Public Records Office, Northern Ireland

5   R M Sibbet, *Orangeism in Ireland and Throughout the Empire*, 2nd ed. (London, 1939); H Senior, *Orangeism in Ireland and Britain 1795–1835* (London, 1966). For interesting primary source background on secret societies, see D W Millar, *Peep O'Day Boys and Defenders* (Belfast, 1991)

6   For a full discussion of the theoretical debates surrounding Orangeism, see E W McFarland, *Protestants First!: Orangeism in Nineteenth Century Scotland* (Edinburgh, 1990), pp. 17–29

7   In recognition of its position as the birthplace of Orangeism in Scotland, a new lodge, L.O.L. no. 0 'Mother Maybole' was instituted in 1929: *Ayrshire Post*, 1 November 1929. J R Cloughley, an official Orange historian, supports the role of the Ayrshire Militia, *Belfast Weekly News*, 23 November 1929. A similar 'military lodge' was formed by the Argyll Fencibles, which Sibbet wrongly suggests was the original Scottish lodge, Sibbet, *Orangeism*, vol. 1, pp. 400–401

8   See Senior, *Orangeism*, for English developments

9   N Murray, *The Scottish Handloom Weavers 1796–1850* (Edinburgh, 1978), p. 212; see also G Walker's valuable piece, 'The Protestant Irish in Scotland', in T Devine (ed.), *Irish Immigrants in Scottish Society in the Nineteenth and Twentieth Centuries* (Edinburgh, 1991), pp. 44–66

10   P Gibbon, *The Origins of Ulster Unionism* (Manchester, 1976), pp. 13–14

11   Walker, 'Protestant Irish'

12   Research is currently under way into the fate of refugee Ulster radicals in Scotland following the '98. There is the intriguing possibility the former United Irishmen may have found their way into the early Orange lodges as shelter or atonement for their political past. See McFarland, *Planting the Green Bough: Irish and Scottish Radicals 1791–1820* (forthcoming)

13   *Irish Poor Report* (1836), 40 xxxiv 427, p. 148

14   *Irish Poor Report* (1836), p. 105, evidence of Archbishop Dr Scott. The first Glasgow lodge was formed in 1813: *Belfast Weekly News*, 23 November 1929

15   There were outbreaks in Glasgow, Newton Stewart, Dumfries and Dalkeith: *Glasgow Courier*, 13 July 1823; *Dumfries Weekly Journal*, 14 July 1826; *Glasgow Herald*, 17 July 1829; Sibbet, op. cit., vol. 1, p. 703. These were usually connected with 12th of July celebrations

16   McFarland, *Protestants*, pp. 47–54; for an example of indigenous No Popery, see E Black, 'The Tumultuous Petitioners. The Protestant Association in Scotland', in *Review of Politics*, 25, (1963), 183–211

17   See T Dickson (ed.), *Scottish Capitalism* (London, 1980), pp. 138–141. Freemasons' lodges of the period faced similar problems: see E Jamieson, *Beith Royal Arch Chapter 1814–1909* (nd)

18   See *Glasgow Herald*, 13 July 1822 and 15 July 1831 for examples of the Scottish authorities' hostile attitude to Orange activities, which were identified with unwelcome public disturbances in general

19   *Report from the Select Committee Appointed to Enquire into the Origin, Nature, Extent and Tendency of Orange Lodges in Great Britain and the Colonies,* House of Commons 1836 [605]; for its findings, see McFarland, *Protestants,* pp. 55–61
20   J McConechy, 'Draft of a Memoir of William Motherwell' (nd), Robertson Mss., University of Glasgow Special Collections
21   *Glasgow Herald,* 17 July 1847, for a typical Ayrshire outbreak
22   A B Campbell, *The Lanarkshire Miners* (Edinburgh, 1979), Appendix 3 for 'Orange and Green Incidents'
23   Walker, *Protestant Irish,* pp. 52–53
24   *Glasgow Courier,* 19 July 1859
25   *Lord Advocates' Papers,* AD 58/70, 'Disturbances between Roman Catholics and Orangemen in Ayrshire', Scottish Records Office
26   *Glasgow Courier,* 17 July 1849
27   *Glasgow News,* 13 July 1875; 13 July 1878
28   W H Marwick, *A Short History of Labour in Scotland* (London, 1967), pp. 60–61
29   J E Handley, *The Irish in Modern Scotland* (Cork, 1947), pp. 93–121. McFarland, *Protestants* pp. 96–101
30   *Glasgow News,* 13 July 1875
31   B Collins, 'The Origins of Irish Immigration to Scotland in the Nineteenth and Twentieth Centuries' in Devine, *Irish Immigrants,* p. 11
32   *Belfast Weekly News,* 23 November 1929
33   I G C T Hutchison, 'Glasgow Working Class Politics' in R A Cage (ed.), *The Working Classes in Glasgow* (London, 1987), p. 129. Note also Walker's judicious reconstruction, using Poor Law records for certain Glasgow parishes, 'Protestant Irish', pp. 54–58
34   McFarland, *Protestants,* p. 105
35   *Greenock Telegraph,* 12 July 1869; for current Scottish participation in the Ulster Twelfth, see *Belfast Telegraph,* 13 July 1992
36   McFarland, *Protestants,* pp. 78–95
37   *Ibid.,* pp. 143–147
38   Sibbet, *Orangeism,* vol. 2, p. 349
39   H Senior, *Orangeism: the Canadian Phase,* pp. 91–92 (Toronto, ND)
40   Sibbet, *Orangeism*
41   A M McDonough, 'Irish Immigrants and Labour Movements in Coatbridge and Airdrie 1881–1931,' BA Dissertation, University of Strathclyde, 1976
42   Handley, *The Irish,* pp. 287–288
43   *Glasgow Observer,* 16 July 1884
44   *Glasgow News,* 10 July 1874
45   *A Report of the Protestant and Orange Soiree held in Paisley on 5 November* (Paisley, 1856)
46   *Ibid.*
47   *Ibid.*
48   *Greenock Telegraph,* 6 November 1870
49   *Glasgow News,* 13 July 1879
50   *Glasgow News,* 8 August 1879
51   See regular freemasonry column in *Glasgow News* 1873–85
52   J Wyllie, *A History of Mother Lodge Kilwinning,* (Glasgow, 1879)
53   See McFarland, *Protestants ,* Chapter 7 for full discussion
54   M W Dewar, J Brown and S E Long, *Orangeism: A New Historical Appreciation* (Belfast, 1967)

55   Gault was the author of *Popery, the Man of Sin and the Son of Perdition* (Glasgow, 1853). For an account of Thompson, see *The Bailie*, vol. xxiii, no. 576 (1883). He attempted to disrupt a municipal banquet in Glasgow in protest at the presence of the Roman Catholic Archbishop Dr Eyre: *Glasgow News*, 6 October 1883

56   McConechy, *William Motherwell* (nd)

57   R F Foster, *Modern Ireland 1600–1972* (Harmondsworth, 1988), p. 387–389

58   B Thatcher, 'The Episcopal Church in Helensburgh in the Mid-Nineteenth Century', in J Butt and J T Ward (eds.), *Scottish Themes: Essays in Honour of S G E Lythe* (Edinburgh, 1976), pp. 98–123

59   J Bullock and A L Drummond, *The Church in Victorian Scotland 1843–74* (Edinburgh, 1975), p. 62

60   Thatcher, *Episcopal Church* , p. 112

61   Diary, 3 September 1848, D.O.D. 880/1, Public Records Office of Northern Ireland

62   *Glasgow News*, 12 September 1881

63   The foundation of a new 'Orange' Church at Greenock in 1876 was justi-fied as follows: 'Large numbers of our brethren who come from the Sister Isle attach themselves to no congregation at all, and we wish to get hold of them.' *Greenock Telegraph*, 21 January 1876

64   See McFarland, *Protestants*, Chapters 9 and 10

65   *Glasgow News*, 1 October 1884

66   J C Beckett, *The Making of Modern Ireland* (London, 1962), pp. 398–399

67   By 1885 Parnell and the leaders of the Irish Parliamentary Party had become disillusioned with their traditional allies, the Liberals, and were prepared to direct their support tactically behind the Tories in return for concessions on Home Rule. See F S L Lyons, *The Irish Parliamentary Party* (London, 1951)

68   Quintin Johnstone to Parker Smith, 8 February 1890, Smith of Jordan-hill Papers, Strathclyde Regional Archives. An anecdote was later circulating in Partick that an illiterate Orangeman had mistaken a polling booth with curtain, for photographic studio: *Partick Star*, 27 July 1895

69   *Glasgow News*, 6 November 1885

70   C Levy, 'Conservatism and Liberal Unionism in Glasgow, 1874–1912', Ph.D. thesis, University of Dundee 1983

71   T Gallagher, *Glasgow: the Uneasy Peace* (Manchester, 1987), pp. 346– 354

72   *Glasgow Herald*, 11 July 1898

73   Note the campaign of Depute Grand Master James McManus in the Glasgow municipal elections of 1896 was fought along these familiar lines: *Glasgow Herald*, 14 October 1896; 3 November 1896; 4 November 1896

74   Collins, *Irish Immigration*, p. 15

75   G Walker, 'The Orange Order in Scotland between the Wars', *International Journal of Social History*, vol. xxxvii, no. 2 (1992)

76   *Glasgow Herald*, 25 March 1929, quoted in Walker, *ibid.*, showed the migration flow already slowing to a trickle

77   See S Bruce, 'The Ulster Connection', in G Walker and T Gallagher (eds.) *Sermons and Battle Hymns: Protestant Popular Culture in Scotland*, (Edinburgh, 1990), pp. 240–249

78   *Ibid.*, p. 201–202

79   Walker, *Orange Order* (1992)

7 Empire, Religion and Nationality

1   The memo was produced by the Committee of the Scottish Unionist Association and was dated 15 May 1914. Bonar Law Papers, House of Lords Record Office, 32/3/30
2   K Robbins, *Nineteenth Century Britain* (Oxford, 1988), pp. 177–178
3   J H Grainger, *Patriotism* (London, 1986), p. 51
4   Quite the contrary in relation especially to the heavy industry in and around Glasgow
5   See A C I Naylor, 'Scottish Attitudes to Ireland 1880–1914', (Ph.D. thesis, University of Edinburgh, 1985), pp. 433–5, regarding the Scots' sense of superiority about their own institutions, also R Mitchison, 'Nineteenth Century Scottish Nationalism: the Cultural Background', in R Mitchison (ed.), *The Roots of Nationalism* (Edinburgh, 1980), re the Scots' delight in teaching the English about such matters as banking and the management of education
6   Naylor, *Scottish Attitudes*, p. 435
7   Quoted in I McLeod, 'Scotland and the Liberal Party 1880–1900. Church, Ireland and Empire. A Family Affair', (MLitt thesis, University of Glasgow, 1978), p. 144
8   For 'Home Rule All Round', see J Kendle, *Ireland and the Federal Solution* (Kingston and Montreal, 1989); there is much material on Scottish Home Rule and Imperial Federation ideas in the papers of Alexander McCallum Scott, Glasgow University Special Collections
9   Quoted in J Adam Smith, *John Buchan* (Oxford, 1985), p. 112
10   *Ibid.*, p. 318
11   See W McGregor Ross, *Kenya From Within* (London, 1927) pp. 95, 454–9
12   For a very different view of the Scots' role in the Empire, see R Miles and L Muirhead, 'Racism in Scotland', *Scottish Government Yearbook* 1986, pp. 108–131. In this article, it is argued that both Scots and English were irredeemably racist and exploitative in regard to Empire
13   See D W Bebbington, 'Religion and National Feeling in Nineteenth Century Wales and Scotland', in S Mews (ed.), *Religion and National Identity: Studies in Church History, Vol 18* (Oxford, 1982), pp. 489–503
14   B Aspinall, 'The Scottish Religious Identity in the Atlantic World 1880–1914' in Mews, *Religion*, pp. 505–18
15   Robbins, *Nineteenth Century Britain*, p. 178
16   See remarks of John Morley on the Scots and imperialism, quoted in L T Hobhouse, *Democracy and Reaction* (Brighton, 1972), p. 65
17   P Gibbon, *The Origins of Ulster Unionism* (Manchester, 1975); D Miller, *Queen's Rebels* (Dublin, 1978); J Loughlin, *Gladstone, Home Rule and the Ulster Question* (Dublin, 1986); A Jackson, *The Ulster Party* (Oxford, 1989)
18   Jackson, *Ulster Party*, pp. 16–17
19   D G Boyce, *Nineteenth Century Ireland* (Dublin, 1990), p. 207
20   Boyce, 'The Marginal Britons: the Irish', in R Colls and P Dodd (eds.), *Englishness: Politics and Culture, 1880–1920* (London, 1986), pp. 230–53
21   See V Bogdanor, *Devolution* (Oxford, 1979), p. 80
22   It should not be thought that pride in being Irish, as opposed to Irish nationalism, was disavowed by Unionists. Many Unionists rhapsodised about Ireland and her beauties. See, for example, speeches delivered at a Glasgow–Ulster Association meeting of Ulster immigrants in Scotland as reported in *Belfast Weekly News*, 25 January 1912

23   *The Covenanter*, 1, 20 May 1914
24   See Grainger, *Patriotisns*, pp. 252–4
25   See Loughlin, *Gladstone*, p. 156
26   See Kendle, *Ireland, passim*
27   Kendle, *Ireland*, pp. 190–1, 196, 208, 238. Carson did react favourably however, to a federal scheme put forward by the Round Table movement in 1914, which excluded the Six Counties from an Irish settlement, and he was impressed by F S Oliver's federal plan in Oliver's *Ulster and a Federal Settlement* (1918)
28   See J Anderson, 'Ideological Variations in Ulster during Ireland's First Home Rule Crisis', in C H Williams and E Kofman (eds.), *Community Conflict, Partition and Nationalism* (London, 1989), pp. 133–166
29   For whom, see R B McMinn, *Against the Tide: J B Armour, Irish Presbyterian Minister and Home Ruler* (Belfast, 1985)
30   Quoted in H Kearney, *The British Isles* (Cambridge, 1989), p. 186
31   See E McFarland, *Protestants First!: Orangeism in Nineteenth Century Scotland* (Edinburgh, 1991)
32   See G Walker, 'The Protestant Irish in Scotland' in T M Devine (ed.), *Irish Immigrants and Scottish Society in the Nineteenth and Twentieth Centuries* (Edinburgh, 1991), pp. 44–66
33   McFarland, *Protestants*, Chapters 9 and 10
34   *Belfast Weekly News*, 18 January 1912, 'Scottish Orange Notes'column
35   *Ibid.* 'Ulster Orangeman' column
36   *Ibid.*, 4 January 1912, 'Ulster Orangeman' column
37   *Ibid.*, 11 January 1912, quoted in 'Scottish Orange Notes'
38   See P Buckland, *Irish Unionism 2: Ulster Unionism* (Dublin, 1973), p. 74, for details of the propaganda efforts of the Unionist Association of Ireland (UAI) in Scotland and England
39   *Belfast Weekly News*, 18 January 1912
40   *Ibid.*
41   Postcard in collection housed by the Ulster Museum, Belfast
42   See H A L Fisher, *James Bryce* (London, 1927) vol. 1, pp. 218–9. My thanks to Professor Paul Bew for this reference
43   *The Witness*, 5 January 1912
44   *Ibid.*, 12 January 1912
45   McMinn, *Against the Tide*
46   *The Witness*, 2 February 1912
47   *Ibid.*
48   *The Witness*, 2 February 1912
49   *Glasgow Herald*, 2 February 1912
50   See full report of Convention in *Belfast Weekly News*, 8 February 1912. I have summarised the resolutions in my own words; the reference to Scotland in number four is as in the original. Quotes from speeches used hereafter are taken from this report
51   See speech by Sir William Crawford
52   See speech by Frank Workman. For a discussion of *Ne Temere*, see D H Akenson, *Small Differences: Irish Catholics and Irish Protestants 1815–1922* (Montreal and Kingston, 1988), pp. 113–4
53   See speech by Rev J C Johnston
54   See speeches by Rev J Gailey and T G Houston
55   For an extended Unionist phillipic against the AOH, see A W

Samuels, KC, *Home Rule: What is it?* (Dublin and London, 1911), pp. 100–9. On page 107 it is claimed that the AOH was spreading rapidly in Scotland

56   See R F G Holmes, 'Ulster Presbyterians and Irish Nationalism', in Mews, *Religion*, pp. 535–48; also Finlay Holmes, *Our Irish Presbyterian Heritage* (Belfast, 1985) p. 134
57   *Glasgow Herald*, 1 February 1912
58   *Ibid.*
59   *Ibid.*, 12 February 1912
60   *Ibid.*, 29 February 1912
61   *Ibid.*, 21 October 1912
62   C Harvie, 'The Covenanting Tradition', in G Walker and T Gallagher (eds.), *Sermons and Battle Hymns: Protestant Popular Culture in Modern Scotland* (Edinburgh, 1990), pp. 88–23
63   *Belfast Weekly News*, 8 February 1912
64   *Ibid.*, 16 January 1913
65   *Ibid.*, 13 February 1913, 'Ulster Orangeman' column
66   *Ibid.*, 6 February 1913
67   Quoted in Holmes, *Ulster Presbyterians*, p. 548
68   J J Lee, *Ireland 1912–1985* (Cambridge, 1990) chapter 1
69   Letter reproduced in T G Houston, *Ulster's Appeal* (Belfast, 1913)
70   See, for example, Griffith's comments in his preface to John Mitchel's *Jail Journal* (London, 1983). Griffith also expressed anti-Semitic sentiments: see T Garvin, *Nationalist Revolutionaries in Ireland 1858–1928* (Oxford, 1987), p. 122
71   See comments of T W Moody, quoted in Holmes, *Ulster Presbyterians*, p. 535
72   See the writings of Pearse in P H Pearse, *The Murder Machine and other Essays* (Cork, 1976), especially 'Ghosts'

8 An Ulster Labourist

1   G Bell, *The Protestants of Ulster* (London, 1976), p. 149
2   D R O'Connor Lysaght, *The Making of Northern Ireland (and the Basis of its Undoing)* (Dublin, 1970), p. 20
3   C Desmond Greaves, *The Life and Times of James Connolly* (London, 1961), p. 210
4   B Ransome, *Connolly's Marxism* (London, 1980), p. 33
5   'William Walker' in J W Boyle (ed.) *Leaders and Workers* (Cork, nd)
6   H Patterson, *Class Conflict and Sectarianism* (Belfast, 1980), p. 56
7   Bob Purdie, 'Red Hand or Red Flag? Loyalism and Workers in Belfast', *Saothar* 8, (Journal of the Irish Labour History Society) 1982, p. 68
8   Austen Morgan, *Labour and Partition* (London, 1991), p. 90
9   Quoted in Patrick Buckland, *Irish Unionism 1885–1923. A Documentary History* (Belfast, 1973), p. 203. The 'McDonnell incident' referred to the Under-Secretary for Ireland, Sir Antony McDonnell (a Catholic) who supported a scheme of administrative devolution. See P Buckland, *Ulster Unionism and the Origins of Northern Ireland* (Dublin, 1973), pp. 43–44
10   Quoted in Greaves, *James Connolly*, p. 39
11   *Leith Observer* 14 August 1909

12 Quoted in I G C Hutchison, *A Political History of Scotland* (Edinburgh, 1986)
13 *Forward* 16 October 1909
14 *Leith Observer ibid.* At an open air meeting when he said that it might be a 'disadvantage to be an Irishman' his fears proved groundless, a voice from the back of the crowd shouting, 'Ye're nane the waur o' that.' ('You're none the worse for that.') *Ibid.*, 21 August
15 *Ibid.*
16 *Ibid,.* 1 January 1910
17 *Ibid.*, 15 January 1910
18 *Edinburgh Evening News* 12 August 1909
19 Reproduced in Ian MacDougal (ed.), *Labour in Scotland – a Pictorial History* (Edinburgh, 1985), p. 156. (The Chinese figures referred to a dispute about indentured Chinese labour in South Africa)
20 *Leith Observer* 14 August 1909
21 *Ibid.*, 21 August 1909
22 *Ibid.*, 25 December 1909
23 *Ibid.*, 20 November 1909
24 *Ibid., Forward* 27 May 1911. In 1900, Ferguson had survived the withdrawal of the Irish vote
25 *Leith Observer* 4 September 1909
26 *Ibid.*, 15 January 1910
27 For accounts of these events, see John Gray, *City in Revolt* (Belfast, 1985); Emmet Larkin, *James Larkin* (London, 1965), pp. 21–35 and Morgan, *Labour and Partition*, pp. 91–117
28 *Leith Observer* 22 January 1910
29 The result was: R C Munro Ferguson, 7,146 (49.6%); Sir R Cranston, 4,540 (31.5%); W Walker, 2,724 (18.9%). The 1906 result had been: R C Munro Ferguson, 7,677; F T Cooper (Liberal Unionist), 4,865 (38.85). In December 1910 Labour did not contest the seat and Ferguson's vote increased by 7.6% on a much lower turnout. In January 1914 Labour got 24.5% and, apart from 1918, this grew steadily until victory in 1945; Walker helped lay a solid foundation in the constituency
30 *Northern Whig* 28 August 1906
31 William Walker, *The Irish Question* (North Belfast ILP, 1908), p. 14
32 *Ibid.*, p. 17
33 See John Holford, *Reshaping Labour: Organisation Work and Politics – Edinburgh in the Great War and After* (London, 1988) p. 149
34 *Report of the Sixth Annual Conference of the Labour Representation Committee* (London, 1906), p. 51
35 *Ibid.*
36 Dr John MacCormick, *Flag in the Wind* (London, 1955), p. 15
37 Sidney and Beatrice Webb, *Industrial Democracy* (London, 1898), pp. 87–88
38 J Dunsmore Clarkson, *Labour and Nationalism in Ireland* (New York, 1925), p. 214
39 See Dermot Keogh, *The Rise of the Irish Working Class* (Belfast, 1982), p. 102–3
40 M Keating and D Bleiman, *Labour and Scottish Nationalism* (London, 1979), pp. 21–58
41 Quoted in David Lowe, *Souvenirs of Scottish Labour* (Glasgow, 1919), p. 117

10 Thin Red Line

1   P Bishop & E Mallie, *The Provisional IRA* (London, 1987), pp. 177–178; also K Kelley, *The Longest War*
2   C De Baróid, *Ballymurphy and the Irish War* (Dublin, 1989), pp. 64–67
3   Former lieutenant, Royal Scots
4   *The Thistle*, 1970
5   *Ibid.*
6   C C O'Brien, *States of Ireland*, (London, 1972), p. 232
7   Former senior officer, King's Own Scottish Borderers, conversation with author
8   Former private, Queen's Own Highlanders
9   Former private, Royal Scots
10 *Guardian*, 13 March 1978
11 Former private, Royal Scots
12 Former private, Parachute Regiment
13 *Queen's Own Highlander*, 1974
14 *Thin Red Line*, 1974
15 Former corporal, Argyll & Sutherland Highlanders
16 Sergeant, Parachute Regiment
17 Conversations with author
18 Corporal in Parachute Regiment, quoted in M Arthur, *Northern Ireland: Soldiers Talking* (London, 1988), p. 63
19 Former sergeant, Queen's Own Highlanders
20 *Ibid.*
21 Former captain, Royal Artillery
22 Former sergeant, Scots Guards
23 *Ibid.*
24 *Ibid.*
25 *Ibid.*
26 *Borderers' Chronicle*, 1970, vol. 35, no. 3
27 *Rose and Thistle*, 28 November 1972
28 *Red Hackle*, 1974
29 *Scotland on Sunday*, 6 September 1992
30 Former private, Queen's Own Highlanders
31 Former sergeant, Queen's Own Highlanders
32 *Ibid.*
33 Former private, Royal Scots
34 Former Royal Marine Commando
35 *Ibid.*
36 *Observer*, 24 September 1989
37 Former Royal Marine Commando
38 *Ibid.*
39 M Asher, *Shoot to Kill: a Soldier's Journey Through Violence* (London, 1990), pp. 119–20
40 Former private, Parachute Regiment
41 *Ibid.*
42 *Guardian*, 15 May 1992
43 Former private, Parachute Regiment
44 *Guardian*, 19 May 1992
45 Private, Parachute Regiment

46   M Dillon & D Lehane, *Political Murder in Northern Ireland* (London, 1973), p. 139
47   *Thin Red Line*, 1973
48   *Scotsman*, 16 January 1981
49   Former corporal, Argyll and Sutherland Highlanders
50   *Scotsman*, 16 January 1981
51   *Scotsman*, 20 January 1981
52   *Ibid.*, 23 January 1981
53   *Ibid.*, 6 October 1981
54   *Red Hackle*, 1974
55   Sergeant, Parachute Regiment
56   *Thin Red Line*, 1973
57   *Ibid.*
58   *Rose and Thistle*, 1 October 1972
59   Former Royal Marine Commando
60   Former sergeant, Queen's Own Highlanders
61   *Borderers Chronicle*, 1972
62   Former sergeant, Scots Guards
63   Sergeant, Parachute Regiment
64   *Borderers Chronicle*, 1990, for an account of this action
65   Former senior officer, King's Own Scottish Borderers
66   *Ibid.*
67   M Arthur, *Soldiers Talking*; D Hamill, *Pig in the Middle: the Army in Northern Ireland 1969–1984* (London, 1985); A F N Clarke, *Contact* (London, 1983); M Dewar, *The British Army in Northern Ireland* (London, 1985); T Parker, *Soldier, Soldier* (London, 1985)
68   Former Royal Marine, 45 Commando
69   *Ibid.*
70   Former private, Royal Scots
71   *Ibid.*
72   Sergeant, Parachute Regiment
73   Former Royal Marine Commando
74   Former private, Queen's Own Highlanders
75   C Hibbert (ed.), *Recollections of Rifleman Harris* (London, 1970), p. 106
76   *Guardian*, 13 March 1978
77   *Ibid.*

In preparing this chapter, I was greatly assisted by the staff of the Scottish United Services Library at Edinburgh Castle. I would like to thank them for their help, also those soldiers and ex-soldiers who talked or wrote to me of their experiences in Northern Ireland.

Notes on Contributors

IAN ADAMSON is a medical practitioner and Unionist Party councillor in Belfast. He has written numerous books and articles on Ulster history.

ROBBIE DINWOODIE worked frequently for the *Scotsman* in Northern Ireland and is now a features writer with the *Herald* in Glasgow.

OWEN DUDLEY EDWARDS is Reader in History at Edinburgh University, and has written, edited and contributed to many books. His biographical work has covered Lord Macaulay, de Valera, Conan Doyle and Connolly, and last year was marked by a new edition of his *Burke and Hare*. He is the general editor of The Oxford Sherlock Holmes (9 vols).

GERRY FINN teaches in Strathclyde University's Faculty of Education and has written widely on sport, society and sectarianism, as well as freemasonry in Scotland.

BILLY KAY is a prolific broadcaster and author with a long interest in Scottish speech and dialect. He edited the *Odyssey* series based on oral history sources.

LINDE LUNNEY is from Antrim and is a graduate of both Edinburgh University and Queen's University, Belfast. She is Editorial Secretary to the *Dictionary of Irish Biography*, based in the Royal Irish Academy, Dublin.

ELAINE MCFARLAND teaches History at Glasgow's Caledonian University. She is the author of *Protestants First!*, a study of the Orange Order in Scotland, and a new book by her, *Scotland and Ireland in the Age of Revolution: Planting the Green Bough*, is due out soon.

SARAH NELSON has worked for the *Scotsman* and the *Herald* and was the author of *Ulster's Uncertain Defenders*, a major work on Ulster Loyalism.

MARCEL O' CONNOR was born in Lurgan, Co. Armagh. His *Boundaries* exhibition was seen in both Edinburgh and Belfast in 1993. He works from a studio in Edinburgh.

BOB PURDIE is a Politics tutor at Ruskin College, Oxford, and author of *Politics in the Streets*, a study of the origins of the Northern Ireland Civil Rights Movement.

GRAHAM WALKER teaches politics at Queen's University, Belfast. Among his many publications are biographies of Harry Midgley and Tom Johnston.

IAN S WOOD teaches History at Napier University, Edinburgh. He is the author of a biography of John Wheatley and was one of the editors of *Forward*, a history of the Labour movement in Scotland.

Index